All
the President's
Kin

All
the President's
Kin

Barbara Kellerman

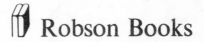 Robson Books

476.780 | 973.92

FIRST PUBLISHED IN GREAT BRITAIN IN 1982 BY
ROBSON BOOKS LTD., BOLSOVER HOUSE, 5-6
CLIPSTONE STREET, LONDON W1P 7EB. COPYRIGHT
© 1981 BARBARA KELLERMAN.

British Library Cataloguing in Publication Data

Kellerman, Barbara
    All the president's kin.
    1. Presidents—United States—Biography
    1. Title
    973.92'092'2   E176.1

    ISBN 0-86051-167-7

Printed in Hungary.

For Jonny

who taught me what I know
about building platforms

Contents

Preface

To talk politics in America is to talk of the president. We have anatomized presidents, dissected the office, and examined all the parts. Or so it has seemed.

But something is missing. For although the president's kin have come to be entrenched in our political culture, we have never given them any thoughtful attention. We have been lulled by the widespread assumption that since they so often decorate, embellish, and entertain, they lack genuine political significance. We have never carefully considered the possibility that there may be more here than meets the eye. We have taken the president's family at face value, as a pleasant bit of background. Despite the fact that nowadays members of the First Family—whether attractive, admirable, average, funny, clever, colorful, cute, eccentric, devoted, devout, honest, modest, or boorish—are regular performers on the political scene, the assumption persists that they are *apolitical*. The rare exceptions prove the rule: in the last fifty years the only presidential relatives widely acknowledged to have political functions have been Eleanor Roosevelt,

Robert Kennedy and Rosalynn Carter. None of the others have yet been taken seriously.

Indeed the tendency has been to relegate the First Family to the popular culture, particularly to the domain of the "housewife." The popularity of articles on the president's kin in magazines aimed at the women's market confirms that this is seen as a nonserious subject for a nonserious audience. Thus, although it seems that we already know more about the American presidency than we ever cared to ask, the president's family *as a political phenomenon* has remained immune to systematic exploration.

Why is this so? Why have political scientists and historians, journalists, commentators, biographers, and even presidents as autobiographers ignored the family? Why is one largely reduced to researching the Chief Executive's family in *McCall's, Ladies' Home Journal,* and *Time?**

Primary responsibility rests with the principal players in the presidential drama, including the presidents themselves. With the exception of Jimmy Carter—who went so far as to announce in an early fireside chat that "I would like to have the opportunity to use members of my family to go and represent me personally, along with professionals who serve the government"—recent presidents have been reluctant to acknowledge that their families might play important political roles. Take the case of Lyndon Johnson. Every Johnson watcher has agreed that his wife Lady Bird was an integral part of his political life. But the president's own book, *The Vantage Point,* although 636 pages long, mentions Mrs. Johnson only a very few times, and then only in passing. Richard Nixon does no better. His autobiography, *RN: The Memoirs of Richard Nixon,* is even longer (1,000 pages plus), but all he manages to do is pay lip service to his wife: "'Heart' is a quality that Pat possesses in abundance. It was her gift to the White House and to the country from the moment she became First Lady." And although we are told how important family support was during the Watergate crisis, and although the record shows that Julie Nixon Eisenhower played no less than a central role during this period, we get little more than brief references to what actually transpired. Gerald Ford, meanwhile, mentions his family—especially his wife—but even here there is no real recog-

---

*For a more extended discussion of sources see the Bibliography.

nition of what a powerful political asset Betty Ford proved herself to be.

The president's kin themselves contribute to the conventional wisdom by, much more often than not, accepting the traditional assignments. First Ladies, for example, usually become active in those areas that are deemed "proper": beautification, education or health. The rest of the family goes along with the act, looking fine for public consumption, behaving as if they were not much more than innocuous bystanders at the political game. (Once again, some members of the Carter clan were exceptions.) Indeed, most of the time they deliberately distance themselves from the substance of politics, leaving what is weighty to "my husband," "my father," "my brother," or "my son."

Opinion makers are also responsible for misconceptions about the presidential family. They manipulate the information on which we base our opinions. Consider this: if an editor at the *New York Times* decides to place an item about Judy Carter's support for the Equal Rights Amendment in the "Notes on People" section (the *Times'* version of *People* magazine), readers will perceive it as a diverting tidbit. If it is placed on the "woman's page" (now labeled "Style"), it will be read as a "human interest" story related to contemporary doings and fashions. If, however, the editor puts the item in the first section, in with the "hard" news, it becomes that itself—news.

While the press and television typically reduce family members to celebrities whose doings are reported with those of the jet set, other opinion makers follow suit in their own way—by dissecting the president or his office, but ignoring his family. In short, the whole spectrum of "experts" have come to the same tacit conclusion as the president and his kin: the First Family is little more than a divertissement.

That leaves us, the public. It is true that we are taught by all concerned to see the president's kin as trivial or almost non-existent. But perhaps our ill-considered consensus on the subject is even better explained by something more fundamental: our political culture has been male dominated and oriented, and Americans have traditionally downplayed the role of the family in the man's professional life.

Although attempts have been made to unravel presidents' personalities, only very rarely have they been considered as husband, son, father or brother. We have scrutinized the Oval Office without seeming to understand that what happens in the White House living room or bedroom can both affect and reveal something about professional performance. This habit of seeing work and home as separate has made us nearly oblivious to the role of the president's family in contributing to, or detracting from, his general well being, and it has hindered us, too, from coming to understand the family's impact on public perceptions.

We have preferred, in short, to cling to time honored notions about what is right and proper, about who belongs where in the White House. The Chief Executive is supposed to be "a family man" (a particularly ubiquitous theme during the 1980 campaign), but he is also supposed to be the head of his household, ruler of his roost. For him to appear overly dependent on his family, or anything less than dominant within it, will not do. Times are changing but departures from the past come hard and come slow; the most popular motif is still the First Family as drawn by Norman Rockwell.

This book breaks old habits by looking at the familiar cast of family characters in a new way. It claims that virtually *all* close relatives of the president play significant political roles; that since the campaign of 1960 these roles have been varied and multifaceted (see chart on opposite page); that the First Family serves four different constituencies (the president, the public, the press, and themselves); and that the political functions (and dysfunctions) of the president's family must now be seen as a permanent part of presidential government.

For better or worse, the candidates' kin have an impact on who gets elected and the president's kin have an impact on how executive power is exercised. At its best—large, active, colorful and variegated—the family is an irreplaceable political plus. And at his or her most powerful, the individual family member cannot be dismissed lightly. Stripped of gossipy anecdotes, the president's kin are seen here for what they are: significant players performing important roles in the non-stop drama that is presidential politics.

The President's Kin: Their Political Roles

Decorations	Jacqueline Kennedy; Caroline and John-John Kennedy; Amy Carter; Patti Davis; family pets
Extensions	Edward Kennedy; Eunice Kennedy Shriver; Patricia Kennedy Lawford; Jean Kennedy Smith; Lynda Bird and Luci Baines Johnson; Tricia Nixon; Michael, Jack, Steve, and Susan Ford; Jack, Chip, and Jeff Carter; Michael Reagan
Humanizers	Rose Kennedy; Betty Ford; Lillian Carter; Billy Carter; Ruth Carter Stapleton; Maureen Reagan; Ron Reagan
Helpmeets	Joseph P. Kennedy; Lady Bird Johnson; Pat Nixon; Nancy Reagan
Moral Supports	Julie Nixon Eisenhower
Alter Egos	Robert Kennedy; Rosalynn Carter
Skeletons	Rosemary Kennedy; Sam Houston Johnson; Donald Nixon; Billy Carter

Acknowledgments

James MacGregor Burns, David Greenwald, Cynthia Macdonald, and Jeffrey Rubin were contributors. Ellen Kellerman, Ken Greenwald, and Tom Greenwald were the bedrock. And Jonathan Greenwald was—is—indispensable in every way.

All
the President's
Kin

CHAPTER 1

Presidential Politics as a Family Affair

Precedents

Billy Carter's indiscreet and foolish dealings with the Libyan government proved one of the political sensations of the 1980 election year. But it was an anomaly, in that the president's kin can normally be counted on to *help* the cause. In that sense the most recent campaign and election confirmed what we already knew: prominent roles in American presidential politics are assigned to supporting players, "surrogates," who tend often and certainly more than ever before to be relatives of candidates—wives, parents, siblings, and children. Moreover, what was underscored during the Carter presidency is that the political influence of presidential kin can be much more than publicity-deep. The era of Rosalynn Carter and the powerful behind-the-scenes influence of Nancy Reagan have provided us with a new (if skewed) perception of the First Lady's role and a fresh reminder that presidential relatives can double as aides, emissaries, and top advisers.

1

The conditions of contemporary America make it probable that presidents' (and candidates') kin will undertake at least one of the two following broadly defined tasks: playing to the public or standing by their man. If assigned the mission of playing to the public, their job will be to win friends in a variety of ways, and to influence people on behalf of the president. If the nature of their relationship to the president is such that their main function is to stay close by, then their mission is to enhance his performance as occupant of the Oval Office.

This making of the president's extended family into something more prominent and more important than ever is a change, or rather an *accelerated development,* in our politics. During the decade and a half of her husband's presidency Eleanor Roosevelt had, of course, a substantial political influence; she is almost as familiar a legend forty years later as FDR himself. But consider too a few other examples—first, Edith Galt Wilson, who was characterized by some as the "first woman President of the United States."[1] Recently married to President Wilson when he had his incapacitating stroke in 1919, she took the advice of Wilson's doctor, Francis S. Dercum, very much to heart. "Have everything come to you," Dr. Dercum supposedly advised Mrs. Wilson. "Weigh the importance of each matter, and see if it is possible by consultations with the respective heads of the Departments to solve them without the guidance of your husband. . . . He has the utmost confidence in you."[2]

As Mrs. Wilson subsequently recalled, she "studied every paper" and tried to present "in tabloid form" the things that had to go to the president. Despite this obviously critical role, she tried to play down her role during this period, and play up the president's. In her book *My Memoir* Edith Wilson wrote that she herself "never made a single decision regarding the disposition of public affairs." Somewhat naïvely, she then proceeded to the heart of the matter: "The only decision that was mine was what was important and what was not, and the *very* important decision of when to present matters to my husband."

Protests against Mrs. Wilson's control over her husband's affairs were to no avail. She was determined to run the show herself.

By far the majority of all letters to the President were ignored . . . but certain matters were acted upon. Over the wide left margins of an elegantly typed letter . . . there were each day penciled notes by a woman who had a total of just two years of formal schooling. . . . Each scrawl began, "The President says" or "The President wants" and there was no one in the world to say that the President . . . did not say or did not want. . . . Eventually the First Lady took to receiving Cabinet members in her sitting room. . . . She would tell the visiting Secretary what the President wanted done about a given problem, the verbal instructions being, she assured her caller, completely representative of her husband's wishes.[3]

In terms of Woodrow Wilson's most cherished goals, the results of all this were catastrophic: the removal of the president from the fight for American membership in the League of Nations, his defeat in that fight, and the subsequent loss of the White House to the Republicans under Warren Harding.

Presidential kin of a different stripe was Milton Eisenhower, youngest of six Eisenhower brothers and essentially a Washington career man. From the Coolidge administration to Richard Nixon's, he played some kind of a prominent role in executive government. Ike's special dependence on Milton stemmed in part from the unusual fact that Ike was a newcomer to politics and a newcomer too to the whole Washington establishment. A military man, Ike assumed the presidency with an astonishing lack of experience in domestic politics. Milton, though, knew the ropes. Combine this resource with filial loyalty, and the relationship between the brothers and the dependence Ike came to have on Milton are all too understandable.

Milton described the relationship himself:

Since my brother and I had worked together intermittently but intimately for twenty years prior to his election to the presidency, it was natural for me to become one of his closest confidants.

We were philosophically compatible. We shared a passionate belief in the American system of representative government. . . .

Our relationship did not change merely because he now occupied the highest office in the land. It may seem incredible, but I did not view him primarily as a leader with great power. I saw him as I always had: a brother with whom I enjoyed an unusually strong affection which, fortunately, was mutual. Our work together had always been, and would be for the eight presidential years, characterized by trust, unqualified openness, and good will.

We had mutually decided, following his election, that it would

be a mistake for him to appoint me to the Cabinet.* It would smack
of nepotism. . . . With this understanding, the White House was my
weekend home for eight years. . . .

I knew President Eisenhower found it helpful to reveal his in-
nermost thoughts and plans to one who was not subservient to him,
was not an advocate of special interests, had no selfish purpose to
serve, and would raise questions and facts solely to help the President think through his problems without pressing for a particular
decision.[4]

Milton Eisenhower also quoted approvingly from articles and
books that he felt captured the essence of his relationship to his
brother: "Milton Eisenhower has served the present administration in so many ways and is known to be so close to the President
that his influence has been compared to that of two previous presidential confidants: Woodrow Wilson's Colonel Edward M.
House and Franklin D. Roosevelt's Harry Hopkins. . . ." "When
Milton is in Washington the two will sit together in the President's bedroom for hours while the President grinds out his ideas
on different subjects. This is the process the President uses ha-
bitually to clarify his thinking and plot the line where he is and
where he wants to go." "The best judgment is that . . . Milton has
become perhaps the most helpful member of the multitude, official and personal, around his brother. . . . Theirs is a relationship
in which neither has to finish a sentence. . . ."[5]

But, as Billy Carter recently reminded us, not every member
of the president's family with political impact has a *positive* impact. All the president's kin do not necessarily *help*. Mary Todd
Lincoln was just such a case: to the degree that she was political,
she was a liability. An extravagant woman, without doubt indiscreet (by the censorious standards of the day) in her friendships
with men, she was, worst of all, tarred by the fact of her own
Kentucky heritage and by being related to a large and extended
Southern family. Mary's youngest brother and her three half
brothers were a part of the Confederate forces; her three half sisters were wives of Confederate officers; and she had eleven second cousins in the Carolina Light Dragoons of the Confederate
forces.

In the overwrought atmosphere of the Civil War, rumors

*Contrast this decision to that made by the Kennedy brothers on the same
subject.

about Mrs. Lincoln grew to the point where it was being said that she was a rebel spy who passed on state secrets to the enemy. So many abusive letters came to the White House addressed to her that she asked one of the staff to screen the mail before bringing it. Never really comprehending the suspicions that swirled about her, she asked on one occasion, "Why should I sympathize with the rebels? Are they not against me? They would hang my husband tomorrow if it was in their power, and perhaps me with him. How then can I sympathize with a people at war with me and mine?"[6]

Mrs. Lincoln was not only a considerable political liability to her husband but something of a personal strain on him as well. She was always susceptible to mood swings, explosions of temper, and unexplained headaches, and after the death of her son Willie at age eleven in the winter of '62, her mental health collapsed completely. She suffered a nervous breakdown and locked herself in her room for three months. Five months after Willie's death the First Lady was still practically unable to speak or write about it.

Lincoln's death was almost more than the First Lady could bear. Her subsequent seclusion was interrupted only by the need to pack and leave the White House, and when she did, nary a friend was present to tell her goodbye. Even then, the attacks on Mary Todd Lincoln did not cease. Until she died, some accused her still of having been a traitor, and others charged her with greed to the point of thievery. When the question arose, toward the end of 1865, of a new appropriation to refurnish the White House for the Johnson administration, it was said that Mrs. Lincoln, upon leaving the premises, had carted off many of the mansion's valuables with her.

Changes

As these short stories underline, in times past *some* relatives of *some* presidents have had political effects and political functions. But until quite recently the family was—for a fascinating combination of reasons of political circumstance, social customs, and technology—less visible and less important than it has now become. In our history, only the occasional presidential relative had a political role. Now only the very occasional relative does not.

Since approximately 1960 there have been dramatic shifts and innovations in every area of our domestic life—social, cultural, political, technological. Together, these changes have made the political impact of the presidential family both broader and more constant than ever before. This is not to argue that Rosalynn Carter had more clout than, say, Abigail Adams. It *is* to claim that it is now difficult if not impossible for the president's kin to withdraw from public life, that our contemporary culture affords them new opportunities to exert their influence, and that recent changes in our political institutions make their at least intermittent participation in presidential government inevitable. Thus our working hypothesis: *families of presidents have more political impact now than in our earlier history.* We can expect, moreover, that *in the future this trend will continue and even accelerate.*

Social and political changes are not announced by the ring of a gong. Rather, they weave themselves slowly, often imperceptibly, into the fabric of our everyday life. When we finally notice them, it often seems as if they had in fact been around for a long, long time. For instance, it is hard to believe that the almost invisible Bess Truman was First Lady less than a decade before superstar Jacqueline Kennedy.

Mrs. Truman had an intense dislike for publicity and hated people to "fuss over her." The President supported her natural proclivity. Harry Truman's daughter, Margaret, remembers that if "there was one thing Dad dreaded, it was the thought of someone in his family getting involved in politics. He felt deeply that the Roosevelts had made a serious mistake in this area." Little better illustrates how times have changed regarding the prevailing attitude on family participation (to which Franklin Roosevelt was a notable exception) than this letter Truman wrote to his sister Mary when she asked his advice about going to an Oklahoma political meeting:

> For goodness sake, refuse it [the invitation]. They are only using you to advertise themselves. It won't help me a bit . . . and it will give these columnists like Pearson and the rest of the gossips a chance to say that my family, particularly the women of my family, are courting the limelight. So please don't go.

Now I don't want to appear to be in the role of a tyrant—but I know politics and political repercussions better than anyone in the family. . . .

I have kept Bess and Margaret out of the political picture as much as I can and I am still trying to keep them from being talked about.

This sort of appearance would give all the mudslingers a chance. I have a lot of pleasant things in mind for you if I can ever get this place to run as it should. . . .[7]

Nowadays, this letter seems as quaint as a Valentine embossed with real lace. We smile at Truman's old-fashioned assumptions: that it is somehow not proper for women to get mixed up in politics; that they should be spared the ugliness of the man's world; that they should be surrounded instead by "a lot of pleasant things"; and that any kind of political event is per se a trap in which his women would more likely than not be victimized by some opportunistic enemy. It was simply not conceivable that a presidential sister, for example, could be turned into a political asset.

How did those days vanish forever? When did this shift in mores and perceptions come about? As good a time as any to place the moment of change is during the presidential campaign of John F. Kennedy. Blatantly, indeed with bounding pride, Kennedy used his family to further his own political ends. Four male relatives served as key political aides, and any and all available female kin were presented like ornaments to be noticed and admired. The impact was dramatic. What had heretofore been frowned on as nepotism, favoritism, self-advertisement, exploitation, interference, and impropriety was, in a sudden reversal of public opinion, being celebrated. Moreover, there was, after the wildly attractive and willing Kennedys, no going back. No president since John Kennedy has been inclined to rein in his family, and no family has wanted to be reined in. And certainly the media and the public were not about to willingly surrender the piece of presidential flesh into which they had, at long last, managed to sink their teeth.

Let us not, however, lay this increased family participation entirely at the doorstep of JFK. In order to effect change, leaders must touch on something for which the time is ripe; and there is no doubt that Kennedy's family made its appearance at the per-

fect moment. After the colorless Eisenhower years, the country
was in the mood for a breath of fresh air, for a national knight
who symbolized the new and different rather than the old and
tried. Around 1960 almost anything John Kennedy did seemed
clever, and if he saw fit to bring his family along with him into
the limelight, it became in short order the thing to do. But the
fact that after Kennedy it became a national habit to mix family
and politics, a matter of routine, suggests that the time was right
in several different ways. The Kennedys initiated the change, but
new and pervasive strains in American life sustained it. For better or worse, the following developments were responsible for the
apparently enduring marriage between family activity and presidential politics: the decline of the party, the increase in the number and importance of primaries, the trends of the office, the
dawn of televison, and a swiftly changing culture.

The Decline of the Party

Kennedy was the first president in our modern history to demonstrate that it is possible to be a winner—of the nomination for the
presidency *and* of the election—without hardline party support.
He was also the first to recognize that the vacuum left by a weak
party structure must be filled by something else. That something
else, the replacement of the party organization in campaign politics, has come to be called the "candidate organization," and it
should come as no surprise to learn that the first requisite demanded of those who staff it is loyalty—loyalty first, last, and
only to the candidate himself.

Surely among the most likely choices for members of such a
staff are those from the candidate's own family—*especially* if that
family is large and multifaceted. Whose loyalty could be more
complete? Whose devotion more total? Whose goals so fully
shared with the main protagonist?

Kennedy won the nomination not because of party regulars,
but in spite of them. He depended almost entirely on the network
he had forged on his own—a network, incidentally, which out-
lasted the campaign and survived intact well into the presidential
years. There is, of course, a wide divergence among candidate
organizations; Kennedy's was among the most effective. The

well-oiled Kennedy machine was in ample evidence at the 1960 Democratic convention.

> The Kennedy organization assigned an individual to each state. . . . These liaison men kept tabs on individual delegates and maintained a running record of the likely distribution of votes. When necessary [they] sent messages to the candidate's headquarters and reinforcements were sent to bolster the situation. . . . Every morning every liaison man attended a staff meeting at which . . . Robert Kennedy would ask each [person] for his estimate of the number of Kennedy votes.[8]

It was a network created to serve the interests of only one man. And who peopled it? Who would stake their entire political investment on the fortunes of one man? In the case of John Kennedy the answer was predictable: relatives, and also friends, almost all of whom had old ties to the Kennedy family. The Kennedy organization was a collective family enterprise: "Not only did his brothers, sisters and parents participate in a big way, but each of them brought his own friends and acquaintances along."[9]

It was brother Robert who pumped the machine. No one who has written about the campaign of 1960 remembers it otherwise. Robert was, in Theodore Sorensen's words, John's "first and only choice for campaign manager," and although Robert had been away from politics for some time, he accepted the assignment with his typically fierce energy and combativeness. His loyalty was, of course, unquestioned, and if he was hardly well loved by Democratic regulars, within the Kennedy organization he was the main propelling force, as well as "generally adored."

But in Kennedy's organization, created not so much to supplement party regulars as to supplant them, Robert was only the most prominent of family members. At least three others had prominent roles: Stephen Smith, brother-in-law of the candidate, who served first as office manager, then as logistics manager, and then as administrative chief; Edward Kennedy, the candidate's younger brother, whose domain became the Mountain states; and Joseph P. Kennedy, the candidate's father, who was pusher, supporter, benefactor, and adviser for all seasons. Of the others who formed the heart of Kennedy's organization, at least three were almost family: Kenneth O'Donnell, a football teammate of Robert Kennedy's at Harvard, Lawrence O'Brien, who, like O'Donnell, had successfully worked for Kennedy in Massachusetts for eight years; and Theodore Sorensen, Kennedy's resident thinker and writer for the preceding seven years. The Kennedy women also got into the act. O'Donnell and David Powers, in their book *"Johnny, We Hardly Knew Ye,"* recalled that Rose Kennedy and her daughters Eunice, Pat, and Jean went to receptions and house parties and rang doorbells on behalf of Kennedy in the Wisconsin primary, and that it was always easier to talk a housewife into giving a party if she was told that Peter Lawford's wife (sister Pat Lawford) would be attending.

The decline of the influence of party regulars on who won the presidential nomination was critical to Kennedy's success. He could never have won under the old system. This pattern has continued. George McGovern used a similar personal network to win the Democratic nomination for president in 1972 (McGovern's group consisted mostly of activists with a special interest in ending our participation in the war in Vietnam), and when Jimmy Carter began his odyssey to the White House, he knew that if he had even a chance of becoming president, it was going to be on the strength of his own organization. Hardly known beyond Georgia, Carter was an outsider not only to party regulars but also to the new breed of issue-oriented purists who had clustered around Eugene McCarthy and McGovern in the late sixties and early seventies. At the 1972 Democratic national convention in Miami Beach, when advisers Hamilton Jordan and Gerald Rafshoon sought to have Carter considered for vice-president, they had trouble just getting in to see McGovern's advisers! Only in 1974 did Carter plant a first toe in the party door; he served as chairman of the Democratic congressional campaign committee. In December of that year he announced his candidacy for the presidency of the United States.

But "Jimmy Carter still had two basic problems.... Not many people knew who he was. And not many people cared."[10] And so he too was forced to depend virtually entirely on his own organization. And he too called on those who were family or very old friends—first, Rosalynn Carter, who advised her husband on problems big and small, serving as counselor and sounding board, and who set out on an aggressive campaign schedule of her own. Rarely during 1975 and 1976 did this husband and wife travel together. "The Carters figured that they could cover more ground if they were in two places at the same time—Jimmy in one, Rosalynn in the other—and that is how they worked it for more than a year."[11]

But again, if Rosalynn was the most prominent family member to participate in the campaign, she was not the only one. Like Kennedy, Carter capitalized on the fortuitous mix between family and politics. Jordan assigned numerical values to indicate what one day of campaigning by each of the Carter-Mondale celebrities would be worth: Carter, 7; Mondale, 5; Rosalynn Carter, 4; Joan Mondale, 3; Jack and Judy Carter, 2; Chip and Caron Carter, 2; and Jeff and Annette Carter, 2. Moreover, the press soon discovered the good copy waiting down home in Plains. In 1975 and '76 names like Lillian and Billy and Amy took on special meaning in our political lore, and reporters clamoring for yet another bon mot from any one of them encountered little resistance.

In sum, the decline of the party has meant a change in the cast of political characters: members of the candidates' families now take on an importance they never had in the days when party bosses ran the entire show.

The Increase in the Number and Importance of Primaries

This century's explosive popularity of the presidential primary is an important reason for the decline of the party. Indeed the primary was explicitly instituted as a reform to counter a system in which if the party organization controlled the convention, it controlled the nomination. Television provided a fresh rationale: by about 1952, presidential candidates began to realize that this new medium could lend great drama to what had previously been strictly local skirmishes. Other reforms, such as the Campaign Reform Act, which channeled the contest into the television studio, have inadvertently had a similar effect. The party is thus gradually being eliminated as an undesirable, costly middleman of sorts, and being replaced now by a more direct tie between the candidate and the voters.

The new importance of the primary as the way to win the presidential nomination also has meant the decline of the national convention as a decision-making body of much significance. The Democratic convention in 1952 was the last to have more than a single ballot (Adlai Stevenson was chosen the third time around), and now the single ballot, for all practical purposes, often does no more than ratify a choice already made before the first gavel falls. Quite simply, the tools of the trade have changed. Once upon a time what a candidate needed was a powerful party organization and a couple of "fat cats." Now, there are new tools—the primary, television, and the opinion poll, for example—that must be mastered by anyone who hopes to be president.

These changes mandate that more than ever before, success in campaign politics depends on the public image of the man. You win big in a primary, or in a television spot, or in a public opinion poll, if you can convince the electorate that you are better than your opponent. The effort is a highly personal one, riding almost exclusively on the actual and perceived political skills and personal qualities of the contender. It is precisely because of the enormous demands on the candidate's own resources, resources that he alone can command, that we are brought back to the family. The primary especially turns his family into a valued commodity in terms of both the image it conveys to the public and the support it lends in private.

Again the pattern began with Kennedy, specifically in the crucial Wisconsin and West Virginia primaries. His sisters and brothers and in-laws and mother—referred to by T. H. White as "in themselves a small troop of unpaid political talent"—roved up and down the roads, operating all across both states. They were, in short, indispensable. The win in Wisconsin effectively knocked Hubert Humphrey from the race; and the victory in West Virginia conquered another problem. "I think," said JFK after that triumph, "we have now buried the religious issue once and for all."

Carter's baptism under fire in New Hampshire was a similar case. It was early in the season of presidential politicking, the cold and lonely February days in the small, rural New England state that prides itself on being the first to pick winners. Jackson didn't trouble to enter that first primary, and Bayh and Udall look back and see mistakes. But Carter, as a good scout should be, was prepared. When he looked back, he saw the New Hampshire win as no accident, but rather as the result of much hard work by family and staff. There was the tightly knit group of long-devoted advisers, and there were the ninety mostly middle-aged and well-heeled Georgians who flew north at their own expense to ring doorbells on behalf of Jimmy; but above all there was Carter, and there were his kin. All exhausted themselves on behalf of his candidacy.

> We contacted 95% of the Democratic homes in New Hampshire. And it was a tedious person-to-person relationship. I went into just about all the shoe factories in New Hampshire and a lot of Beano games. I guess if you went to the stores and the restaurants and jewelry shops, coffee houses and barbershops and beauty parlors in New Hampshire and the media centers, at least it would be hard for you to find one of those places where one of my family hasn't been. Chip or Caron or Julie or Jeffrey or Annette or Sissy or Ruth or any of them.[12]

The fact that primaries now play the critical role in who gets the presidential nomination means that a resource of no mean value is a candidate's family, especially if the family is large, willing to work, and broadly appealing. The most ardent of disciples, relatives spread the gospel, person-to-person, beyond anything the candidate could possibly do alone. Furthermore, they are magnets to the media; they themselves become celebrities and hence generate valuable publicity. Finally, they provide their man with those symbols of unity and stability that make him more credible to a public sometimes just beginning to get acquainted. In a day when the people's visceral response counts for more, the value of the family in securing the nomination is greatly enhanced.

The Trends of the Office

Three seemingly irresistible trends are of particular importance to the increased impact of the presidential family: the personalization of the office, executive expansion, and the weakened Cabinet. "Personalization of the office" simply means that more than ever we elect a president on the basis of his personal attributes rather than, for example, ideology or party label. How smart is he? How honest? How industrious? How stable? How courageous? How affable, healthy, dutiful, devoted, devout, and disciplined?

Once again, the family serves: it becomes an integral part of the quasi-information, replacing hard facts, which we are fed during the months preceding the election. First, we are reassured by the ever-present family that the candidate is a devoted family man. That makes him a stable person, and a caring one. Second, we are treated to the spectacle of the family going all out in support of their beloved hero. That makes him a good organizer, as well as an evocative leader. And third, we come to know different members of the family as if important in their own right. Their fame enhances their glamour, and draws our attention to each of them as individuals.

All of this sets the stage for a system that puts great store in the personal qualities of the man who occupies the presidential office. This is yet another outgrowth of the decline of the party and the ideological fuzziness that is one of the decline's most significant by-products. We come to believe that the personality of the president is the all-powerful determinant of how our government works. Good policy, this line of reasoning goes, comes from a good man. And just as the family is used during the campaign to convince us that we are in the presence of a worthy leader, so it functions during the president's term of office. The great man on whom so much is thought to depend is set off by his family. Like the royal court of old, they surround our president and make him somehow larger than life.

Executive expansion has occurred on two fronts, in the growth of the federal bureaucracy and the "swelling" of the presidency. The first hatched the second. As one gradual result of the enormous increase in domestic activity by the national government, more power came to reside in the Oval Office. Meanwhile, the United States also evolved into a world leader. Certainly after World War II our role at the forefront of "the free world" crystallized and the White House became an international seat of power.

Inevitably, as our national government took on more tasks, the presidency gained greater attention. The Chief Executive assumed new roles, and our fantasies soared accordingly. Who, we now ask, if not the president, "is going to prevent the communists from burying us, pollution from choking us, crime and conflict from destroying our cities, oil-producing nations from freezing us to death, and pornography from slipping into our neighborhood bookstores and theatres?"[13] Presidents themselves contributed to the mythology by appearing to embrace the impossible demands. Lyndon Johnson, for example, cultivated the identification between himself and the "Great Society." Single-handedly he, at the helm of the ship of state, would be the great provider. Nixon's self-aggrandizement took a different form. The epitome of the "imperial president," Nixon too regularly inflated his presidential authority.

I do not want to suggest that, for example, Nixon lurched through his presidency with a Machiavellian wife, daughter, or brother at his side. Rather I propose that this huge concentration of power at the center bestows a *vicarious* importance on anyone near the president and a *real* importance on anyone near him who is directly involved with politics. Several analogies come to mind. Think of the old Hollywood that was so completely geared to the star system. One was an attraction, an object of curiosity, as the child or spouse or even maid of a star. The interest was in both the satellite and what he or she could reveal about "the great one." Or think of the court of the absolute monarch. One was an object of fascination to all the rest if only a distant member of the royal entourage — and a principal in one's own right as the king's counselor, adviser, or *eminence grise.*

The sequence was probably inevitable: an enlarged federal government, heightened public expectations, a turn to the president as the personification of how these might be realized, a new attention to the man, a setting in which "the life of the White House is the life of a court,"[14] a system in which the public is intrigued by all those close to the one being lionized and grows gradually used to the idea that they too have a proper role in governing. Robert Kennedy leaps over heads to become the attorney general. Lillian Carter represents the president at state occasions (e.g., Tito's funeral). It has come to be understood that when the president wills it, his family may quite freely practice politics.

The weakened Cabinet is important to my point because in a system in which the president is remote from the heads of the executive agencies, he depends more on his personal staff—a corps entirely of his own making.

It is true, of course, that throughout our history the ideal of a Cabinet serving as a coherent and loyal body of key advisers has been lived up to only intermittently. Still, at no time has the Cabinet been so consistently weak as in the modern presidency, when it is, theoretically at least, relied on more than ever before. (Reagan is trying to reverse this trend.) Of our recent presidents only Eisenhower upgraded the Cabinet. As for the rest: "President Kennedy regarded the idea of the cabinet as a collective consultative body largely as an anachronism. . . ." Under Johnson, complained one White House aide, "the cabinet became a joke; it was never used for anything near what could be called presidential listening or consultation." And Nixon's centralization of power in the White House was considered "an apparent vote of no confidence in his cabinet members."[15]

So we now have a situation in which it has become entirely possible for the president's inner circle to be penetrated by his (blood or extended) family. Whereas once the main presidential policy-making group would have been the Cabinet, now it is most likely to contain those on the White House staff who are close personal assistants to the president. These lieutenants have no loyalties other than those to the president, no responsibilities other than those assigned by the White House, and no outside constituency to call them to account. Indeed, they often form adversary relationships with their counterparts in the executive departments. Among the most publicized in recent years was Henry Kissinger and Zbigniew Brzezinski of the president's National Security Council vis-à-vis William Rogers and Cyrus Vance of State; and the two Teutons, Robert Haldeman and John Ehrlichman, Nixon's top aides, vis-à-vis Walter Hickel of Interior. Unchecked, this tendency toward isolation of the president and White House personnel led in the Nixon years to monumental miscalculations and flagrant abuses of power. Yet even in the post-Watergate era the structure of the system remains much the same. Jimmy Carter's closest aides were not members of his Cabinet or newly appointed advisers, but rather those on his immediate staff who had been with him since his days as a Georgia politician.

The potential consequences for family members are almost self-evident. Since no legislature must ratify the president's appointment of his personal advisers, the opportunities and temptations for the president to draw on the counsel of his family are enormous. Opportunities abound because decisions are made in an insular setting in which old ties and friendships count for more than experience or expertise. And the temptations are great because there are no longer any outsiders—read Cabinet members—with whom immediate and challenging interactions are anticipated. (Robert Sherrill wrote, apropos "leaked" minutes of the Cabinet's meetings from March 14, 1977 to March 13, 1978, that "these meetings have a way of deteriorating to the level of a park-bench bull session."[16]) It does not surprise, then, when the president closets himself almost exclusively with his own kind, or when the First Lady is rumored to have major influence. Nowadays, the group that runs the government is, after all, generally not too different from that which engineered the successful campaign. The mix that led to triumph then is, barring a long history of obvious failures, unlikely to be much altered now. Remember how hard it was for Carter to dump Bert Lance, who was "like a brother" to him?

The Dawn of Television

According to the newest almanacs the average American watches about five hours of television a day. He is, then, voluntarily or involuntarily, going to be exposed to *some* news program—if only because of its accidental place before, between, or just after Monday night football, for instance. And indeed since the 1947–48 season, when NBC and CBS first won sponsors for their main newscasts, the evening news especially has become a staple of the American TV diet. Now we have reached a point where networks allot the national news thirty successive minutes each day and local news up to another two hours.

Television has also proven itself magnificently capable of covering the special political event—national conventions, for example. And so it is that science and our boundless fascination with one of its more ubiquitous products have conspired to make the tube an important agent in our political life.

John Kennedy remarked that "we wouldn't have had a prayer without that gadget," television, and well he might have. The first year in which television was said to have literally determined the result of a presidential election was 1960. Specifically, there were the "Great Debates" between Kennedy and Nixon, debates which may have, as Henry Steele Commager suggested, glorified traits having little to do with the presidency, but which nonetheless made a tremendous impact on voters' perceptions, and which were to the incalculable advantage of Kennedy. More generally though, it was the TV persona of the handsome senator from Massachusetts that was the smashing success.

The campaign had suddenly thrust a new personality on the consciousness of television audiences. Like Lucy and Van Doren and
the *Bonanza* group and *The Untouchables,* John Kennedy had
caught on suddenly with a spectacular rise in ratings. . . . He had
wit and drama. He went after an adversary with style. . . . In the fall
of 1960 his vitality crackled from the television tube.[17]

But again the cameras did not depend on the man alone. It
was Kennedy's great good fortune to be surrounded by a large
family that would seem to have been dreamed up just for the campaign by central casting. Television made it possible for us to
become extensively acquainted with a candidate's family for the
first time, and what a fortuitous moment it was—for the Kennedys. In contrast to Nixon's already familiar and none too exciting
Pat, Tricia, and Julie, Kennedy introduced a multifaceted clan
equipped to please celebrity watchers of every age and taste. We
came to know the attractive parents, the wholesome siblings, the
glamourous wife, and the winning child in an instant, in our very
own living room. Soon we knew each and every member of this
enormous and enormously engaging troupe, and our curiosity,
once sparked, never waned. And the Kennedy kin did not disappoint even once.

From that time on, Americans have taken a proprietal interest
in the president's kin. The Kennedys and the tube joined forces
to make it impossible for succeeding families to be private; just
as the president was public property, so now were his relatives.
Indeed, in 1976 a candidate's wife, Rosalynn Carter, appeared as
a guest on the deadly earnest Sunday morning interview program
"Face the Nation."

I have talked more about the importance of television in the
politics of winning the office than in the politics of holding it.
The emphasis was not accidental. It is, in fact, during the campaign that television provides us with the most information about
the personalities of the presidential contenders, and about the
persons and places that have, over the years, influenced them.

This is not, however, to suggest that family members have a
diminished role as TV stars during the actual White House years.
Indeed, their symbolic functions are well served by the tube.
What more ordinary and all-American, for example, than television scenes of presidential blue jeans, ball games, and public
schools? Furthermore, television maximizes the impact of family
members, who come to have a special relationship with the pub-

lic. It allowed instant and repeated transmissions of the cuteness of Caroline Kennedy, the steady devotion of Pat Nixon, the wit and wisdom of Lillian Carter. What television gradually effected, then, was no less than a sequence in which huge numbers of us were first introduced to all the president's kin, then accustomed to having them participate in presidential politics, and finally convinced that they were no less than bona fide celebrities and political actors in their own right.

Changing Culture

476.780 | 973.92

When we talk about the advent of television, we can be specific about when things happened: in January 1947 the opening of Congress was televised for the first time, in 1956 we had the first videotape of a presidential inauguration, by 1969 a television set was owned by 88% of American families, and so forth. Changes in manners, pastimes, values, and mores are harder to pin down, their presence among us less clearly defined. So any consideration of how these shifts connect to the increased visibility and impact of the presidential family must of necessity be general. Ideas can be put forth only because they are suggestive. Still, and with that proviso, there are, I think, no less than six changes which came upon us over the last decade and a half or so and which can be pointed to as having some influence on the behaviors of, and on our perceptions of, the First Family. They are the women's movement, the youth cult, gray power, people power, attitudes toward sex, liquor, and drugs, and a new openness and straightforwardness in American life (otherwise known as "letting it all hang out").

1. The women's movement has made it legitimate for First Ladies, and for that matter all female presidential kin, to behave in other than the traditional ways. This is not to say that this leeway has been exploited. On the contrary, there is still a considerable respect for propriety and precedent, and very few presidents' wives broke with tradition before there was a social movement to sanction their choice. But as two of the most recent First Ladies have shown, as well as Ruth Carter Stapleton, the presidents' women are carving out more independent roles for themselves. The ways in which these three women have used this new space differ. Betty Ford broke precedent with her honesty about

sex and cancer (and later about drugs, alcohol, and cosmetic surgery). Rosalynn Carter was her husband's independent equal during the campaign, preferred subsequently to be considered his full partner, and assumed an active role as political adviser to, and defender of, Carter's administration. Ruth Carter Stapleton is said by brother Jimmy to have been a key figure in his spiritual life—it was she who fostered his "born again" conversion—and she is a successful and attractive (Jules Witcover referred to her as a "sexy blond mother"[18]) career woman in her own right. It seems clear that while the White House has not exactly been a hotbed of "women's lib" activity, its recent female denizens have tended to be sympathetic fellow travelers: both Betty Ford and Rosalynn Carter actively supported the Equal Rights Amendment. Nancy Reagan is, of course, much more of a traditionalist. But the clout she is rumored to have with her husband belies some of her more old-fashioned posturing.

2. Since the late sixties and the Vietnam generation, America's youth has had an ever brighter place in the sun than before. As is symbolized graphically by the ratification of the Twenty-sixth Amendment to the Constitution (1971), which gave eighteen-year-olds the right to vote, our young people demand and get an attention and respect denied them in other cultures. Our interest in them, including our desire to look like them and emulate them, suggests a mild fixation of which one result is that we are fascinated with even the most trivial things they do. Three of our recent presidents have had teenaged children during their time in the White House, and we were, or so it seemed, not spared the details of a single date. Lynda Bird and Luci Baines Johnson, Trician and Julie Nixon, and Jack, Steve, and Susan Ford all regaled us with their very modest exploits, and when on occasion they were engaged in a more serious endeavor, we bestowed on them our earnest interest. Luci's conversion to Catholicism, Julie's marriage to David Eisenhower, and Jack's confessional on the subject of marijuana were all big news. The assumption that what young people do is of inherent value and interest has melded with our curiosity about the First Family to guarantee presidential youngsters a large and rapt audience. Indeed, before Ronald Reagan was even inaugurated, his son Ron's wedding to Doria Palmieri rated a picture on the front page of the *New York Times*.

3. One of our newer fads is the notion that old people should be taken seriously. This latest idea derives, of course, from the

growing recognition that the nation's elderly are now so numerous that they are both consumers and voters to be reckoned with. The result?

For the first time in many generations American businesses and government are catering to those over sixty. Another result? Lillian Carter evolved into a "First Mother" like none other in our history. When her son the president decided to send her on a goodwill tour to drought-stricken areas of Africa, or to our own grass roots on whistle-stop tours for Democratic hopefuls, none questioned, at least not out loud, the logic or justification of such forays. To doubt the appropriateness of Miss Lillian's activities would have been to doubt the fitness of all who are gray and lined, and so hardly a protest was raised, hardly even a snicker was heard.

4. People power has its roots in the mythology of democracy—government by the people and for the people—but in the sixties and seventies it took on a new cast. The belief that every citizen with a grievance has the right, nay duty, to shoot off his mouth and shoot from the hip probably received its most recent impetus from the civil rights and stop-the-war movements. The last ten years have witnessed loud protests from groups—blacks, students, and gays, for exmaple—that were heretofore perceived as powerless. Clusters formed around a shared identity or goal and tried, then, to exert their collective muscle. Some of the older groups have by now lost steam, but the syndrome has assumed yet another form in the public interest group—ordinary people joining together on some issue of mutual concern to fight the power elite. I am suggesting that something of this new mood of sympathy and empathy for the common man has colored our perception of the president's kin—perhaps in combination with Watergate, after which a conscious attempt was made to "de-imperialize" the presidency. The most obvious case in point here is the phenomenon of (the early) Billy Carter. The celebration of Billy was a celebration of the common man. Indeed it was an unabashed expression of delight in his vulgarities, vulgarities which we all share to varying degrees but which in our recent history have not been in evidence around presidents. The enormous popularity of naughty Billy must be explained not only by his own idiosyncratic behavior but also by the fact that it tapped something in us. More than Jimmy, Billy *was* us, or at least he was that part of us that still rebelled, that sneered at the trappings of power, that felt equal and even superior to those who held it,

that desperately wanted "in" and was smug about being "out" all at the same time.

5. The fact that we have shed our Victorian postures toward sex, done away in most parts of the country with attempts to regulate the drinking habits of private persons, and taken strides toward the decriminalization and even legalization of marijuana indicates that we have gone far toward stripping away the veneer of what was once considered polite society. One effect of this liberalization is to remove social barriers: when our last two presidents acknowledged that they had sons who smoked "pot," they brought themselves down, in that moment, to our level. Similarly, we learned that Betty Ford—just like a lot of other mothers—had come to terms with the idea that her daughter might actually engage in premarital sex, that Chip and Caron Carter—just like a lot of other all-American couples—had major marital problems, and that the Reagans' younger son had up and married his roommate in quickie hippie fashion at City Hall— *without* his parents in attendance.

The agents of this leveling are almost always members of the president's family. Ford and Carter did not smoke marijuana. Nor did Ford worry aloud about his daughter's virginity. Nor did Rosalynn and Jimmy separate. Still, public confession does hit home, close to the president himself. Yet rather than condemn him for the house he built, we tend now to empathize, relieved perhaps that we live in a time when even presidents are touched by "sin" and none of us have to wear a scarlet letter forever.

6. The last sociocultural change to affect the impact of the president's family—a new honesty, a fuller expression of personal feelings—is implicitly tied to the aforementioned liberalization of attitudes. We can afford to be open only if we can count on a public acquittal. But the new honesty also has roots elsewhere, perhaps most prominently in the trendy but astonishingly influential "encounter groups" in which therapeutic success was said to depend absolutely on the members' willingness to share their most intimate thoughts. "Rap sessions" became the order of the day, "letting it all hang out" a talent and virtue, "coming out of the closet" an act of personal courage, and spilled beans and guts a highly valued means of exchange. Again the effect on the presidential family is indirect, but again it is there to be discerned. To an extent this new mode of interacting has reached the White House, and also, once again, it falls largely to the presi-

dent's kin to practice it. Our last two presidents have both been "blessed" with outspoken relatives. I hardly need chronicle the long list of Betty Ford's shared confidences, and as for Carter's relatives, well, if it was straight talk you wanted, all you had to do was to nab Miss Lillian, or Billy, or Ruth. You might even have tried Rosalynn or Jimmy (of "I've committed adultery in my heart many times" fame) when the moment was right. The reserved and careful silence that characterized presidential families in the past is no longer necessary, or even desirable. The president's kin have been unmuzzled, and the net effect is that they have "up-fronted" themselves right to the forefront of our political and popular culture. Even the Republican Reagans are not immune. Nancy Reagan is decidedly *not* one to disclose all; indeed her autobiography is a veritable model of 1950s reticence and propriety. But the four Reagan children are something else again. Maureen is, within limits, politically outspoken, and Michael has revealed that he has at times felt "left out" of his father's entourage. Patti Davis' life history as part of the "counterculture" is in good part a matter now of public record, and there is every indication that she will attempt, at least, to be open in her newfound role as a show-biz success. (When she found herself in sudden demand after her father's 1980 triumph, she felt compelled to concede that "the extra exposure will help my career.") And although he tries earnestly not to embarrass his parents, Ron Reagan, a ballet dancer, is, by virtue of his chosen profession and life style, a quite public figure.

Roles

If it's here to stay in a big way, we ought to reconsider it. What precisely *is* the First Family?

On the one hand, it is, like all families, a cluster of individuals each of whom is linked to each of the others by blood or marriage. When a president first takes office, he ushers in a new cast of family characters just as he brings in a new administration. They have their own particular relationship to the president, as well as their own particular relationship to the public.

On the other hand, the president's kin are more than an assembly of individuals: they are also a unit. The president's image makers take care to display the First Family as a unified whole, a tribe, a clan, a block held together by affection and for protection. The Kennedys epitomized the point; the many descendants of Joe and Rose were as one. Gatherings of the Irish-American brood that made good still linger in the mind's eye: assorted clapboard houses at the Hyannis compound clustered together, the homes themselves a symbol of family closeness. We were mesmerized not only by the wealth and power gathered here, but by the startling fact that these were enjoyed within a passionately strong family community. Kennedy was the least alone of our recent presidents. At work, inevitably, there was brother Robert. And at play, inevitably, there were numberless relatives gamboling close by. It was, we sensed, a strength.

But to see the president's family as a collective, we need not resort to the most obvious example. Stop for a moment. Close your eyes and see the president away from his desk. From all the evidence at our disposal, the White House has been occupied by only the most dedicated of family men. Eisenhower was the last president to go out and play (golf) with the boys unabashedly and often, and by the time he was in the White House his one son was grown and away from home—like the four children of Ronald Reagan. In the evenings the presidential family watches movies together (when the president is not working late) or reads by the fire together. On weekends the family stays home together, or goes to Camp David together, or to church together, or wherever together. On longer holidays there is an *en famille* migration to the chosen spot—Hyannis or Palm Beach, a ranch by the Pedernales, Key Biscayne or San Clemente, Aspen, down home in Plains, or a ranch 2,400 feet up in the Santa Ynez Mountains. Snapshots abound: the family united in a moment of triumph or tribulation, winning or losing, smiling, weeping. From that moment in the convention hall, when arms are joyously linked in the wake of the winning of the presidential nomination, it is clear that America is about to gain not just a president but also his family. The moment is an early indicator that presidential politics is, like it or not, a family affair.

The sometime evidence notwithstanding, presidents are human. Families provide them, as they do the rest of us, with something they need. Presidents, in fact, usually lean on their families more than most. The reason: "the splendid isolation" of the Oval Office. Lyndon Johnson made the point in the preface of his autobiography: "It has been said the Presidency is the loneliest office in the world. I did not find it so. Even during the darkest hours of my administration, I always knew that I could draw on the strength, support, and love of my family and my friends."[19]

The president's family provides him with all the support any of us receives from our parents, spouse, children, and siblings. But in addition his family helps to fend off the isolation peculiar to his job, lends an ear and may provide advice and analysis, and offers an unswerving loyalty to one frequently under attack.

One-to-one relationships within the family are equally important. They can provide the president with sound advice and loving support, while the relative, in turn, gains a real access to political power. To take the most obvious recent example, virtually every observer of Jimmy Carter the man and the Carter presidency has commented on the unusual intimacy between husband and wife. Although neither elected nor appointed, Rosalynn, through her special relationship to the president and his evident respect for her political intelligence and skill, affected the Carter presidency.

Interestingly, though, in order for presidential relatives to have political impact, they need not have special access to the president—or even be anywhere near the White House. If they can develop a special public appeal, as they easily do, the fact of the kinship is enough to evoke a fervent and widespread public interest. The actual political result will depend, of course, on how ready kin are to make themselves available to the public, and how skillful they are in drawing positive (albeit vicarious) attention to the president. The line between the benefits of publicity and charges of opportunism can be fine. But more often than not the public appetite for presidential relatives in the flesh or on the gossip pages is insatiable, and the president's kin appear increasingly willing to oblige. Until John F. Kennedy came onto the national scene, Jacqueline Bouvier Kennedy was known only to those in the know. But by the time her husband became president, she was transformed into nothing less than a star. At the very least, the glamorous appeal of "Jackie" provided the president with a constant, benign publicity. At the most, this interest translated into good will, support, and even votes.

More specifically, the president's family is a living example of what we may call the symbolic use of politics. Consider the following postures.

The Family as Symbol of Unity

It is hard to say whether the First Family is so often represented as being uncommonly close because it is thought that family unity will serve as a metaphor for national unity or because it is presumed that we will trust the man more if he is the patriarch of a brood in which everyone gets along splendidly with everyone else. In either case, the pressure on presidents to make their families "work right" was evidenced by the January 1979 flap over Billy Carter, who was transformed into, in William Safire's words, "Billy the Problem." Russell Baker wrote, "A child getting divorced, a cousin having a fling at greed, a brother making a fool of himself, are all seized as evidence that the President can't even make a family work right and, by a leap of illogic, that he therefore must be incompetent to preside over the government."[20] Certainly, while the man is a candidate or in office, we are not allowed to see any open conflict within his nuclear family. The "mutual love and respect" among Nixon family members was "reflected in almost everything they do."[21] The executive mansion under the Fords was marked by a "new informality" in which the atmosphere was "happy, free and open."[22] And under Carter, the ideal was realized: "When Jimmy Carter found himself in the White House, sons Chip and Jeff and their wives were right there with him. For the first time since the days of Franklin and Eleanor Roosevelt, the mansion on Pennsylvania Avenue houses an extended family."[23] Even Ronald Reagan's nuclear family—as loose a unit as we've had recently in the White House—joins hands when it really counts.

The Family as Symbol of Stability

Here the family has a twofold function. First, it is trotted out to demonstrate that the president is stable, that is to say that he is a mature and loving man, capable of leading the kind of monogamous, responsible family life Americans typically associate with a healthy male adulthood. The president as playboy will never do, and so that part of him, if it exists, is not to be revealed—at least not while he is president. (Neither will the presidential candidate as *Playboy* portrayed Jimmy Carter in 1976 do. Candidate

Carter received much flack for trying to fit Hugh Hefner's cloth: "I've looked at a lot of women with lust. I've committed adultery in my heart many times."[24]) The president's role as father is sacrosanct. How many endless shots have we seen of Kennedy and Caroline, of Johnson and his "darling daughters" ("Far and away the girls' biggest fan is Daddy . . ."[25]), of Nixon and Tricia or Julie, of Ford and Susan or Jack, etc., and, of course, of Carter and Amy? Every one of our presidents seems to have been to fatherhood born—even the more distant Mr. Reagan, whose virtues as a parent were touted by his wife in her autobiography.

Second, the family comes to symbolize stability insofar as stability implies tradition and predictability. None of us wants an erratic president, and family men are less erratic than those who are fancy free. Perhaps nowhere is this so much in evidence as in our preoccupation with what the president does on any major holiday. Invariably he does the right and same thing, whether that means going to church or to the tomb of the unknown soldier. Invariably, too, he undertakes these traditional activities ensconced in the bosom of his family. Remember these presidential Christmases?

> President and Mrs. Johnson and their older daughter Lynda, 21, began their Christmas day by attending St. Barnabas Episcopal Church. . . . Mr. Johnson gave his wife a camera. Luci's gift to her father was a belt and a buckle. And Lynda gave her parents an album of prints by Hogarth. . . . Christmas dinner, including turkey with cornbread dressing, sweet potatoes with marshmallow on top, vegetables and fruitcake and eggnog, was served at the ranch at 6 P.M. . . .[26]

> President and Mrs. Nixon celebrated Christmas quietly today at the White House with their family and Mrs. Dwight D. Eisenhower. The first family opened their Christmas gifts and their red Christmas stockings, bulging with other presents, in the yellow Oval room of the White House. . . .
>
> Then they gathered for an early roast turkey dinner with Mrs. Eisenhower, their daughter and son-in-law, Julie and David Eisenhower, and their other daughter Tricia. . . .
>
> The President hinted that he wanted lots of books and gave away the secret that he would be giving his wife and daughters jewelry, as was his custom. . . . The President and his family went by helicopter to Camp David late this afternoon. . . .[27]

Offering prayers for peace in the Middle East, President Carter celebrated a traditional Christmas at home with his family. There was
breakfast at his mother's house and Christmas dinner at his mother-
in-law's. . . . The President said that his Christmas presents included an Irish tweed jacket, . . . a pair of binoculars, books, record
albums and two shirts. . . .

Mr. Carter then drove home, changed out of blue jeans and
sweater to a dark blue suit and drove to bible class. . . . Later the
President and his family returned to Mrs. Smith's home for a dinner
of roast turkey with giblet gravy and cornbread dressing, candied
sweet potatoes, green beans, a cheese ring, cranberry sauce, hot
rolls and fruit cake.[28]

The family unit, then, and those shared occasions of celebration
ensure that we the American people know, at least sometimes,
what comes next. The certain knowledge that from year to year
both cast and menu will stay roughly the same is reassuring.

The Family as Symbol of King/Commoner

Depending on the temper of the moment, recent presidents and
their families have been either more royal or more ordinary.
Roughly, we can divide presidents since Kennedy into two
groups: pre- and post-Watergate. The pre-Watergate era culmi-
nated in the "imperial presidency." Not surprisingly, the royal
nimbus rubbed off on the family and on its life style. The Kennedys were not only as beautiful a family as the kings and queens of
fairy tales, they were as rich. In Hyannis and Palm Beach and
Washington, they lived the glamorous life of the beautiful and
powerful people without embarrassment. And after John Kennedy's assassination, his widow "*wanted* Camelot to top the story
[of his presidency]. Camelot, heroes, fairy tales, legends were
what history is all about."[29] The Johnsons, although led by an
earthy patriarch, were nonetheless not quite like the rest of us. It
was well known that they had become millionaires, and when
they left Washington for rest and recreation, it was to reside in
Texas-sized splendor at their huge ranch. When daughter Luci
married Patrick Nugent, the *New York Times* described the ceremony as "unmatched in size, splendor and ritual by the wedding
of any other Presidential daughter in American history."[30] The
Nixon proclivity for the high life is by now well known: from a

Fifth Avenue apartment into the White House, and from there on to Key Biscayne and a Western mansion in San Clemente. There was also a formality here. Tricia and Julie, for example, offered a striking contrast to the then current draft-card burners and hippies. If either of them ever wore slacks (not to speak of jeans!), we certainly were never privy to the secret.

All of this came to a hasty end with Watergate. The Ford and Carter presidencies had a studied modesty about them which is neither coincidental nor, as the Fords subsequent building of a Palm Springs estate indicates, necessarily an honest preference. These most recent presidents emphasized not the differences between them and us, but the similarities. The Fords moved to the White House from an ordinary suburban home where the pool, the press allowed, "swallowed up the whole backyard." Betty was like other housewives, sacrificing for husband and children—children who were wholesome, athletic, and clad in denim. Time off was spent in a ski condominium in Aspen where the style was less luxurious than sporty. And parties at the Ford White House were "warm and genial—like a party in a private house, not a formal function in an official residence."[31]

The Carters probably carried all of this as far as possible (though later the president and his family retreated from the initial stance of "just folks"): Carter himself in blue jeans running peanuts from the farm through his fingers; the family strolling down the street casually, unceremoniously, just after the inauguration; Amy noisily enrolled in a public school; Carter addressing the nation by the fire clad in a knit cardigan; retreats from Washington confined to (government-owned) Camp David or the family home in Plains; Chip and Caron openly admitting marital troubles (and then reconciling and then separating again); entertainments limited (at first) to aperitifs and white wine, with menus in English and early-to-bed hosts; and a family at large notable for idiosyncracies which seemed to epitomize what is commonly thought to be the common man.

Nancy and Ronald Reagan give early indications of a shift back (or forward) to a greater emphasis on style, fashion, and social activity. The Reagans are accustomed to living well, dressing well, and eating well. For the time being, the apex of the down-home presidency has been reached: the country is ready for, and is getting, a return to a more traditional, lofty elegance in the White House.

The way we see the president's family is a by-product of the way we see the president. Our earliest tendency, as children, is to idealize him. The adult counterpart is our wish to see him as endowed with superhuman powers and to demand from him a superhuman performance. As part of this our leader becomes also a sort of quasi-king to us. It is really not terribly surprising, then, that our curiosity vis-à-vis his quasi-queen and all the other royal relatives is endlessly piqued. We have only to look at the English and their tireless fascination with the births, deaths, marriages, divorces, beddings, and petulances of the royal family to see another, classic example of this passion—a passion which, as we are about to see, is manifested in idealized expectations, rose-colored perceptions, and finally, sometimes, hurt disappointment.

Why, just before a new president is about to take office and in the early months of his first administration, do we so ache to exalt the man and his family that we find qualities in them that they do not have? Clearly our ignorance then is bliss, and we can vent the urge to crown and deify. It is a period of rebirth, of optimism and foolish hope, when "any journalist worth his salt writes at least a couple of articles about the new political era and new political style, and even journalists not worth their salt, though oppressed by their shortcoming, manage nonetheless."[32]

With similar verve, they write about an idealized family: Nixon's family was "close with mutual love and respect";[33] when Ford was first made vice-president, his family was described as "the closest in Washington";[34] and a few months after Carter had taken office, the *New York Times* noted admiringly how "Carter's Extended Family Puts a Southern Tradition to Work."[35] Even the relatively fragmented Reagans (a situation fostered in part by the fact that the two older offspring are from an earlier marriage to actress Jane Wyman) fell into line: the four children, *People* magazine avowed in its July 21 issue just after the 1980 Republican convention, "show an unmistakable fondness for and loyalty toward their father."

It is noteworthy that even as the president becomes tarnished by time and decisions, his family remains relatively unscathed. Gallup's list of "most admired women" is perennially laden with First Ladies past and present and other women relatives of the president. According to the Gallup Opinion Index of January 1975, during 1974 six out of the ten most admired women were related to Chief Executives. And in a cumulative survey of the most admired women of the last fifteen years, Jacqueline Kennedy places first, Mamie Eisenhower second, Lady Bird Johnson fourth, Pat Nixon fifth, Rose Kennedy sixth, and Ethel Kennedy tenth. While perhaps this list says more about the lack of female role models than anything else, it is also a symptom of our weakness for gods—and goddesses.

But many of us come not to idealize the president's family, but to praise it, seeing it not as a paragon of virtue, but simply as a good group that made good. This state of grace is apt to last at least as long as the man is in office, as if, although the president is fair game, his family is not. This syndrome too is most prevalent at the beginning of a new administration: in the first blush of love, warts don't register.

Soon after Gerald Ford moved into the Oval Office, *Vogue* featured an article titled "As American as Betty Ford":

> Households in every town, city, and especially suburb in America are wived by Betty Fords, pre-liberated women of intelligence and talent who have accepted motherhood as an ideal, the fostering of a husband's career as a duty. They draw their self-image and satisfaction from their families, often not without cost to themselves—a price they have paid willingly.[36]

Although this statement seems ironic and sad in light of later revelations about Mrs. Ford's problem with drugs and alcohol, it typifies our tendency to see quick good in those who accompany the president to power—especially First Ladies. Even family members remote from Washington get such hype. To wit, what *Time* said about Billy Carter just after his brother was elected:

> Billy is also a family man; the beer hour never prevents him from sitting down to dinner with Sybil and their six children who range in age from six months to twenty years. He is also a bang-up businessman who in the past six years has raised the gross of the family peanut business from $800,000 to $4 million plus. . . . He [also] reads from Georgia papers each day as well as three books a week (Faulkner is a favorite).[37]

In fact, the tendency to praise presidents' families goes back even further, to when the man first emerges as a viable candidate. Again the Carters illustrate the point. In the summer of 1976, *Time* ran an article on the entire clan, "The Carters: Spreading like Moss." It was a fairly long essay and carried nary a discouraging word about anyone. Rosalynn: "a comely woman with soft,

almost feline movements and hazel eyes to match" whose performance as the First Lady of Georgia was "nearly flawless."
Miss Lillian: a "redoubtable personality who would have fascinated William Faulkner and Bertolt Brecht." The three Carter
sons: all quality chips off the old block—Jack, although a law
school graduate, "has yet to try any cases because he is too busy
working for Dad"; Chip, according to a Carter aide, "is smart,
has good instincts and works harder than the rest"; and Jeff, although shy, was dedicated and "working on a degree in government . . . and wants to become an urban planner." Amy, the cherished only daughter and youngest child: "a frisky, freckled,
strawberry blonde who looks like Huck Finn's kid sister with the
inevitable Carter smile [and who] basks in all the attention without letting it turn her head." And Carter's three siblings provided
their earnest brother with an earthy glow. Ruth Stapleton: the
"one-time high school beauty queen who has by no means lost
her looks [and who] discovered the healing powers of Christ during a period of bleak despair in the early years of her marriage."
Gloria Spann, Jimmy's oldest sister: the "clan cutup" who enjoyed "teaching art, decorating jeans with paint and decals and
roaring around on one of her two Honda motorcycles."[38] And as
for Billy, well, we have already seen what *Time* thought about
Billy—at least then.

The president's family, though, gets all the attention and
praise only at a price: adherence to unspoken yet nonetheless
quite clearly extant rules of behavior. The rules change over
time, as we have seen, but only gradually, so that even in this era
of liberation we basically expect family members to behave in a
certain way. If they do not, someone will yell. The rules shift
according to the fads and temper of the year, the perceived personality of the presidential relative, the age and sex involved, and
the nature of the relationship to the president. But if we could put
them under a single heading, that heading might be "DECO-
RUM." We expect of the president's family propriety of behavior,
speech, dress, values, and morals. If there is a deviation from the
requirements of polite society, and if this deviation does not have
the blessing of youth, fashion, or amusing idiosyncracy, fault will
be found. (How happy for the Reagans that son Ron wed his
roommate *before* the inauguration!)

The praise heaped on Betty Ford and Billy Carter has its cor-
relate here. When Moreley Safer of CBS's "60 Minutes" asked

First Lady Betty Ford how she would respond if her daughter
came to her and told her she was having an affair, and Mrs. Ford
began her answer with "Well, I wouldn't be surprised, I think
she's a perfectly normal human being like all young girls," and
continued in the same moderate vein, she provoked an outcry.
(Jimmy Carter, who was funnier before he became president, said
in response to the same question that he would be "shocked and
overwhelmed. But then my daughter is only seven.") To be sure,
the president's wife received widespread support (60% according
to a Harris poll). But all she was doing was supporting the norm.
All the more remarkable, then, that a considerable minority was
outraged.

> A number of remarks made by Betty Ford in her CBS interview . . .
> represent a manifest abuse of her position as First Lady. They con-
> stituted a failure of taste that reflected a failure of understand-
> ing. . . . Mrs. Ford ought to know that it is not up to her to rewrite
> the Ten Commandments over nationwide T.V. . . .[39]

Although she had scarcely been radical, given the prevailing
moral code, this kind of negative reaction indicated once again
that speaking freely is only under certain circumstances an acknowledged prerogative of the president's family.

Billy Carter was turned from paragon to pariah before the
worst had even come. Although, like Betty Ford, he had his ad-
mirers, the press quickly got fed up. *Time*, the former fawner,
epitomized the switch:

> Never in U.S. history has a presidential relative engaged in such
> aggressively crass exploitatic ¯ of a genetic coincidence. . . .
>   Something is decidedly wrong with the spectacle of Billy
> Carter. . . . He is, after all, the President's brother, and his attraction
> depends on that presidential nimbus. Watergate discredited the
> presidency, but it does not follow that the office therefore deserves
> to be treated cheaply. . . . Billy Carter is hardly subverting the Re-
> public by being tacky, but the psychodrama of his celebrity does not
> add much shine to the leader of the free world.[40]

Once again, a presidential relative had violated the unwritten
code of behavior. For being a money-hungry publicity seeker, he
was called to task.

But there is an important caveat here: the family tends *not* to
be blamed in matters that might be considered of *real* significance—as long as these are confined to the private sphere. (If

First Family "sins" spill over into our public affairs, the response will be different—as in "Billygate.") Whatever the press knows about the private failures and flaws of family, it tends to mute or even suppress them while the president is in office. There was no hint while Ford was president of the real nature of some of Betty Ford's problems. We heard more often than not about a "pinched nerve" keeping her out of commission, and even a more honest account, such as this rare one in *Newsweek,* left the reader to infer:

> Her movements [after a year in the White House] often seem stiffer and more deliberate than before, her pauses longer, and there are new signs of strain under her eye make-up. What her ups and downs in Europe suggested was not a recurrence of her cancer but a reminder that she is, beneath her obvious good spirits and her apparent good health, a fragile woman—and that the stamina she could bring to a presidential campaign and a full term in the White House remains very much an open question.[41]

There was further evidence in the virtual concealment, during the early years of Carter, of the fact that the son of his "cutup" sister Gloria Spann, William Carter Spann, was doing time for armed robbery in a California penitentiary. In line with the overwhelming inclination to idealize and praise the president's family, there is a powerful disinclination for the press to publicize, and the public to perceive, serious flaws. This disinclination is more than good manners. It grows out of a reluctance to undercut one of the few remaining preserves of traditional values.

By this time it should be apparent that presidential parents, wives, children, and siblings do, nowadays, play *some* kind of a role in presidential politics. But surely they don't all play exactly the same role. Nor would it even be logical to assume that all First Ladies play the same role, all children the same role, and so on. On the contrary: as the presidents' kin became familiar and the literature was canvassed, what emerged were six different ways for family members to contribute positively to presidential politics—*six functional roles,* if you will—which were independent of age, sex, and relationship to the Chief Executive. Consider our first examples, in Chapter 2: In fine detail Jacqueline Kennedy and Amy Carter have precious little in common. Yet in their broad political strokes—in what they did for the president (for his candidacy and presidency) and to the public—it is the similarities that are striking. In functional terms they were much alike.

The six roles have been labeled Decorations, Extensions, Humanizers, Helpmeets, Moral Supports, and Alter Egos. Although they go far toward helping us to see how family members exercise political impact and how they come to serve the president's ends, they should not be seen as rigorously distinct. They are designed to illustrate modes or types of political activity. They are not boxes into which any single individual (not to speak of two or more) will fit exactly. The claim for the scheme is built on the following common-sense notions: presidential relatives who have political impact take on their particular roles early in the administration, even during the campaign; these roles differ from each other just as the personalities and interactions of all concerned must differ; these differences, though, given the constancies of both family life and the Oval Office, are circumscribed; and, finally, although the roles are not mutually exclusive, that is, any relative can assume aspects of roles other than the one to which he/she is assigned, one type of political activity will emerge as predominant.

The following six chapters will present the six roles in order of ascending political importance and consider how our cast—characters such as the young Edward Kennedy, the four children of Gerald Ford, Lady Bird Johnson, Julie Nixon Eisenhower, and Robert Kennedy—performed in them. It is of special interest to see specifically and exactly how the president's kin exercised a positive political impact, and to that end we will look at two people in most of the six roles. Seeing ostensibly different types such as Betty Ford and Billy Carter play the same part will allow us to see the idiosyncracies of their performances right alongside the remarkable similarities.

The six chapters on the functional roles will be followed by one titled "Skeletons." It will discuss four different relatives (of four different presidents) who were considered to be *dysfunctional,* and who were as a consequence hidden from public view.

Finally we will question "The Family Legacy." Who does it serve? Is it good? And what, in the increasingly popular game of family politics, can we look forward to?

CHAPTER 2

Decorations

Decorations make the president more attractive. They enhance the man, make him and his administration at the most more glamorous and at the least more appealing. They add nothing to the substance of the presidency but a great deal to the style. They lend an intangible aura of pleasure to the grit of day-to-day politics; their presence alone lends grace. At their best, Decorations are in fact quite removed from politics. In what would appear, but only at first glance, to be a paradox, it is this distance that allows their charm to exert its political impact.

Jacqueline Kennedy and Amy Carter are Decorations. They must, then, by definition, "make the president more attractive." But to whom? To the public, of course, a public that craves anything beautiful, stylish, or winning, and relishes it all the more when the object of attention is close to the epicenter of political power in America. Our reaction to Decorations is uncomplicated: a simple delight that comes from seeing something nice. They need never be heard. To be glimpsed is enough, and the picture, therefore, is the message. The Decoration must be *seen*—on television, in the newspapers, in magazines, or in person.

The president can be a passive bystander in this exchange. While he is the actual magnet—after all, this other person is the *president's* kin—his actual presence is immaterial to the attraction a Decoration gradually comes to hold. For a Decoration to have political impact, the president need not be around, or even nearby; the two do not even have to interact very much. Yet the president is plainly the most important beneficiary of the positive fallout. A glamorous wife lends glamour to the president, and indeed to the entire administration. A funny, winning child lends him appeal.

How does someone qualify to be a Decoration, and then actually become one? The chief requisite is to be physically appealing. Since the communicating between a Decoration and the public is done largely through pictures, these must reflect something to which great numbers of people are immediately and repeatedly attracted. Moreover, there must be an idiosyncratic aspect; to be pleasantly attractive but average will not suffice (though to be a young child is idiosyncratic enough in the adult world of presidential politics). A Decoration must stand out just enough to become an instantly recognizable symbol of sorts, so that even a momentary glance will evoke both the pleasure which defines the role and the association with the husband, father, or brother who is president.

Decorations should also be removed from politics. To evoke pure pleasure, they have to remain unsullied, hence separate from the grubbiness of *Realpolitik*. Indeed, it is the contrast between the apparent chasteness of Decorations and the infestation of the political world from which they seem to have emerged unscathed that allows for the uncomplicated public fascination. They are *of* presidential politics but not really *in* it. And from their perch, outside and above, they bestow a grace.

Finally, Decorations must make public appearances. Not too many, for too much of even a good thing will satiate soon. Rather, public displays—access if you will—must be scheduled and programmed, spaced out in time, and staged to attract just the right amount of attention. Furthermore, the ideal must be realized with almost total consistency. For a Decoration to be seen in an inappropriate guise or manner, even once, is to rob people of their fantasy. In fact, a Decoration is a fragile commodity: unless it works really well, it does not work at all.

A timely reminder: *decorations play a functional role.* I have said that they add nothing to the substance of the presidency (at least nothing we can point to with certainty). But they do add to the style of an administration; they do temper the climate in which it is received; and they do adorn the president himself. Obviously, then, any president with one or more Decorations in tow can count himself lucky indeed.

Children are the most likely Decorations. While Kennedy

was president, daughter Caroline was certainly the most photographed child in the world, and infant son John-John was the
object of boundless curiosity and good feeling. (Ben Bradlee reported that the Kennedys were "appalled by the national hunger
for news and pictures of [Caroline] and John-John and wonder if
they can keep them unspoiled."[1]) The cuteness of these two leapt
out of the simplest snapshot, and their innocent appeal separated
them from the stolidly adult world of presidential politics—of
which they were nonetheless a part. Like most young children,
they could be shown off or kept from public view at the discretion
of their parents. And when they were on display, they could usually be counted on to do something unpredictable and, given the
setting, really quite funny.

Animals have also served as Decorations; in fact, they have
served very well. And why not? What could be more removed,
innocent, and unpredictable than an Irish setter? Dogs do indeed
abound in the White House, and unless a president is foolish
enough to pull them by their ears (as Lyndon Johnson did with
his beagles), they will invariably win the Chief Executive some
sympathy. A pony will do the same. Mrs. Kennedy's social secretary recalled, "Perusing this mail made one realize that there
were thousands of little souls praying to God that the pony Maca-
roni was not suffering from the snowstorm that had just passed
through Washington. . . ."[2]

For an adult, though, to be a Decoration, as Jacqueline Kennedy so clearly was, is uncommon. The mix of instant physical
appeal and a thoroughgoing distance from real-world politics is
rare in a presidential parent, wife, or sibling. Perhaps that is why,
when it happened, in the person of the reigning queen of Camelot, its impact was so great.

Jacqueline Kennedy

Contemporary historians have found it difficult to discuss, not to
speak of assess, the relationship between President John F. Kennedy and his wife Jacqueline. Partly out of tact, partly out of ignorance, and partly because it was in the tradition to do so anyway,
most serious observers have treated the issue by avoiding it.
(This is in contrast to "pop writers." See, for example, Kitty
Kelly's *Jackie Oh!* if your passion is for a gossipy account of the

Kennedys' marriage.) And now, perhaps as a reaction to what is seen as the excessive romanticism of the Kennedy era, our recollections of that marriage are being crowded out by newer and more sensational stories of the president and his extramarital escapades. These tales, some of which have the ring of truth, have fit perfectly into the world of the late seventies and early eighties, in which a realistic appraisal of America has become equated with the expectation of its decline. The net effect, though, has been to wash away, or worse yet to mock, the memory of what the marriage was really like.

It is in fact not important to this particular enterprise to know "the Truth" about the interaction between John and Jacqueline Kennedy. But it is important to remind ourselves of what it, and the two people themselves, *appeared* to be. T. H. White remembers trying to write an epitaph of the Kennedy administration, one week after the assassination, in the presence of the president's widow:

> At 2 A.M. I was dictating the story from the Kennedy kitchen to two of my favorite editors . . . who, as good editors, despite a ballooning overtime printing bill, were nonetheless trying to edit and change phrases as I dictated. Maness [one of the editors] observed that maybe I had too much of "Camelot" in the dispatch. Mrs. Kennedy had come in at that moment; she overheard the editor trying to edit me, who had already so heavily edited her. She shook her head. She *wanted* Camelot to top the story. Camelot, heroes, fairy tales, legends were what history was all about. Maness caught the tone in my reply as I insisted this had to be done as Camelot. . . .
>
> So the epitaph on the Kennedy Administration became Camelot—a magic moment in American history. . . . Which, of course, is a misreading of history. The magic Camelot of John F. Kennedy never existed. . . .[3]

This avoidance of reality in favor of a chocolate-coated sweet may seem regrettable and even wrong now. But then we not only swallowed the sweet whole but savored the taste.

To understand the political impact of Jackie Kennedy as a Decoration, we must travel back to that (seemingly) simpler time when appearances were enough. I have said that Decorations provide the artless pleasure which comes from "seeing something nice." Thus it is no coincidence that the single adult who qualifies as a Decoration served an administration in which appearances played a large part. Kennedy and the men around him

appeared to be "the best and the brightest." And so did the First
Lady. While she was in the White House, no woman seemed to
be better at what women were then supposed to be good at; the
star of no other woman in America shone as brightly.

Jackie Kennedy's function was to adorn, and in any case,
whatever the relationship between the President and Mrs. Kennedy, it seems safe to assume that it did not include much hot
debate about political matters. In John Kennedy's life, the world
of work was populated virtually exclusively by men. Women were
to assume the traditional roles. His wife's political impact was
derived from the fascination she had for an endlessly entertained
public and from some men in positions of political power who
found her equally enchanting. Thus John Kennedy was extra-
neous to his wife's political life, although he was certainly its
main beneficiary.

From the beginning, Jacqueline Bouvier Kennedy was not
like other Kennedy women. Born in 1929 to a family of class and
wealth, she had had a good cosmopolitan education (she was at
Vassar for two years; her junior year was spent in France; and she
received her B.A. from George Washington University) before
taking a job as the "Inquiring Camera Girl" for the *Washington
Times-Herald.* "Her natural habitat was the international world
of society and art . . . and her response to life was aesthetic rather
than intellectual or moralistic."[4] The Kennedys were more nar-
rowly based. Their exposure to the social discrimination against
the Boston Irish was recent; their experience with family triumph and tragedy intimate and binding; their affiliation with the
Catholic church strong; their passion for politics all-consuming;
their ambition extreme; and their dedication to clannish togetherness a major determinant in how they lived their lives.

Although the Kennedy women themselves did not participate
in politics, it was an old family tradition that they should be right
alongside their men who did. Mother Rose Fitzgerald Kennedy
had set the pattern. Raised in very comfortable circumstances,
attending exclusive private convents in Europe, she took to public life like a duck to water: as the daughter of the legendary
mayor of Boston, John Francis "Honey Fitz" Fitzgerald, she had
tooled around the city by his side even as a young child. Subsequently, she served as the model companion to Joseph P. Kennedy in his varied careers in business and government. It was an

ideal both her daughters and daughters-in-law were expected to
follow, and by the time John Kennedy ran for president, it was
clear the lesson had been learned well. Rose Kennedy and three
of her daughters—Eunice Shriver, Patricia Lawford, and Jean
Smith—were all on hand to help campaign. All four were the
politician's perfect woman: ready, willing, and able to serve.
Serving meant appearing in public, often, at any time, if necessary on short notice, smiling, shaking hands, many hands, saying
nothing of substance, praising the candidate, remembering short
appealing family-type anecdotes, and, above all, being prepared
to follow the instructions of the men in charge on where to go,
what to do once there, and when to do it.

But as I said, Jacqueline Kennedy was different. Not only did
she not share the upbringing of the Kennedy women or their robust competitiveness or their clannishness; above all she did not
share their lusty ease in the manly world of politics. Although
she had been forewarned—upon their marriage in 1953 John
Kennedy was already an up-and-coming senator from Massachusetts—there was never really any time when Jacqueline was terribly interested, involved, or busy participating in her husband's
political career. Whatever the motivating forces, there had always
been a distance, perhaps even an alienation from the politics
which so entranced almost all the other Kennedys. Ben Bradlee,
a long-time Kennedy family friend, recalls Mrs. Kennedy in the
late 50s:

> I remember most watching Jackie, and the almost physical discom-
> fort she showed as she walked slowly into this crowded hall to get
> stared at—not talked to, just simply stared at. Her reaction, later to
> become so familiar, was simply to pull some invisible shade down
> across her face and cut out spiritually.[5]

In spite of Jacqueline Kennedy's problems with the public,
she was enormously successful with it—and indeed I am suggesting a causal relationship here: much of Mrs. Kennedy's appeal to the people derived from her distance from them. Objec-
tively, according to the measures of beauty, class, wealth, and
proximity to power, she was above most other people. And sub-
jectively, it seemed she saw herself as, at least, different from
them. This interplay between reserve on her part and effusive
acceptance on ours is strikingly illustrated in this recollection by
a California politician:

I came to the conclusion that [Mrs. Kennedy] really didn't like politics very much and she didn't really like politicians or people connected with it very much. She was, of course, always perfectly
charming to everybody. . . . I found out quickly that she didn't want
to go into a room that was full of people. . . . My own feeling was
that she was really shy about this kind of people, that she couldn't
relate easily to the miscellaneous sorts of individuals that you'd find
in the political context. . . .

[She made an enormously favorable impression by] just the way
she walked into a room or the way she stood up at a table when she
was introduced and smiled; that was all she ever had to do. Oh, they
adored her, but I don't think she knew who they were, any of
them. . . . She didn't seem to want to be present when political matters were discussed, as though this were not a part of her life. . . .
She was a very private kind of person basically, with charm and
brains and infinite capacity to win people without doing anything
much more than just standing up and sitting down.[6]

Yet even by the time Mrs. Kennedy found herself wife of the
president-elect, she had had precious little contact with the public. In fact, her role in the 1960 campaign was minimal. Although her pregnancy was a mitigating circumstance—the Kennedy's second child was born just weeks after the election—it is
nonetheless striking that in perhaps the most complete record of
that campaign there is virtually no reference to Jackie.[7]

As of January 1961, things changed. When John Kennedy became president, Jacqueline Kennedy's aesthetic, almost ethereal
qualities were finally used, by all concerned, to real advantage.
Occupying the throne suited her better than fighting to gain it.
She was, it immediately seemed, to the position of First Lady
born. Mrs. Kennedy was not like you and me, or like other political wives or other Kennedys, and with the prize of the presidency
in hand these differences came to be an advantage. It was not
overstating the case to write that this was a "First Lady of such
beauty, elegance, taste, and culture that her effect during her husband's time of office was to influence, for the better, the culture
of the country."[8]

The reason we were able to accept Mrs. Kennedy's extravagant style so quickly and uncritically was that we saw her first of
all as a devoted, responsible wife and mother. She publicly labored to turn her husband's home into the perfect presidential
domicile, and although we knew that she had a bevy of nannies
and maids to help cope with the children, she laid so much stress

on her maternal duties that we believed her: "My major effort must be devoted to my children. I feel very strongly that if they do not grow up as happy and secure individuals ... nothing that I could accomplish in the public eye would give me satisfaction."[9] The combination, then, was of homebody and fantasy figure. The second image was dependent on the first, and the responsibilities of motherhood especially were used to explain the very inaccessibility which allowed the fantasy to survive for so long.

I have spoken of Decorations as being primarily a creation of their own appearance, and so it is only fitting that with Jacqueline Kennedy, we begin with how she looked. Unadorned she was lovely. Called everything from "reigning beauty" to "charmer," she had an unusual handsomeness that also bespoke her monied, upper-class origins. Her voice (when we heard it) was barely above a whisper, and her body movements seemed always tenuously balanced between those of a child and those of an assured, well-bred race horse. No coincidence perhaps. Horseback riding was a favorite activity of Jacqueline Kennedy, and there were many pictures of her in riding gear. For all this femininity, however, there was also a steely quality here. This apparently delicate, quiet woman never seemed anyone's fool, and indeed there was more than a touch of imperiousness. A photographer from *Look* remembered feeling that "Mrs. Kennedy had a kind of way with her that sort of strikes terror to your heart. She was a very strong-minded girl and very tough."[10]

As everyone who hasn't been living in a cave for the last two decades knows by now, Mrs. Kennedy did not depend on her natural assets alone. She made a supreme effort to clothe and present herself in the best way that money and impeccable taste made possible. The effort paid off. Not only was the woman herself perfectly ravishing in virtually every public appearance, but the women of America, and indeed the entire "civilized" world, were so impressed, that they took on her style as their own. Not even the Soviet bloc could resist. The Polish magazine *Swiat* named Jacqueline Kennedy among those setting the tone and style of the sixties for women around the world. The "Jackie look" grabbed feminine fancies and, for the duration of John Kennedy's presidency and beyond, would not let go.

By Inauguration Day, Mrs. Kennedy's dresses, suits, coats, gloves, shoes, purses and hats were sweeping across America and around the world. Almost overnight, America discarded the last of its ruf-

fles, tight belts and bows. Millinery shops sold the largest collection
of back-of-the-head pillbox hats in their history. Beauty shops reported that women . . . wanted their hair artfully teased into the
bouffant Kennedy coiffure. Stores found themselves selling the
low-heeled shoes, alligator handbags, little white gloves, and elbow-
length kid gloves, great coats and small furs that Mrs. Kennedy favored. . . .[11]

And in addition to making every "ordinary" public appearance an
event only by dint of her own appearance, Mrs. Kennedy made
certain that on special occasions she would not disappoint.

Her clothes [on a 1961 trip to Paris with her husband] were sensational. . . . For the gala at Versailles she wore a white satin Given-
chy ballgown, with matching coat. . . . Her photograph, judging by
the press clippings sent to us, made the front page of every gazette
from Madagascar to Outer Mongolia.[12]

There was a powerful corollary to Jackie Kennedy's personal
style in the way she breathed new life into the White House. During the Truman and Eisenhower administrations, 1600 Pennsylvania Avenue had not exactly been a hotbed of social activity, nor
had it been a trend setter in anything. As of early 1961, all that
also changed. Perhaps the fact that the appointment of the famed
French chef René Verdon to the position of head chef at the
White House made the front page of the *New York Times* says it
all. The story was, like all the stories on Mrs. Kennedy's clothes,
as fluffy and evanescent as a cumulus cloud. Yet the positioning
of such an item on the front page of our most prestigious newspaper was no accident. Such happenings were seen as no less than
symbols of an optimistic new era, and of America's coming of age
in a fresh time of cultural and artistic maturity.

Social events at the White House were not only upgraded,
they were modernized. Now there was bright, happy music by the
Marine Band. Drinks were passed around on trays. Social aides
were hired to get everyone talking. Fresh paint was washed on
the dining-room walls. Round tables for from eight to ten were
installed. And new, low floral arrangements became the order of
the day. (Pamela Turnure, Mrs. Kennedy's press secretary, had
earnestly announced that "Mrs. Kennedy wants the White House
to look more like a country home with dainty arrangements. The
flowers must not look as if they had come from a florist. . . ."[13])
The net effect was to impress and delight. After one White House

dinner, *Washington Star* columnist Betty Beale was moved to summarize the prevailing opinion: "[There should be] an end for the time being to any question as to who is now the number one hostess in Washington. First Ladies have always held this title in name, but Jacqueline Kennedy now holds it in fact."[14] Historian Arthur Schlesinger, Jr., hardly one to gush, concurred. State dinners became "elegant and cheerful parties, beautifully mingling informality and dignity," while the smaller dinner parties were "blithe and enchanted evenings."[15]

What gave White House entertaining during these years its really special éclat, however, was the overall guest list. It was studded with names of persons both great and famous, most exceptionally from the worlds of art, music, and literature. Guests ranged from Carl Sandburg to Igor Stravinsky, from Aaron Copeland to Robert Frost, from Leonard Bernstein to Andrew Wyeth. One evening was given over to winners of the Nobel prize only. And the entertainments were, it was said, something to behold: orchestras, opera singers, Shakespeare, and an evening with master cellist Pablo Casals that has since become legend.

Every modern First Lady also has a special project of sorts, and Mrs. Kennedy managed to find one perfect for her particular skills and interests: the restoration of the White House. It was, moreover, a task that was wonderfully appropriate to the position of the president's wife as she had come to define it. It would keep her around the (White) house, and it was in an area suitable for a woman of her taste and culture. It would also enhance the image of her husband and his administration, yet at the same time maintain her own posture as one completely removed from politics.

As in her personal appearance and her entertaining, Mrs. Kennedy excelled. She was actively involved in the project only some of the time, but when she was not, her interest and blessing alone were enough to give it the necessary momentum. There were some who criticized the effort to recover from around the country the old objects with which past presidents had furnished the White House, but the First Lady was firm: "The White House does and must continue to represent the living, evolving character of the executive branch of the national government. Its occupants have been persons of . . . different . . . backgrounds and tastes. . . . It would, therefore, be inadvisable . . . to fix on a single style . . . for a building that ought to reflect the whole history of the presidency."[16]

The Congress was persuaded to designate the executive mansion as a national museum. Personal campaigns were undertaken to secure gifts of furniture and dollars to the cause. And three commissions were formed: the White House Historical Association, Committee of the Fine Arts Commission for the White House, and the Advisory Committee to the Fine Arts Commission. "Every gallery and museum in the country, it seemed, was laying its treasures at Jackie's feet for her to pick and choose from."[17] An administrator for the General Services Administration (who thought Mrs. Kennedy did a "fantastic job" at the White House) remembers "Mrs. Kennedy calling me to see if we had, at Archives, busts of Presidents Jackson, Roosevelt and Jefferson to use in the little niches above the doorways in the Cabinet Room. She always had a great interest in all of these details."[18] Much publicity was given to her discovery—apparently in the White House basement—of a great carved oak desk from the timbers of a British frigate. It was promptly installed in the president's office. And *Life* was satisfied to do no less than an eleven-page cover story on how the First Lady was bringing "history and beauty to the White House."[19]

Because of her evident taste and cultural interests, Jacqueline Kennedy also became associated in the minds of many with the arts in America. She was made honorary national chairman of the National Cultural Center, and her name was used to drum up interest in the notion of bringing culture to Washington, which had heretofore been considered something of a cultural backwater. Interestingly, the effort met with some success during that time, but this was more the result of the concern Mrs. Kennedy stimulated than any specific activities she undertook. She had created the necessary climate, and that was almost sufficient. The actual tasks were left to others. August Heckscher, then special consultant to the president on the arts, remembers her reluctant but nonetheless effective role:

> [With respect to the arts, Mrs. Kennedy] was a somewhat ambivalent figure. In the first place, she was devoted to [her] private life . . . and yet, on the other hand, she found that she was becoming more and more the representative of a bright flame of cultural interest in this country. Sometimes she seemed to draw back as if she didn't want to get too much involved. . . . Mrs. Kennedy . . . was much too wise to be busy every moment promoting the arts. She would do one thing with superb taste and it would have tremendous impact.

Although promising "anything for the arts," she added, "But, of course, I can't be away too much from the children. . . . After all, I'm not Mrs. Roosevelt."[20]

She had, of course, only to mention "the children," who were themselves enchanting Decorations, to give the perfect excuse for not being more involved.

Probably no single thing Mrs. Kennedy did during her tenure as First Lady did as much to focus attention on her and her particular interests—the restoration of the White House and the arts in general—as her televised tour of the new White House in February 1962. There were a few naysayers—Norman Mailer wrote in *Esquire* that she walked through the program "like a starlet who is utterly without talent"—but on the whole, the show met with great personal success. It was agreed that it was an extraordinary program that raised a great deal of popular interest in Mrs. Kennedy and the arts and the president himself, and Heckscher recalled a moment during the show which wonderfully illustrates Jacqueline Kennedy's withdrawal from "the real world of politics" and her concomitant impact in those areas which she had carved out as her very own:

> I remember at the time, the reporter asked Mrs. Kennedy, as they were walking through the White House, looking at paintings and all, "Mrs. Kennedy, what do you think the government's relation to the arts ought to be?" And she answered it so perfectly. She said, "Good Heavens, that's much too complicated a question for me to answer. But look, here is a painting that I think is very beautiful."[21]

We have conflicting reports on the president's reaction to all the excitement this show aroused. Arthur Schlesinger writes that Kennedy "viewed the program with great satisfaction,"[22] while Ben Bradlee, who watched it along with Kennedy in the White House, remembers that the president "was obviously not particularly pleased" with his own small role on the show, or with his performance in it. Bradlee's wife concluded, as he put it, that the president was "actually jealous of Jackie's performance and the attention she got as a result."[23]

The reputation of Mrs. Kennedy as a star attraction seemed to increase geometrically as time went on. Whether the chicken or the egg came first doesn't much matter, but her successes on her travels abroad either contributed to or benefited from this burgeoning attention. Her command of Spanish and French helped,

and on trips to Canada, France, Austria, England, Greece, Venezuela, Colombia, India, Pakistan, and Mexico, as soon as she
came, she conquered. Her first trip to Europe, in the company of
her husband scarcely four months after he became president, set
the startling pattern. In country after country she had no less
than a personal triumph—all of which was, of course, promptly
relayed to the folks back at home.

France was the epitome, predictably perhaps, as Jacqueline
was a devoted Francophile. Some of her ancestors had been
French, and her taste for French food, clothes, and culture was
well known and truly felt. Immediately there was a resonance
here, a resonance between the French people and this young,
beautiful American woman, married to the president, who
seemed to personify the possibility that not all Americans were
Philistines. "The Parisians cheered the President, but it was now
apparent that it was his wife whom they adored. . . . It had the air
of a startled rediscovery of America as a new society, young and
cosmopolitan and sophisticated, capable of aspiring to the leadership of the civilized peoples."[24]

A trip to India and Pakistan in March 1962, on which Mrs.
Kennedy was accompanied by her sister, Lee Radziwill, made a
similarly stupendous impression. This voyage was undertaken
without the president; the focus, therefore, was on the First
Lady. Here she was called "Amerika Maharani," the Queen of
America; and above all, again, she looked the part. She had taken
along a dazzlingly large and extravagant array of clothes. In every
appearance she provided a unique vision to people who had traveled from all over the country to see her. *Time* reported that she
"paraded across India in triumph, more than making up by her
charm, good looks and splendidly attired figure for three post-
ponements."[25] And *Life* again reflected its fascination with the
First Lady by covering the "storybook journey" in a long photo-
story heavily laden with brilliant color shots of this exquisité
woman representing America in this exotic setting.[26]

Mrs. Kennedy's travels also allowed for special interactions
with key people. Generally, when she got along particularly well
with someone in political life, he would hail from a foreign country. There are exceptions, of course, but the record shows that the
major impressions were made on men who were not American.
President Habib Bourguiba of Tunisia found her "fascinating";
President Abboud was so impressed that "he jokingly said that

the President could visit him in the Sudan only if he would bring
Mrs. Kennedy along"; Nehru found conversation with John
Kennedy "heavy going" and in conversation displayed "interest
and vivacity only with Jacqueline"; Khrushchev "turned a heavy,
waggish charm on Mrs. Kennedy . . . and became for a moment
almost cozy";[27] with French Minister of Culture André Malraux
a special friendship was formed (he dedicated his autobiography,
Anti-memoirs, to Mrs. Kennedy); and a singular impression was
made on the elusive Charles de Gaulle.

> Privately, [President Kennedy] gave Jackie the credit for establish-
> ing an easy and intimate understanding between himself and de
> Gaulle. . . . De Gaulle was captivated by Jackie's knowledge of and
> interest in France, and by her fluency in the subtleties of his lan-
> guage. Acting as his interpreter, she drew him into long and enter-.
> taining conversations with her husband that probably made him
> more relaxed with Kennedy than he had ever been with another
> head of a foreign government.[28]

De Gaulle told Kennedy that his wife knew more French history
than most French women, and Mrs. Kennedy was also much
taken with de Gaulle. Correspondent Peter Lisagor recalled that
President Kennedy had a problem with Mrs. Kennedy and de
Gaulle. "You know, Mrs. Kennedy was so kind of . . . she loved
de Gaulle so much and the French and everything that she used
to complain that people were beastly to de Gaulle. . . . It created a
small problem apparently."[29]

It is clear that Kennedy gradually came to realize what an
enormous political asset he had in his wife. There were a few
stories of particular appearances around the country that made an
immediate difference—such as the time she came to the home of
civil rights leader and presidential adviser Belford Lawson: "Because she was such a charmer, here was a chance, as we saw it, to
get her to know some Negroes that night, real quick. She just
stormed the place with her personality. That reception helped to
dissipate certain attitudes toward Kennedy which existed in the
community. . . ."[30] But more generally it was that Jacqueline
Kennedy was an absolutely integral part of the fresh, optimistic,
self-confident, ubiquitous national sentiment that was perhaps
the most singular political creation of the Kennedy administration. As people clamored to catch a glimpse of Jackie, to know
what she did and how she did it, to copy her taste and manners,
they began to identify warmly with the Kennedy presidency. And

as she added an ever-increasing luster to her husband, he began,
as months wore on, to take increasing note. On his last day in
Dallas, he gave a waiting crowd chanting "Where's Jackie?
Where's Jackie?" what was by then a typical answer: "Mrs. Kennedy is organizing herself. It takes her a little longer, but, of
course, she looks better than us when she does it." Some minutes
later, when Mrs. Kennedy made her appearance at a Chamber of
Commerce breakfast, 2,000 Texans "went wild, standing up on
their chairs to get a better look at her, and cheering." In response,
Kennedy started his talk by saying, "Two years ago I introduced
myself in Paris by saying that I was the man who had accompanied Mrs. Kennedy. . . . I am getting somewhat the same sensation as I travel around Texas. Why is it nobody wonders what
Lyndon and I will be wearing?" As always, the small joke with
Jackie Kennedy at the center of it went over well. In Houston, on
that same fated Texas trip, Dave Powers told Kennedy that his
crowd was the same as last years—but that "a hundred thousand
more people came out to cheer for Jackie."[31]

Earlier I said that to understand the political impact of Jacqueline Kennedy as a Decoration, it would be necessary to travel
back to the apparently "simpler time" during which she was the
First Lady. To further recapture the mood, here is an excerpt
from *Time*, published in the middle of John Kennedy's administration. It is from an article titled "Reigning Beauties."

> More than any other reigning beauty, John F. Kennedy's Jacqueline
> has set the pace for new First Ladies. . . . During nearly 17 months
> in the White House, she has gone far toward recreating and refur-
> bishing the serene, classically elegant residence that Jefferson in-
> tended it to be. She has helped, too, to awaken the sometimes dor-
> mant American respect for excellence, be it in food or poetry, decor
> or dance.
>
> Not since Dolly Madison has the chatelaine of the White House
> dressed as elegantly, entertained as imaginatively, or so clearly seen
> both functions as a creative contribution to the success of an Ad-
> ministration. . . . Few men or women in the world today exercise
> such influence."[32]

It is clear, even from this effusive excerpt, that if we try to
explain Jackie Kennedy's impact by what she actually did, we
will be hard pressed. To be sure, there was the successful effort to
restore the White House. But all the rest is quite amorphous, dis-
connected from politics, and more reminiscent of a perfect social-

ite than anything else: domestic responsibilities dutifully performed but, of course, with a retinue of servants to help; ultra-elegant attire; an interest in "doing something for the arts"; a gracious, cultivated, entertaining manner; adeptness at appearing at home when abroad; a flair for charming, not too serious conversation with men of position and power. All of this is not to detract from what was accomplished. No First Lady has ever been better at providing us with "the simple delight that comes from seeing something nice." And no First Lady has ever contributed more to the pervading style of her husband's administration. It would be a mistake to consider these accomplishments as either trivial or extrapolitical.

Jacqueline Kennedy became such a powerful political asset because she successfully defined the role of First Lady to match her own particular proclivities. The tasks and privileges of the First Lady are redefined with each new administration; the contours of the position remain vague. Thus presidential kin who "work the public" actually create the public's expectations of how they will, and indeed should, behave. Intuitively, Mrs. Kennedy understood both these verities, and soon after her husband took office, it seemed to the American people that she filled the role of the president's wife exactly as it was supposed to be filled. (Therefore, to criticize Jacqueline Kennedy from the perspective of the "liberated woman" of the seventies and eighties is somewhat besides the point. How relevant would June Sochen's 1974 critique have seemed in 1962? "Jacqueline Kennedy did nothing for the cause. . . . She had no interest in social welfare, only in social taste. . . . She did not become a desirable role model. . . ."[33])

That things worked out this way between Jacqueline Kennedy and the public was both her luck and her genius. As a Decoration she provided us with a host of appearances, both literal and figurative, and if in retrospect it seems that we were on more than a few occasions deceived, perhaps that was because we wanted to be.

Amy Carter

In the days of vaudeville, no self-respecting performer went on stage just after an act featuring dogs or children. It was a sure way to flop. It was not at all important to know what it was these dogs or children actually did, nor did it allay fears if their turn was in fact terrible. Very simply, it was a show-business axiom that a dog or child had only to appear to put the audience neatly into the palm of its hand (or paw).

Almost invariably, dogs and children can be counted on to be sure-fire crowd pleasers—and presidential politics is no exception. For example, the very young Amy Carter.

In order to understand the impact Amy had as a Decoration when her father first began to become nationally known, she must be placed in the context of her nuclear family. It hardly seemed she belonged. While Rosalynn Carter appeared young and trim enough, Jimmy Carter was clearly no longer in the first blush of manhood—his hair was a steely gray and his face visibly lined—and, more important, the other three children of the Carters were children no more. They were all male, all grown, indeed all married, and one of them would soon make Rosalynn and Jimmy grandparents. Amy had been born a considerable fifteen years after youngest son Jeff, and so, if only by virtue of her unexpected youth and gender within the context of the Carter family, she stood out.

The father's response to this special child confirmed her unique position. In his autobiography Carter wrote that he had always loved children and wished that he and Rosalynn had ten of them. For more than a dozen years Rosalynn was unable to have another child, but shortly after an operation to remove a tumor from her uterus, she became pregnant. The Carters "began to pray for a daughter."

> Amy came.
>
> It was after twenty-one years of marriage. . . . Amy has made us young again, rebound our family together, and been a source of joy, pride, and delight. Her three brothers are so much older that it is almost as though she has four fathers, and we have had to stand in line to spoil her.
>
> Amy was three years old when we moved into the governor's mansion in early 1971, and she has had a rapidly developing life among adults. She is probably the most photographed member of our family, being interviewed and photographed continually at a young age and being actively involved in all sorts of state activities.[34]

Carter, who has said that the night Amy was born was the "greatest night" of his life, caught, in this excerpt, the two strands that made Amy such a focal point for those who would cover the president: she was extraordinary within the family (and known to have brought it extraordinary joy), and she was, from the earliest age, allowed by her parents to be highly visible. Consequently, on countless occasions Amy also provided the public with the "simple delight that comes from seeing something nice" — a delight that was derived from the mere fact that she was a young child.

Amy Carter was born in October 1967. That made her seven in 1975 when Carter was early in his presidential run, eight in 1976 when the campaign was in high gear, and nine during her father's first year as Chief Executive. She came in, in other words, just under the wire. If Americans have a place in their hearts for little girls, they are more resistant to those in the throes of early adolescence — a period in which most youngsters are a little less than wildly winning. But during the important years Amy served well. Her childhood coincided with the time when Carter needed someone like her the most, (this also includes the time when he was most active in state politics), and she filled the role of Decoration admirably.

The national press discovered Amy's potential during the early months of 1976. By July of that year *Time* could already conclude that she was a "distinct political asset."[35] The early focus, as is proper for a Decoration, was on how she looked.

A frisky, freckled, strawberry blonde who looks like Huck Finn's kid sister with the inevitable Carter smile. . . .[36]

Amy Carter is . . . a freckle-faced strawberry blonde with a quick smile, a perky nose and silver blue eyes that give away all her secrets. . . . [She is] a veritable Becky Thatcher with a hundred Tom Sawyers at her elbow. . . .[37]

Halloween Magic. Rosalynn Carter watches as her daughter Amy has her face painted to scare away the bravest goblin or ghost during a Halloween party at Poe Elementary School in Houston.[38]

This last item appeared with an accompanying photo just a few days before the presidential election! Stories on Amy were inevitably accompanied by a photograph, and often there were photos of her without a real story, or simply shots of Jimmy and Rosalynn with Amy in tow.

Since the visual image of Amy was becoming so familiar, reporters were obviously feeling pressure to tell us what the child was really like. Surprise, surprise: she was well-nigh perfect! She basked in all the attention without letting it turn her head; she was incredibly well adjusted even while "Secret Service agents, journalists, members of her father's growing entourage and the scores of tourists were transforming her pleasant, placid, pastoral hometown into a beehive of curiosity seekers"; and she was a straight-A student who also liked to cook, play the piano, ice skate, and roller skate. Above all, she was just a regular little girl. She looked forward to going to an all-girls school in Washington—"Girls are much more fun. They like to giggle and whisper. Boys are no fun. . . . They won't even pass notes"—but she didn't want to leave her friends in Plains, and she was lonely when both her parents would disappear on the campaign trail for long stretches of time.

> Carter was working on a group of well-wishers when someone trying to make conversation asked, "How's Amy?" It was the sort of question that is usually responded to with a standard "Fine, just fine." But instead, Carter offered a candid glimpse of the problems of a family on campaigning.
>
> "Amy cried the last time we left home," Carter said. . . . "Now she's home all day without us . . . and she misses us. It's hard for her."
>
> Rosalynn Carter remembered the incident as well. "She just kind of cried," Mrs. Carter said. "It was very unusual. She was two when Jimmy ran for governor and she's never done that. . . ."
>
> The incident was unsettling on both parents [and] from then on Carter's mother would come and stay in their home with Amy whenever both Jimmy and Rosalynn had to go out campaigning.[39]

A campaign was clearly on to transform Amy from the village darling into the nation's darling, and while some might have questioned some of her parents' decisions with regard to their young daughter, the Carters were at least quite open about some of the problems that all of this attention and confusion entailed.

By November 29, 1976, Amy Carter had arrived. As the nation's "First Kid" she made the front page of the *New York Times:* "AMY CARTER WILL GO TO A PUBLIC SCHOOL NEAR THE WHITE HOUSE." The story of the president's decision to put his daughter in a public school was big news for some weeks. For reasons both symbolic and real, the public was curious.

Amy would be the first president's child to attend a public

school since the time of Theodore Roosevelt. She was to go to one right near the White House which had been built in 1868 for the children of freed slaves. The school was named for Thaddeus Stevens, a congressman from Pennsylvania with a powerful belief in public education and an even more powerful belief in the abolition of slavery. (To satisfy the sudden curiosity in Thaddeus Stevens, the *New York Times* included an Op Ed article on him, "If You Wondered About Thaddeus Stevens."[40]) It had 215 pupils from twenty-six countries and was integrated—60% black, 30% Oriental or Hispanic, and 10% white. Rosalynn Carter was reported by the *Times* to be "very pleased with the quality of the school, the attitude of the staff and teachers, and the friendliness of the students." Amy's future teacher was quoted as promising, "I'll adjust and she will be just like the other 20 girls in the class." And Amy, after one quick visit to the school was mollified about leaving Plains: "I think we're going to have fun in Washington."

The *New York Times* of November 30, featured a long article headlined "Well-Wishers Besiege Amy Carter's School," which revealed among many other things, that students there had been assigned to write on "why we are pleased that Amy Carter might be coming to Stevens," and was accompanied by six different photos of happily integrated Stevens children at work and play. (The story was, of course, also heavily covered on television.) The attention to this (non)event was so frenzied that humorist Russell Baker felt compelled to take to paper.

> The Carters [have] decided to send Amy to a Washington public school. For Washingtonians, this may be the most revealing development of the entire Carter administration.... If [the President] reads "James Bond," as Kennedy did, you read "James Bond" and talk about it. If he is suspicious of people who live in Georgetown, as Johnson was, you look for quarters elsewhere. If he sends his children to public school, you begin to re-examine the public school scene. You certainly don't want to come right out in the middle of dinner with a confession that you send your own kids to private school.[41]

By the time Amy actually started school in January, the story had begun to play itself out. But it was still good for front-page photos of Amy arriving for her first day at school, and items such as the fact that she was late on Monday but on time by Tuesday. And her new teacher, we learned, was satisfied: "Amy was very unaffected, very natural, very independent and she fitted in just beautifully."[42]

Around this same time there was another story, with similar overtones, that also swirled around Amy. It concerned Mary Fitzpatrick, a thirty-two-year-old black divorced mother of two who was serving a life sentence for the shooting of a man in an argument seven years earlier. As a prison trusty, Ms. Fitzpatrick had served as Amy Carter's nurse when Carter was the governor of Georgia. (Several Georgia prisoners worked at the governor's mansion.) Now she was being asked to attend the inauguration and to serve thereafter in a similar capacity while the Carters occupied the White House. Her good fortune was labeled a "modern day Cinderella tale," and Ms. Fitzpatrick was quoted as saying that she never imagined that she would leave Georgia again—not to speak of attending a presidential inauguration. The relationship between Amy Carter and Mary Fitzpatrick was depicted as too good to be intruded on by either past history or bureaucratic formalities.

Stories such as those about Amy's attending an integrated public school, or having a convicted murderer as a nursemaid, have symbolic functions. Whatever the Carter's real motivations, the net effect of decisions like these was to make Amy serve a political end. Amy was a Decoration. We never had a passionate interest in what she—who was, after all, only a child—said, or even specifically in what she did. The appeal was in her little-girlishness. And the fascination was with the juxtaposition between this girlishness and the hectic political environment in which it was being displayed. But just as Jacqueline Kennedy's style could not help but come to stand for the style of the Kennedy administration itself, so the would-be liberalism and modernism with which Amy was promptly enveloped was taken to be an indicator of the intended direction and mood of the Carter presidency. By 1977 Amy's blond hair and freckled young face evoked instant recognition. They had only to be momentarily glimpsed in a shot of her holding hands with a black classmate as they were paired to take a tour of the National Portrait Gallery for the point to be made.[43]

Of course, most of the time Amy was only used to stand for whatever it is a typical American child stands for. Consequently, most of the stories about her tended to dwell on whatever child-like impulses and activities could be mustered.

During the inauguration ceremony she "yawned once during a prayer." In the festivities immediately following, she "caused the parade to pause twice, once to fasten a button, once to tie a bootlace." When she was baptized, the minister "put his arms around her and lowered her completely into [the] water." She was photographed frolicking with Grits, part springer spaniel and part "neighborhood dog," who had been given to her by her new teacher. Grits was named "First Canine" by the president of the Voice for Animals, who observed, "Our gesture is not as silly as perhaps it seems . . . because Amy is now the idol of millions of America's children." (Lest cat lovers feel neglected, I should also note that Amy's cat, Misty, was named "First Feline" by the Voice for Animals.) She formally accepted the gift of a baby elephant from Sri Lanka on behalf of the children of America. She toyed with an Easter egg with her name on it given to her by the Atlanta Children's Hospital. She had a party in the tree house designed by her father. (Shortly thereafter, numberless callers were bombarding the White House with requests for presidential tree-house plans. They were quoted as saying such things as "My kid wants an Amy Carter tree house.") She did or did not write a letter to August Stern, the son of a Jewish doctor jailed in the Soviet Union and then freed to emigrate. (The purported letter was shown by Stern to reporters, but the White House denied the story.) She took a reading enrichment course and studied the violin according to the Suzuki method. She invited the daughter of a Republican congressman whose vote Jimmy Carter needed on the bill to deregulate natural gas to play at the White House. (Rumor has it that this same child had two earlier letters to the White House go unanswered.) She played hostess to nine-year-old Caitlin West, a perfect stranger just paying a tourist's visit to Washington, but who pretty soon felt at ease because Amy was "very relaxed about the whole thing and friendly." She had a tenth birthday party Halloween style, complete with pumpkins, a horror movie, hamburgers, and fourteen boys and girls. At Christmas she got a pair of reindeer from Finland (which, fortunately, landed at the National Zoo in Washington), and when calls came pouring into the White House to find out what else it was that little Amy had set her heart on, the well-wishers were told to send their gifts to needy children.

Time celebrated the new residents of the White House in early 1977 by putting Amy and Grits on its cover.[44] The photo, in living color, of child nuzzling dog was perhaps the high point of Amy's career as a Decoration. But already there were hints in the accompanying article that her days as one who could "lend an intangible aura of pleasure to the grit of day-to-day politics" might be numbered. Mrs. Carter's press secretary reported that Amy "needs to get her feet on the ground and be treated like any other nine year old," and the new president ruled out any more Amy press conferences. (The idealization of Amy was, typically, an outgrowth of our early fascination with the president. Gradually, the press turned to some of her problems. The same issue of *Time* which featured Amy on its cover also reported a *Washington Post* description of her as "forlorn—a baffled and beleaguered public figure.") Of course, as long as Amy was even remotely childlike and occasionally visible, she would continue to serve as the inevitable crowd pleaser and sometime symbol. Even this much of a role as Decoration, though, was being threatened by that insidious force adolescence.

In 1980, as Miss Amy Carter neared thirteen years of age, she was no longer quite as adorable a sight to behold as when, some years before, she had sold lemonade in Plains for 5 cents a glass. Nor, with her more grown-up manner, which appeared indeed to be that of a quite serious rather than giddy young lady, was she any longer such an immediately apparent exception within her own family. In short, the days when she could be counted on, sight seen, to add to the appeal of Jimmy Carter, were already over. She was an effective Decoration when it mattered most, in the very early days when Jimmy Carter needed above all to become nationally known. But Decorations enhance even presidents, including those with their own panache—and no one ever accused President Carter of a surplus in that department. Therefore, the fact that this child became a victim of increasing age had to be seen as a considerable loss by all who counted themselves in the Carter camp. (Not to exaggerate the case, there was life in the young girl yet. Well past her peak, Amy-freaks could buy a book about a child called Amy Love and/or a matching three-foot-high rag doll with blond hair, blue eyes, and glasses.)

Amy suffered a somewhat ignominious political end. President Carter tried to bestow on her a last hurrah when, during his preelection debate with Ronald Reagan, he said that he had asked Amy "what the most important issue was." Her answer, he claimed: "Nuclear weapons and the control of nuclear arms."

America snickered at what was seen to be a clumsy attempt at homiyness. Johnny Carson the next night promised that "this will be a significant monologue because I asked Amy Carter what she thought were the most important issues to make jokes about." And the director of the Reagan-Bush campaign in Connecticut ordered 2,000 red and white buttons reading "Ask Amy." The president should have known better than to try and mix Decorations and bombs.

Icing on the Cake

At first glance, Jacqueline Kennedy and Amy Carter bear each other little resemblance. They appear to have in common only the obvious fact that both are female relatives of a president; differences between them obscure other similarities. But I hope that by now we have all gone somewhat beyond the proverbial first glance, gone beyond it to the point where we can begin to see that what Mrs. Kennedy and Miss Carter did for the president and the presidency is similar in nature—as there is a similarity in how they each related to the public. As Decorations, both of them served the primary purpose of selling the president to the public, a job each could perform so well because she had the two prerequisites: a place in the American political culture derived from her position as a relative of the president (or president-elect or prominent presidential candidate), and an aspect of personality or presence which soon evoked virtually instant visual recognition.

Jackie's stunning looks and style were without exception a lovely sight to behold; and in Amy's salad days, one snapshot of this "Becky Thatcher" was enough to launch a thousand smiles. The activities of both the president's wife and the president's child were reported eagerly—even though in neither case did they contribute a thing to the substance of a candidacy or presidency; and even though in neither case (with the single exception of Mrs. Kennedy's White House labors) did they themselves have much political substance. No matter though. What we look for in Decorations is exactly style and not substance, a style which can impact without the president around, and which gratifies America's collective eye without making any demands in exchange.

How, still more precisely, was the political impact exercised by Jacqueline Kennedy and Amy Carter similar? Both had an active relationship with an interested and affectionate public. Both communicated with the public primarily through pictures of themselves in newspapers, in magazines, and on television. Both permitted themselves controlled public exposure. (Amy's parents were unusually permissive in this regard, especially early on. Amy's reduced visibility from around the age of ten seems, from what we can tell, to have been in part her own doing.) Both enlisted sympathy for the president: Jackie lent John Kennedy glamour; Amy lent Jimmy Carter her appeal. Both stood out even within their own families. Both radiated an uncomplicated grace because they appeared to be totally removed from politics. Amy was separate by mere virtue of the fact that she was a child, while Jackie, the more interesting case in this regard, made certain to hold herself above and apart. In both cases, the particular quality of the political impact depended on this apparent political innocence.

Precisely because Decorations are seen to be such babes in the woods, they can also, occasionally, be used to send messages that are blatantly political in content. President Kennedy was not above using Jackie to address, in Spanish, some veterans of the Bay of Pigs fiasco. Nor did President Carter resist the front-page headlines of Amy's attendance at a public school that was 60% black. Decorations, I might point out, although popular in their own right, are also implicit reflections of the president. What they do, therefore, although apparently innocuous because of who is doing it, can have symbolic political value for the president. Presidents must be careful, though, not to use Decorations as subliminal messengers too often. Innocence is a credit that is easily spent.

We can probably assume that by the time John Kennedy died, his relationship to his wife was marked by some mutual respect and affection. And we can presume to know that one of the great pleasures of Jimmy Carter's middle adulthood has been his daughter Amy. But neither Jacqueline nor Amy ever contributed much if anything to the political persona or administrations of their respective presidential kin. Rather, their contribution was indirect. Both would first capture and beguile the audience, and then turn it over, already primed, to him who was really seeking the thunderous applause.

CHAPTER 3

Extensions

Extensions are the president when the president cannot be there. They have little identity of their own. Indeed, their value as Extensions is derived not from who they are, but from what they are: close relatives of the president. What they say is only minimally important. Recognizing this, they usually say very little. When it is anything more than a pleasantry, we know it is the president speaking through a trusted mouthpiece. Extensions allow presidents to win friends and influence people without really trying, often without even being there. The very best Extensions bear a physical resemblance to the president, for they are, in effect, his stand-in.

Fifteen of the presidential kin listed in the front chart are Extensions: Edward Kennedy, Eunice Kennedy Shriver, Patricia Kennedy Lawford, Jean Kennedy Smith, Lynda Bird and Luci Baines Johnson, Tricia Nixon, Michael, Jack, Steve, and Susan Ford, Jack, Chip, and Jeff Carter, and, provisionally, Michael Reagan. How come so many? Why, especially when a president has a large family, does it seem that they, clones gone awry, are everywhere?

Before investing the reasonably obvious with a special mystique, consider the requirements. There is really only one. Extensions need not, no *must* not, have a separate identity. "Their value as Extensions is derived . . . from what they are: close relatives of the president." And that, to be blunt, is enough. The public, that constituency that bestows on Extensions their political import, must merely be made aware of their blood or marital tie to the president.

Extensions need not have any endearing traits—not looks, not charm, not wit. Nor, indeed, must the public be convinced

that Extensions have a particularly intimate interaction with the
president (although when Extensions are presidential offspring,
it is assumed that the relationship is a good one). It may fairly be
said, then, that simply to exist will do—to exist, anyway, in a
state of blessed kinship to the Chief Executive.

James Monaco begins his book *Celebrity* by talking about a
case that illustrates the phenomenon we are addressing here: the
remarkable story of Joyce Brothers' mother.

> The commercial opens on a close-up of a pleasant, middle-aged
> woman in her kitchen, talking to the camera:
>> I'm Dr. Joyce Brothers' mother. Even when Joyce was little, I
>> knew she was going to be a psychologist. I'd say, "Joyce, come
>> to dinner." She'd say, "What do you mean by that?"
> We cut to a close-up shot of a plate of Mueller's Tuna and Noodle
> Casserole and Mueller's package. The narration continues:
>> Then I'd say, "But Joyce, I made your favorite! Mueller's egg
>> noodles with tuna!"
> Cut back to mother.
>> She said, "Fine. Very often a good, hot meal establishes a feel-
>> ing of security in a growing child."
> The announcer delivers the tagline:
>> Egg noodles and tuna are one reason mothers say . . . Nothing
>> goes with everything like Mueller's.
> Very nice ad. The Needham, Harper & Steers agency did a little
> research. . . . To capitalize on the traditional connotations of the
> product, they developed a series of . . . spots featuring mothers of
> celebrities. . . .
>> Estelle Bauer has not yet hit the talk-show circuit, but it's only
> a matter of time. She is a member of that rare breed, the "parace-
> lebrity." . . . Paracelebrities are well-known for being known by
> people who are well-known for their well-known-ness.[1]

Now I am not trying to say that presidents are celebrities because
they are "well-known for their well-known-ness." (The phrase is
Daniel Boorstin's.) One can draw only so many parallels between
Joyce Brothers and, say, Lyndon Johnson. I am, however, claiming that the paracelebrity syndrome—the circumstance in which
those close to the famous become themselves objects of interest—is the explanation of why Extensions have political impact.
The public is curious about them. It will go to see them in person; it will buy magazines with them on the cover; it will watch

them on the tube; it will listen to what they say. And make no mistake: when I speak of the public, I refer not only to readers of *People* and devotees of "Laverne and Shirley." I refer to anyone who has ever spent one moment listening to a campaign pitch by postpubescent presidential progeny—or followed the exploits of same with even a modicum of interest.

What makes Extensions different from other presidential relatives—we are just as interested, after all, in Decorations or in Helpmeets—is that they have absolutely nothing to recommend them *except* the presidential tie. And precisely because they lack all peculiar markings, they, more than any other kin, *are* the president when the great man himself cannot be there. Very occasionally, Extensions will do or say something to distinguish themselves from the president. But if they do it too much, by our own definition they become something else, a Humanizer perhaps. Thus Extensions spend a good deal of their time just standing there, so to speak, appearing before the voters to remind them of just who that man in the White House is, and how clever he must be to have in tow such a devoted and affable sister or brother, daughter or son. Mostly they say very little of substance; apolitical pleasantries permit the positive association to continue uninterrupted. When Extensions do talk about real life, they can be counted on to echo the president. To the extent that they speak at all, they are his trusted mouthpiece.

The ideal Extension, then, is more than a little like the old-fashioned notion of the ideal child. To be a lot seen and not too much heard is just about perfect. It is truly perfect if the Extension and the president bear a strong physical resemblance to each other so that every posture, gesture, and inflection of the former remind the public of the latter.

It is probably true that Extensions have their peak effect during the presidential campaigns. Their prime time—when every appearance is measured in possible votes—occurs quadrennially between about February (the beginning of the primary season) and November of a presidential election year. That is not to say that their impact in the years in-between should be discounted. As we will see below in the case of the four children of Gerald Ford, their activities during the administrations of their presidential kin serve a variety of important functions. But it is during a campaign that Extensions become an invalauble asset, an asset for which the claim can reasonably be made that it has, in at least two out of the last five elections, contributed mightily to who won and who lost.

This wholesale use of the family during the campaign was, of course, pioneered by John Kennedy. As we saw in Chapter 1, family members were not altogether invisible before that, but a presidential relative *cum* celebrity was the exception rather than the rule, and most presidents still thought it somehow unseemly to use their kin as pitchmen. Not so John Kennedy, who learned this particular lesson from his mother. Rose Kennedy, you will remember, had tooled around Boston as a young child by the side of her mayor father, "Honey Fitz" Fitzgerald. And since she had been taught that even as a woman you were a lot more useful politicking than knitting at home by the fire, when John Kennedy's time came, she and her three healthy daughters were actively involved in his political life.

Rose Kennedy was too strong a personality in her own right to be labeled an Extension, (see Chapter 4), but Eunice Shriver, Patricia Lawford, and Jean Smith all behaved like the very models of Extensions. All of them campaigned actively for brother Jack; but despite the fact that they were in the limelight frequently and over a long stretch in 1959 and '60, they appeared to us to have no identities of their own. They were no more and no less than the candidate's sisters. Still, they were powerful attractions indeed. A tea that featured Pat Lawford was a sure-fire sellout.

Eunice Shriver looked the most like her brother Jack. They were also "physiologically alike" in that they both had Addison's disease.[2] And she was the first of the sisters to work for him. As far back as 1946, in Kennedy's first congressional campaign, Eunice was putting in appearances at "house parties." They were an old tradition in Boston politics: "A campaign worker would invite the candidate to his or her house to meet twenty or thirty neighbors, serve coffee and sandwiches, cookies, cake and ice cream. After meeting everyone, the candidate usually gave a little talk. . . . The Kennedy machine utilized the house party more intensely than any candidate in memory. Eunice (and later Pat and Jean) participated in these festivities."[3] Eunice was also assigned the town of Cambridge, and she was the first to get involved in national politics. In 1956, she toured the delegations in Chicago, along with Robert Kennedy, on behalf of Jack's attempt to secure the Democratic nomination for vice-president.

If Eunice was the trailblazer, the other two sisters followed close behind. From the earliest days in Boston, it became clear how much ground they could cover together. An old Boston pol remembered it this way:

> We'd set up six to nine parties—or more—for a single evening with anywhere from twenty-five to seventy-five people at each. Jack, Pat and Eunice would set out for party number one. They'd drop Pat or Eunice at number one. Then Jack'd go to number two and drop another sister. Then Jack would go alone to number three. The sisters would circulate, shake hands and talk. Then we'd backtrack to number one, pick up the sister, and take her (and Jack) to number four and drop her and so on and on, carrying this on for hours.[4]

The system did not change all that much when John Kennedy ran for president. The main difference was that he was around less, and his sisters more. Now the Kennedys tried to blanket not one district in Massachusetts, but every district in the land. And since the candidate himself was at an absolute premium, his sisters too became more valuable.

They were joined by the wives of Jack's brothers and all of them were given extensive assignments, especially in suburban areas. Eunice, Pat, and Jean also appeared with the senator in their husbands' home states of Illinois, California, and New York. "In preparation for this campaign," said the senator to those audiences, "I had sisters living in all the key states."[5] For the important Wisconsin primary, Robert Kennedy had it arranged so that each of his three sisters was scheduled to attend nine house parties a day, for a total of twenty-seven parties a day in every town over a period of two weeks. O'Donnell and Powers remember the juggling:

> In another town we talked the wife of a funeral director into giving a party in her living quarters, in the rear of the funeral home. When she gave the party, with Jean as the honored guest, there was a wake going on in the funeral parlor down the hall. The mourners left the wake and came to the party, and after Jean talked with them and drank a cup of tea with them, they went back to the wake. That afternoon I got Jean to give a talk at a cattle auction. We found out that it was easier to talk a housewife into giving a party if we told her that Peter Lawford's wife, Pat Lawford, would be coming to her house. Peter Lawford had a weekly comedy show on television then, and he was a much bigger celebrity in Washington than Jack Kennedy. After a big crowd of women gathered at the party to get a peek

at Pat Lawford, I would appear with Eunice and Jean and explain with profuse apologies that Pat couldn't make it. Of course, I didn't mention that Pat was at another party in the next block.[6]

After Kennedy demonstrated how valuable an Extension could be, every president had (at least) one. They played at being everything from Queen of the Apple Blossom Festival to head of the March of Dimes Teen Age Program; but always, of course, they were primarily campaigners and publicists.

The Carter clan from Georgia gave Extensions new respectability. Heretofore Extensions had mostly been lightweights. Since they were denied identities of their own (in any case they never claimed them publicly) and since they spoke only echoes or inanities, they were in growing danger of appearing altogether too frivolous, even irrelevant, and therefore of losing some of their political impact. When along came Jimmy Carter. With the intuition of the born politician, Carter updated the model and turned his Extensions into a semblance of serious, reasonably competent individuals. Make no mistake. None of them were so individual that they were actually separate from the man who would be president. Still, they seemed to be more than mere appendages.

During the campaign each son and his wife—Jack and Judy Carter, Chip and Caron Carter, and Jeff and Annette Carter—were assigned (by Hamilton Jordan) a 2-point value for one day of campaigning. Each of the couples took a share of the work load, and while they all came across as fervently devoted to Jimmy's cause, they also managed to emerge slightly from behind his shadow, in part at least because they had more substance than the Extensions of old. The trend continued once Carter took office, a trend for which he gets the credit—assuming credit is due. In an early fireside chat Carter stated his intention to use members of his family as extensions of the presidential office: "I would like to have the opportunity to use members of my family to go and represent me personally, along with professionals who serve the government." And he did so, and so it was no accident that it was during the Carter administration that the role of the Extension received a certain legitimacy. As a sign of this, shortly after Carter came to Washington, his son Chip made his political activism official by signing on as an $8,000-a-year man for the Democratic National Committee.

Chip, then, became the New Extension. He was still seen more as his father's son than as his own man. And he was still only a trusted mouthpiece for the president. He *was* Jimmy Carter when Jimmy Carter was elsewhere. Yet he earned a salary for what he did. And he was emissary to more than the Apple Blossom Festival. Domestically, he carried out assignments that ranged from consoling frozen souls ravaged by winter blizzards to raising funds for needy candidates to putting out political feelers for the 1980 "run again" campaign of his father. He also made the foreign scene. Some of the great capitals of the world have been graced by Chip, representing his father at an array of ceremonial occasions. Sometimes he was sent by his father on a mission of real importance. In March 1978 he accompanied Zbigniew Brzezinski to Saudi Arabia and Jordan to seek their support of the Egyptian-Israeli peace treaty. The *New York Times* said on March 16 that "the presence of the President's son in the delegation is meant to underscore the President's personal interest in success of the mission."

It is possible that Chip is the prototype of the Extension of the future. It is possible that Extensions will in the future be less willing to hide their entire light under the President's bushel; that, if they are over eighteen or so, they will demand better conditions, especially for regular work after the campaign season. Of course, if Extensions get to the point where they become utterly respectable and very active on the president's behalf, they become something else. For it is the very essence of Extensions that even with some retooling, they remain, at the base, no more than paracelebrities.

Edward ("Ted") Kennedy

Go back in time to when he was angular-looking, a couple of months out of law school, and completely unknown. Go back to 1959 when even Senator John Kennedy had not yet been imprinted on our national consciousness—and when his youngest sibling's main claim to fame was to be known as the "kid brother." Go back to the presidential campaign of 1960 when the Democratic candidate was so Irish-lucky that one of his many Extensions was a double.

To get "Ted" Kennedy in those years was the closest thing to getting the president (or candidate) himself. He was so low in the hierarchy of the Kennedy family that he almost never did anything to distinguish himself from his brother, and so any audience could relax, sit back, and imagine it was John Kennedy whom they were hearing and seeing. Precisely because Teddy was so innocuous, because he made so sure to be in the image of his oldest brother, the strong physical resemblance had a powerful effect. No one missed it.

> [Their campaign styles were] similar. Teddy . . . . raced through everything. He spoke terribly fast. His brother also spoke at a rapid-fire clip. Their styles were somewhat similar.[7]

> Hubert Humphrey complained about the Kennedy invasion [in the Wisconsin primary]. "They're all over the state, and they look alike and sound alike." Humphrey said, "Teddy or Eunice talks to a crowd, wearing a racoon coat and stocking cap, and people think they're listening to Jack. I get reports that Jack is appearing in three or four different places at the same time."[8]

> [Teddy made] the most of the Kennedy name, the Kennedy looks, the Kennedy manner. He had the familiar thatch of thick brown hair, the outthrust jaw, the meat chopping gestures, the flat Boston accent. A voter could close his eyes, listen to the talk of "Cuber" and "Asier" and swear the President was on the platform.[9]

But to understand how, in that male stronghold otherwise known as the Kennedy clan, Teddy could occupy such a humble place, fill a role of no greater stature than Extension, we need to do two things: first, reconstruct the family ties as they existed in 1959, and second, consider the position of Edward Kennedy at the age of twenty-seven.

We have heard it intoned a million times that the Kennedy family was very close. But of the nine offspring of Joe and Rose, some were closer than others. It seems clear that among the surviving brothers, a team was formed by Jack and Bobby from which Teddy, as very much the youngest, was largely excluded. The difference in age between Jack and Ted was fifteen years; it was too great a gap to ever be fully bridged. And so when John and Robert undertook the quest for the presidency, it was altogether natural that they should do so as partners, while Edward was expected to join them to do what he was told. It was much as if all three were in a backyard touch football game—with Jack serving as quarterback, Robert as running back, and Teddy as an ever-ready but only occasionally used substitute. Indeed, there is no doubt that during the time of John Kennedy's candidacy and presidency, Teddy had no access to power. Although he was given credit by the family for his political talents—they called him, in fact, their "best politician"—they were crediting merely his ability to charm voters in record time. When the hard decisions of the campaign and of the Kennedy presidency were being made, Edward Kennedy was no more than an interested spectator.

Of course, he was still very young. And very inexperienced. It was true that he had been the nominal head of Kennedy's campaign for the Senate in 1958, a campaign which resulted in a win by the largest margin ever given a candidate in any party in Massachusetts. But it was also true that this was largely an honorary role to which he had been assigned to gain some political experience, that the real planning and deciding were done by Kennedy stalwarts Lawrence O'Brien and Kenneth O'Donnell, and that Teddy was supposed to return to law school before election day even dawned. By the time he graduated from the University of Virginia Law School in June 1959, the planning for the presidential race was well underway. Thus he came into a situation in which the political scenario was already all worked out, and he himself was still moist behind the ears. For John Kennedy's purposes, it was as if brother Ted had been to the role of Extension born.

The first goal was to win the nomination. Ted Kennedy's domain was the Rocky Mountain and Western states, where he, under the tutelage of Hyman Raskin, a long-time Democrat and Chicago lawyer, scouted delegates for his brother. Mostly it was a laborious task. Teddy did not have the clout to do anything other than carry out instructions from back east. Nor did he have the experience or knowledge to carry much weight in personal meetings with party leaders. Nor was he assigned to an area in which John Kennedy was destined to have a particular appeal. "Most state and local party chieftains were linked closely to long established leaders like Lyndon B. Johnson and governors such as Pat Brown of California were not going to offer support without strong commitments by the candidate."[10] And there were lessons to be learned—sometimes in a funny way. In October 1959 *Time* reported the following incident, in which Ted was described as John Kennedy's "strapping (6 ft. 2 in., 200 lbs) kid brother . . . serving as a sort of general evangelist for the candidacy of his eldest brother." One snowy night before an audience of a mere fifteen Young Democrats at the University of Denver's student lounge, Ted Kennedy "blissfully answered some blunt questions unaware that a reporter from the *Rocky Mountain News* was in the room." He declared that his brother was in an all-or-nothing race to be the Democratic nominee, and that although as recently as last June he might have considered the vice-presidential spot, now he would not. The Democrats, he went on, would be foolish if they nominated Stevenson once again. He was a "brilliant but ineffectual man who would make an admirable Secretary of State." Of Stuart Symington, Teddy observed that "he is not in a position of particular leadership," and Hubert Humphrey, he thought, "will not be a significant threat at the convention." After the *News* reported his comments, to the considerable discomfort of the Kennedy camp, Ted replied, "Adlai Stevenson, ineffectual? I can't imagine my saying it."[11]

There was a moment of glory for Edward Kennedy at the convention in Los Angeles. He had been cultivating the Wyoming delegation since the early fall. As the countdown in the huge hall wound down, Ted persuaded the Wyoming delegates to vote unanimously for JFK. When they did, they thereby put Kennedy over the top. And it was the "kid brother" who stood smiling broadly amid the Wyoming delegates as their crucial fifteen votes were announced.

But immediately thereafter it was back to the Western mines for Ted, to a situation now improved only slightly by the fact that he was campaigning for the Democratic party's official nominee. Of all the Western and Mountain states for which Ted Kennedy was nominally responsible, the Democrats took only New Mexico and Nevada. No one in the family ever put any special blame on Ted, and in fact there were good, objective reasons for the dismal showing, reasons which might well not have been made to disappear by even a more experienced campaigner. Yet to look back at this fiasco is to conclude that a lightweight, an Extension, was given the job of a heavyweight. It was no wonder that the job was done poorly—although it was not the fault of the twenty-eight-year-old who was twelve months out of law school. The only equipment Ted Kennedy had for the work to which he had been assigned was the natural appeal of his own personality, and the only credential he had was his relationship to the candidate. No wonder that people took kindly to him but did not take him seriously.

In all the *New York Times* references to the Kennedy campaign between July and November 1960 there is only one mention of a time when Edward Kennedy did anything specific, and that was only to correct a mistake of his brother's. "Senator John F. Kennedy made a 'slip of the tongue' if he suggested he did not want the support of rank-and-file teamsters and longshoremen, his brother Edward said tonight. 'I am sure he does want the support of all the honest hard-working union people throughout the country.'"[12] Other times when young Teddy was part of a story, he was a "legman" or a "general factotum" or an "awed onlooker." Here was a boy being sent out to do a man's job, and for all the effort Edward Kennedy put into getting his brother elected president, there was but one positive legacy: the memory almost everyone who came into contact with him had of an eager and winning very young man.

There are a few recollections of Teddy Kennedy during this time, and they are remarkable for their similar tone. All agree that he was like a naive Jack. And all agree that as stand-ins go, he was just about perfect.

> Teddy, who came out to take charge of the western states for the campaign, also didn't have any real "feel" [for the California political situation]* although he did quite well. He made a great public impression out here. . . . I think he was quite young and quite inexperienced and, I think, not too effective. . . . But he found his way along pretty well. . . . His presence was very good; he was a great substitute for his brother in speaking. . . . Every place he went, he drew great crowds of young people and, I think, generally, increased interest in the campaign quite a little bit.[14]

> They loved Jack and at the Armenian Democratic Liberal Union's convention in Swampscott in 1959, Jack was invited to speak, and since Jack couldn't come, Steve Smith promised me that he'd have a

---

*It was in reference to California that the *Times* said of Teddy that he was an "awed onlooker." "For more than a week he has been threading his way through a functional battlefield, trying to put together a state campaign organization whose principles would marshal more enthusiasm than alienation."[13]

member of the Kennedy family there. And young Teddy came and spoke there and he opened the speech in Armenian and the crowd roared.[15]

They assigned Ted to handle the western part, you remember. . . . He came to the opening of our headquarters. He was so cute, just 28 years old. . . .[16]

I had a great deal of contact with Ted Kennedy during those days [in California in 1960] including a lot of campaigning. I must say that he certainly had his brother Jack's magnetism and vitality and drive. . . .[17]

Bob called me and asked if I would sponsor a cocktail party for Teddy Kennedy, who was coming here on his brother's behalf to drum up some enthusiasm. . . . I agreed to . . . and I am happy today that I supported it and we had our cocktail party and . . . it was a very successful event.[18]

When they were not directly campaigning in the west, Robert and Ted were here and were very effective. They had their wives with them and they knew how to greet people . . . and West Virginia people liked them. It was just a very happy circumstance.[19]

Well, this has been quite a few years ago, and Ted was sort of fresh to the political arena. So they all liked him, a likeable young guy. . . .[20]

I think for the most part [Edward Kennedy] was very effective because of his personality, his manner, his approach. . . .[21]

Despite the fact that Teddy should not have been given all that responsibility out west in the first place and despite the fact that he did perform well in the modest role of Extension—he won a lot of friends and influenced a few people for John Kennedy—there is some evidence that the kid brother felt badly about the poor showing in his territory. Bobby is quoted as saying, "I'm worrying about Teddy. We've lost every state he's worked in out West. Jack will kid him and that may hurt his feelings."[22] And Ted himself wired the victor whimsically but also wistfully, "Can I come back if I promise to carry the Western states in 1964?"[23] But during the inaugural weekend Jack took gentle (and prescient) note of what could have been turned into bad feeling: he gave Edward Kennedy a cigarette box engraved with the words "And the Last Shall Be First."

During the first year of the Kennedy administration Teddy continued to perform as an Extension, if only because he had nothing else to do. His future had not yet been determined, and although he took a job of sorts—as an assistant district attorney of Suffolk County in Massachusetts at $1 per year—1961 was clearly waiting time. It was decided that he would serve the new president as he had the old candidate. But now instead of winning a lot of friends and influencing a few people on the home front for votes, he would do so abroad on behalf of Kennedy's foreign policy. Soon after the election Edward Kennedy went on a "fact-finding tour" for the president-elect to Africa. The following May he toured Europe. Unlike other assistant district attorneys of Suffolk County he got to meet with luminaries such as the Vice-President of Yugoslavia and the President of Italy, and he had a thirty-minute audience with the Pope. In July he took off for the rural and depressed areas of Latin America. The trip was termed "strictly unofficial," and Mr. Kennedy was reported as saying that "we will be especially interested in housing programs as they effect the middle classes."[24] Why he might have a sudden, special interest in housing programs for the middle class was never explained.

In February 1962 Edward Kennedy began his major tour to date: three weeks in Western and Eastern Europe and the Middle East. In Belgium he met students, labor leaders, officials of the European Economic Community, and heads of U.S. businesses operating in Belgium. He was met by a special representative of King Baudouin, and he dined with Paul-Henri Spaak, the Belgian Foreign Minister. When pressed, Teddy described his trip as "personal" and denied that he was representing President Kennedy on the tour. But it was also known that when, for example, the kid brother met with American businessmen, he asked them about the consequences of President Kennedy's program for trade agreements with the Common Market. And so it went: an hour in Israel with Premier David Ben-Gurion, in Greece lunch with Crown Prince Constantine and dinner with Premier Constantine Karamanlis, and a trip to Germany that *Pravda* felt compelled to attack as a "cold war" activity.

On February 25 the *New York Times* featured a front-page photo of the Chancellor of Germany, Konrad Adenauer, and the two Kennedy brothers, both of whom were in Bonn at the same time. Teddy caused a brouhaha simply by crossing the border into East Berlin. The Communist authorities were delighted by the gesture, regarding as a sign of their new legitimacy the fact that the president's brother had stepped on their soil. According to the *Times* report on February 24, they rejoiced that Edward Kennedy "respected in every way the sovereignty of the German Democratic Republic." President Kennedy's personal representative on the scene, General Lucius Clay, responded that it was he who had especially asked Kennedy to go to East Berlin: "I wanted him to have the chance to see the contrast between the two parts of the city himself." Teddy, in any case, learned what he was supposed to, since upon his return from the East Zone he commented that the "faces show the despair" of life over there, which is "no life, no action" and "sterile." Incidentally, just as he was poised to cross into East Berlin, it was learned that he lacked the requisite currency declaration. Somehow, when it was explained that he was the brother of the President of the United States, it was decided that he might pass through without it.

Perhaps we should pause for a moment to ruminate about what was going on. The trip was officially described variously as a "fact-finding" tour, a "strictly unofficial" trip, and a "personal" investigation abroad. Odd definitions of "strictly unofficial" and "personal!" Surely it was a bit unusual for an unelected local official from a New England state to be received by royalty (both secular and religious), to chat with heads of state, to cause *Pravda* to redden. But also we can probably assume that John Kennedy did not assign his youngest brother any secret missions of major importance. No, Teddy Kennedy was, in 1961 and early '62, acting as a "goodwill ambassador" — a term we reserve for those who go abroad to please everyone and offend no one in the name of Uncle Sam. Of course, in this case Edward Kennedy was a goodwill ambassador not just for his country but in particular for his brother's administration. It was the perfect job for an Extension. Teddy was young and pliable; he said only what was trivial or what he had been told to say; he reminded all who met him of the president himself; and all who met him knew that because of the sibling relationship anything they said to Ted would get back to John. And Teddy was the perfect Extension *cum* goodwill ambassador: sunny but not dopey, and looking for all the world like the President of the United States in a different time zone.

But on March 14, 1962, something happened to change the nature of Teddy Kennedy's public life. He announced his candidacy for the United States Senate. (He ran for the Massachusetts seat vacated two years earlier by Jack.) We have to push hard to remind ourselves of the furor that ensued. To virtually everyone outside the Kennedy family, Edward was no more than the kid brother, no more than an Extension. He was nothing in his own right, and he was running for the upper house even though he had never before run for anything in his life.

The tone of the attacks was predictable. Charges of nepotism peppered the air as if shot from a rapid-fire machine gun. In a debate with his rival for the Democratic nomination, Edward McCormack, Teddy heard the accusation to his face. When McCormack's turn came, he turned to Kennedy and said, "You have never worked for a living. You have never held public office. You are running on a name; you're not running on your own. . . . You say you 'can do more for Massachusetts' and what does that mean? It means you have connections; you have relations. . . . If your name were Edward Moore instead of Edward Moore Kennedy, your candidacy would be a joke."[25]

But it was not only Kennedy opponents who were dismayed. Many who might have been expected to be more sympathetic were equally upset. In August, the National Committee for an Effective Congress issued the following report: "Teddy's undistinguished academic career has not been followed by a record of serious personal accomplishment. . . . The fact that Teddy's candidacy involves exploitation of the reputation of the President is arousing widespread resentment. Virtually everyone in public life has been approached by friends who are deeply troubled by the implication of nepotism and disregard of precedent in this candidacy. Their loss of respect for a President can have a profoundly damaging effect upon his ability to lead the country." And the cartoonists, of course, had a field day. Mauldin got in his licks with a drawing of Ted looking terribly young and terribly like his oldest brother, sitting before the president (who was ensconced behind his desk in the Oval Office) and explaining, "I *AM* WORKING MY WAY UP THROUGH THE RANKS. I'M STARTING WITH THE SENATE." And Herblock had a man on the dais during a political function launching loudly and confidently into a pro forma introduction but then stumbling: "It Is My Great Privilege To Present A Man Who—Uh—Has A Brother Who—"[26]

The official White House line was to keep hands off. And to

an extent the White House did. A statement was issued that said the president "prefers that this matter be decided by the public of Massachusetts—and that the President should not become involved." And even privately Jack Kennedy was not inclined to fight all of Ted Kennedy's battles. When it came out that Teddy had been expelled from Harvard for cheating, the president asserted, "He's got 6 months to fight his way out of it. It's just like my Addison's disease. It's out, and now he's got to fight it."[27] But remember, as John Kennedy did, the fraternal connection. When he ran for president and certainly during the first year of his administration, Ted Kennedy was his Extension. There was no way the president could, even if he wanted to, amputate now. To a considerable degree his own prestige and power were on the line in that Massachusetts race, and so, for professional as well as personal reasons, John Kennedy wanted Edward Kennedy to win that Senate seat and win it big.

Thus, despite the disclaimers, there was support from Washington. As one presidential adviser hints, there was no obvious reason to break an old habit: "[Teddy] talked to his brother on numerous occasions during the pre-primary convention and during the primary. . . . He had been so used to asking his brother for advice . . . that he continued to do so at that time."[28] In addition, Theodore Sorensen and other close Kennedy aides were sent to Massachusetts to dispense general advice and to coach Teddy on how to deal with particular issues. And there were all those billboards with the coy suggestion that a senator with a brother in the White House could "do more for Massachusetts"—a suggestion that the White House did nothing to slap down.

The president's reaction, meanwhile, was quite interesting. Some of the stories about the prospect of a Kennedy dynasty angered him, but he did not completely lose his sense of humor. "He told the Gridiron Club jokingly that he had announced that 'no presidential aide or appointee would be allowed to take part in that political war in Massachusetts,' but that, 'of course, we may send up a few training missions.'"[29] Nor was the president unduly upset by the notion that the Kennedy brothers might really be an unparallelled force in American politics. His friend Ben Bradlee quotes him as saying, "The idea [of a dynasty] is not only legitimate but fascinating."[30]

By now the Kennedys knew how to mount a political campaign, and in 1962 in Massachusetts there was all the evidence of

organization, money, and a highly marketable candidate that had
for some sixteen years been the hallmarks of Kennedy politics in
the Bay State. But the size of Edward Kennedy's victory in the
primary against an attractive young candidate, also from a family
well known in Massachusetts for its Democratic politics, was
truly enormous. He beat his opponent by a margin of more than
two to one. And in the general election in November he beat
Republican George Lodge, scion of another prominent New England family, by close to 300,000 votes.

The voice of *the* people had been heard. The voice of *some*
people still had a mighty cranky tone. Just after Kennedy's election, the *New York Times* editorialized:

> Mr. Kennedy won nomination and election despite a monumental
> lack of relevant experience. His campaign boast that "He Can Do
> More for Massachusetts" had the idealism of a promissory note,
> with no collateral other than consanguinity. A dazzling smile, a tire-
> less handshake and a great deal of native political acumen pretty
> much completed his arsenal of qualifications. . . .[31]

But the deed was done and on January 9, 1963, Edward M. Kennedy was sworn in as senator from Massachusetts. Can it fairly be
claimed that after that day, one on which he became an elected
official in his own right, he was still only an extension of the
president? There are only eleven months of evidence, but they
suggest that within that period no full transition to something
else had yet taken place. Teddy Kennedy was still the novice, the
learner, the younger: there was no doubt that the administration
could count on support from the junior senator from the Bay
State (except perhaps in some few cases where the interests of
Massachusetts and the nation were in conflict); those who
viewed the youngest Kennedy still saw him more as his brother's
brother than as an independent political power; and Teddy himself apparently felt that although some things changed, others
stayed much the same. Years later he commented, "By the time I
arrived in the Senate and he was President the sense of great age
difference had almost disappeared. What would never disappear
was the fact that he was the older brother and I was the younger."[32]

Earlier I wrote that Jimmy Carter's son Chip was the New
Extension, that is, something decidedly more than just a trivial-

ized version of the president. But Chip Carter, who followed his father to the capital, did have one role model to follow: Teddy Kennedy. Both of them first became known as kids around the candidate. And both of them worked to upgrade their tasks and images to the point where people could gradually start taking them seriously for what they themselves had accomplished. The next step seems almost self-evident: to establish an independent image, or at least to establish an identity independent enough to serve as the basis of a fledgling political career. Ted took his opportunity, and it seems safe to speculate that at some future moment Chip Carter will try mightily to do the same.

It is clear, in any case, that young persons related to presidents potentially have a long head start in professional politics. It turns out that to be an Extension is to be an apprentice. Extensions learn about politics from their presidential kin, and they also derive from them an exposure that would be impossible to duplicate any other way. Without Teddy Kennedy's special problems in the area we've come to call character, he might well have been the first Extension to become president himself. Indeed, it is still possible that he will be. Perhaps John Kennedy had a premonition of just that. When he came up from Washington in 1962 to vote for his brother in the Massachusetts primary, he quipped to a grinning audience, "I will introduce myself. I am Teddy Kennedy's brother."

Michael, Jack, Steve, and Susan Ford

It is not that the Ford kids were off an assembly line. It is not that they all served as Extensions of Gerald Ford to the same degree or in the same way. The chances are, in fact, that you have in your mind's eye a couple of pictures of Susan Ford but can barely remember that Michael Ford exists, not to speak of what he looks like. But when we suddenly found that Ford, whom we had not elected to any executive office, was our president, we wanted to know him, and one way we could know him was through all his four children. And when Ford staked a claim to the White House for another four years, one way he made his case was through all his four children. It might be said, in fact, that the Ford kids came in especially handy during two distinct phases—phase 1, "Getting to Know You," and phase 2, "I'm Dreaming of a White (House) Christmas."

Who *are* these four children of Gerald Ford? The point is, of course, that as excellent Extensions, the Ford offspring lacked their own identity, never did anything that really stood out, and now, a scant few years after their photos dotted the "People" section of *Time* with what some would insist was depressing regularity, are only rather vaguely recalled. (The exception to this is Susan Ford, who has managed through a variety of tricks, such as marriage, to stay dimly in the public eye.) But although now they are rather a blur, during the Ford era they *were*, at times and in certain ways, the president. They were he when he could not be there, at political rallies, for example. They were he in that those traits that they did display were seen as reflections of what he was, and of what he would approve. And they were he in that they, through the much-heralded intimacy of the family circle, were an integral part of his whole. Seen another way, they constituted the family unit of which he was a part.

This last point is crucial. In order for us to buy the Ford offspring as Extensions, we had to be sold a bill of goods on how close they were to their father. A rebellious son will not an Extension make and so, particularly since these were still unknown quantities, the first thing we heard (even when Ford was still vice-president) was how tightly knit a family circle this really was.

All four children feel unusually close to their father. Explains Jack: "He never tried to mold or direct us. He allowed us room to explore for ourselves, to find ourselves." Exclaims Susan: "He's the perfect Father."[33]

"We're exceptionally close to one another," Betty Ford explains. "Even though the two older boys are away, we talk to them constantly on the phone. . . . And as much as Jerry travels, he never fails to call me when he gets to his hotel room. . . . He calls and wants to know how I am and how the kids are. He's truly a family man. . . .[34]

Both Mom and Dad have always been willing to listen. We haven't always agreed, but it would be pretty dull if we did. My parents encouraged us to think for ourselves. . . . Mother wasn't too happy about moving to the White House in the beginning, but she is basically very adaptable. That's why it's easy for her to adjust to the idea that my father will run for reelection in 1976. If he's happy, we're happy.[35]

Another point that had to be established early on was the similarity between parents and children. We have seen that the very best Extensions actually look like the president. Failing that, being the same type helps, so that the audience to whom the Extension is playing will confuse the two, that is, will automatically think of the winning daughter, for example, as reflecting her winning father. And so early in the Ford presidency we came to learn that his three sons and one daughter were their parents' true offspring; the younger generation bore the traits of the older. Physically, indeed, they all resembled their father. Susan was quite large and blond; and Michael, Jack, and Steve were over 6 feet tall and graced with their Dad's husky and athletic build. The children's interests, too, mirrored those of their parents. All four were sports buffs as we knew father had always been, and Susan was a dancer like her mother, who, every tot learned, once studied with Martha Graham.

"Outdoorsyness" got a particular play. The president was pictured as an ardent swimmer and skier, and the children followed his trail. Michael was quiet and devout, like his mother, but he also played tennis and gardened. Jack turned full-time aide to his father, but only after giving up plans to become an environmentalist. Steve went all out. He worked on a cattle ranch, rode bucking broncos, and studied grizzly bears in Montana and animal husbandry in California. And when Susan decided to pursue a career as a photographer, she chose as an early mentor the reknowned student of nature Ansel Adams.

This unit of six Fords, then (Michael Ford married Gayle Brumbaugh one month before Gerald Ford was sworn in as president), was an absolutely terrific family, or so we were sold. And the children were like the parents: self-reliant and independent, but within the confines of tradition, shared values, and mutual affection.

Perhaps the most important task of the Ford children during phase 1, "Getting to Know You," was to help differentiate Ford from his predecessor. Gerald Ford could not possibly, no matter how hard he worked at it, do the job of separating himself from the Nixon stench alone. And so, in this matter of style and tone, the Ford Extensions came to have important roles. They responded as if in unison to the plea articulated by, among others, columnist David Broder, who was quoted by *Time* two weeks after Ford became president: "We can play a helpful part in bringing the presidency back to human scale . . . if we back off just enough to let Jerry Ford have room to himself. . . . The Ford family should be spared the massive publicity that has made their predecessors a version of American royalty." All their early efforts were toward normalcy. And all the early talk was of how the Fords would live in the White House much the way they would live anywhere else. The idea was that this wholesome bunch of middle-class, all-American kids would, after their father had served as president, still be a wholesome bunch of middle-class, all-American kids. Blue jeans were symbolic of the new order. Who had ever seen Julie or Tricia in denim? Susan was different. On moving day (from the suburbs to the White House) she wore jeans as defiantly as another would hoist a revolutionary banner, demanding to know, "What else would you wear on moving day? Anything else would be silly and artificial."[36]

Perhaps the word that best describes the note commentators struck when they first wrote about the Fords is "neighborly." It was as if good friends of ours had had a stroke of great fortune and we believed as we hoped that it would not change them or our relationship to them. Betty Ford, we were told, "is intent on ensuring that the White House is a lively home for her family,"[37] and their friends, it was reported, "do not expect the Presidency to change the Fords any more than the Vice Presidency did, which is to say, not at all. . . ."[38] Susan sustained the hope by asserting, "I am the same old Susan and I don't expect to change,"[39] and continuing to baby-sit at a dollar an hour.

Certainly no one could claim that the interests of the Ford children were "highfalutin." Before the year was out, we were told that Susan's main preoccupations were her diet, homework, plants, friends, and sports (the order of priority was not specified), that Steve and Jack had gone to some effort to catch Evel Knievel's attempt to vault the Snake River in a rocket-powered motorcycle, and that Jack, himself just a forestry major at Utah State University, had former Beatle George Hamilton to lunch at the White House.

During 1975, the four Ford children grew to be distinguishable from each other even though they still came in a bunch. Articles were titled "The Fun Fords"[40] or "White House Youngsters — Frank, Free and a Lot Like Their Mother."[41] But enough interest had been generated that the media did the sorting for us. Michael, we learned, was different from Jack was different from

Steve was different from Susan—and they all mirrored different parts of their parents.

Of course, the shared traits were still central—their "candor," their "outdoorsyness," their "independence," their "interest in today's issues," their "closeness to their parents." But by giving each a bit of local color, writers could make the Ford Extensions appeal to a much wider audience. Conveniently, in terms of public appeal, they ran the gamut from preacher to playboy. Michael, the eldest, was the quietest, the most serious, and the most removed from public life. He and his wife lived in Massachusetts, where he attended the Gordon-Conwell Seminary in pursuit of a master's degree in theology. He was described as reflective and devout and planning a career in Christian youth work. Jack, who was twenty-three in 1975, enjoyed two images, one as White House nightlifer and the other as political apprentice. More on the second below, but as for the first, one mention of experience with marijuana and a session or two with such types as Bianca Jagger and Andy Warhol were enough to convince the nation that it had a swinger loitering by the Oval Office. Steve was the lonesome cowboy, and a photogenic one at that. He dabbled from time to time in school, but mostly there were shots of him bulldogging, bronco busting, and calf roping. He was the type of whom Slim Pickens could say, "The kid rides real good."[42] And then there was Susan, the apple of her father's eye, and the Queen of the Forty-eighth Shenandoah Apple Blossom Festival, to which she wore a long white gown with a long white and gold train. An indifferent high school student, she turned semiserious upon graduation in pursuit of a career as a photographer—even to the point of taking summer employment with the Topeka, Kansas, *Capital-Journal* at $115 a week. Susan was the Extension of our closest scrutiny. We learned about her boyfriends (e.g., a ski patrolman from Vail), about her graduation prom (it was old-fashioned), about her eighteenth birthday party (there were hot dogs, hamburgers, and a rock band), and about all her late adolescent escapades (*cum* public relations happenings— e.g., "President Ford's daughter Susan plummeted down a 260-foot water flume today to open River Country, a new attraction at Walt Disney World. . . ."[43])

There was something very reassuring about the Ford children in 1975. Just as the president was the nice guy next door, they were the nice kids next door—guy and kids to be sure who had stepped up in the world, but who didn't get stuck-up about it. Susan, in fact, proved the point. For several months running she wrote a column for *Seventeen* called "White House Diary" in which her rampant averageness shone through. One month she toyed with thoughts about her future—would she or would she not combine having a family with a career? Another month she told us that "my mother is a very special person. . . . My mother really cares about people. She made a point of going down to the White House switchboard room and personally meeting all the operators." And still another time we learned that in spite of her brothers' jokes and teasing, Susan "always looked up to them and counted them as friends. . . . My brothers are good-looking and fun, and they've got it together."[44]

To be sure, the Ford boys were not just snakes and snails and puppy-dog tails, and Susan was not pure sugar and spice. The Ford children had slightly more color than their predecessors; unlike Tricia Nixon, for example, they did not seem middle-aged painted young. They were Extensions in that they, like their father, were Everyman, that is, typical of other Americans their age. And so it was hardly surprising that around Jack and Susan Ford, the president's most visible offspring, there was some excitement about "pot" and sex.

Jack 'fessed up in October 1975—just as his father's campaign for election to the presidency in '76 was getting into gear. *Time* said that "he brought it into the open because he, along with some White House advisers, worried that his father's political opponents might try to make use of rumors about his freewheeling bachelor life, which have been swirling through Washington like smoke at a rock concert."[45] Jack said, "I've smoked marijuana before and I don't think that's so exceptional for people growing up in the nineteen-sixties."[46] And the president said that he had never tried marijuana himself but that he was glad that his son had been honest about his experience with it: "I can disagree with what some of the children do . . . as long as they are honest with us and give us an opportunity to give our views. . . . They have been brought up to be honest with their parents and honest otherwise."[47]

Susan became the focus of attention not because of what it was she did, but because of what it was she might do: have an affair. During a television interview Betty Ford quite reasonably observed that she would not be surprised if her daughter had one, an affair that is. The uproar that resulted was astounding (see Chapter 4). Susan, though, handled the whole thing like an old pro, assuring the worried nation that she had no interest in having an affair "as yet," and rushing to the defense of her mother who "talked about things people should talk about like abortion."[48]

It is worth noting once again how effective all these goings-on were in terms of publicity for the president. Every time one of his Extensions was in the news, he was in the news, and by having four of them in different shades, he could please a broad spectrum of people. For example, in the affair about Susan's affair, there was Michael Ford to counterbalance his racy mother. He announced that he was not sure he agreed with his mother's relative calm about the subject of sex, saying, "I guess I'm more old-fashioned." But it must be emphasized again how these intrafamily problems never seemed to us to be anything other than normal for an all-American family of six, and never seemed to rise above the level of healthy, honest disagreement. If there was any real anger or conflict here during the presidency of Gerald Ford, we were not privy to it.

As 1975 went on, one of the four Ford Extensions started to separate himself somewhat from the others. Jack Ford began to mix his play with serious politics. Jack has been, certainly as far as his mother is concerned, the most difficult of the children. Although she considers him "the best read and most intellectual," she also wrote that he can "be impossible to live with," that he was "filled with resentments," and that he "has been the last to find himself."[49] One of the places he looked was in politics. Labeling himself "by far the most politicized" of the Ford children, he returned to Washington in the summer to start work as a campaign aide. He was scheduled to help line up delegates pledged to his father, and in preparation for the task he sat in on meetings of the White House senior staff, attended conferences with congressional groups, and joined smaller sessions with his father and a few key advisers. It was said that sometimes at day's end, father and son "settle down in the private study off the Oval Office and discuss everything from matters of state to whether or not to breed the family's female golden retriever, Liberty."[50]

There is no evidence that Jack Ford was a match for Ted Kennedy or even Chip Carter as far as being an Extension of substance goes, and indeed the early intentions appeared to wane

a bit during 1976. Jack never fully transcended the image of
White House bachelor-in-residence. But the story of his tentative
try is illustrative. It suggests how close to policy-making situations presidential kin can get if they half try. And it suggests how
tolerant professionals and public are of such an effort as long as it
is not downright embarrassing.

Perhaps because of the prominence of Jimmy Carter's family
during the period when he was just starting to be taken seriously
as a presidential contender, it was during this same time—the
long campaign of 1976—that the Ford family really blossomed.
All four children worked hard at being Extensions. In fact, they
worked so hard that by March 1976 it was being written that as
campaigners, "they are coming on like 'Gangbusters.'"[51] Together with their mother they seemed to be everywhere, selling
their father as they sold themselves—with the vigor and apparent
candor that does a first-rate job with breakfast cereal.

During these months there was a spate of articles extolling
the virtues of togetherness on the hustings. The *New York Times
Magazine* had "Fords for Ford";[52] *Newsweek,* "All-Americans";[53]
U.S. News and World Report, "Ford's Campaign Will Be a Family Affair";[54] and *Time,* "It's a Clash of the Clans."[55] The theme
of all these essays was much the same. The family that had been
described in an early White House press release as "outdoorsy,
sports-loving, close-knit and informal" was using its natural appeal to attract attention to and gain support for the incumbent.
Said Jack, "Since the character of the candidate is so important
in this campaign, those of us in the family have some important
impressions to convey about him."

At first, Mike and Steve laid low. The latter was quoted as
having said, "Politics is not for me, it's my old man's game." But
all the kids showed and cheered at the convention, and from that
point on they all participated. Much was made of the independence of the four, but the independence did not, it seemed, extend to ideology. Barring the occasional disagreement on the
subject of marijuana, or on just how evil Richard Nixon really
was, when the Ford offspring fielded questions, they did so in the
image of their father. Jack especially, as the best and most-in-
formed speaker in the family, "took it upon himself," as his
mother put it, "to see that the 'real message' about Jerry got out.
Jack could really do it, talk about the economy, foreign policy,
energy conservation."[56] The other three talked less but smiled as

much. Mike Ford finally got involved in the campaign "because it was his Christian duty to do so." Susan, smiling like a beauty queen, was "dispatched to march down Main Streets at the first roll of a drum," and when asked why vote for her father, answered, "Because he's a great American. He's doing a good job on the economy and pulled the U.S. out of the hole." And Steve lived up to his title as "Man on the Trail" (bestowed by the Girls Rodeo Association) by traveling around making small talk in the Far West.

Perhaps it is easiest to convey the extent to which the Fords were involved in the campaign—along with the Carter clan—by the unease it occasionally evoked. We were, it seemed, blanketed by the candidates' kin, and *Time,* for one, didn't like it a bit.

> Should a presidential election begin to sound like Book CXXXV of "One Man's Family"?
>
> In a sense, the trend is understandable. The family campaigners can extend the candidate's image far beyond what he could achieve alone. . . . They can appeal to generations and interest groups by whom the candidate might not be welcomed or understood. They ensure constant exposure of the candidate's name. . . .
>
> Until recently, the political family had quite a different view of its proper function: it should be seen only occasionally and heard not at all. . . .
>
> Should families skulk back to the home and suppress their need (if it exists) to express themselves? That is one possibility. But even short of such drastic action, it might be useful to remember that it is the candidate who is running for the presidency.[57]

But for reasons already discussed in Chapter 1, there is no turning back. Offspring such as the four children of Gerald Ford are simply too important an asset. Think of it this way: if you were a politician, that is, one of a species with an insatiable appetite for positive publicity, would you pull back Extensions like Mike, Jack, Steve, and Susan?

The Extended Family

Although some of the Extensions are blessed with extraordinary traits, it seems clear, after considering the performances of Ted Kennedy and the Ford offspring, that these do not come into play during the time they serve the president. Extensions have only one job and only one way of doing it: selling the president to the public by conforming to, and indeed confirming, the image of the man the public already has. Extensions do not incite or excite. They reaffirm what we already know, or think we know—sometimes by adding bits of information, sometimes by only repeating what the candidate or president has already said before.

The media, of course, are the primary means of communication for Extensions. And precisely if somewhat paradoxically, because Extensions are so bland, they do not get chewed up. None of them have ever suffered from media overkill; they are simply too uninteresting. As long as they stay in their accustomed role, they have a long and useful life—even beyond the time when they have a tie to the White House. One way ex-President Ford has managed to stay in the public eye since his departure from Washington in January 1977 is through the exploits of his four children, who, though receding from memory, still seem to make good enough copy. Within a two-week period in June 1978, for example, the *New York Times* saw fit to print an article on Susan Ford, "Trying Life on Her Own," and an item on Steve Ford as a member of the Los Angeles Rough Riders professional rodeo team.[58]

Which brings us to the last point: playing the role of Extension is an excellent entrée to a political career of one's own. The fact that Extensions lack their own identity makes entry into politics relatively easy. Fame is already theirs; they are "well-known for being known by people who are well-known." But their record is a clean slate. Ordinarily, people who enter politics need to have acquired a reputation for something they have done, or something they have said, or something they stand for. None of this is necessary in the case of Extensions, who, at their point of entry, are famous without having offended a single soul.

But we are getting ahead of our story. For now it will suffice to affirm that candidates and presidents with extended families full of Extensions have a valuable resource. Effective, hardworking Extensions generate the kind of good publicity that P.R. persons dream about. And it's all free.

CHAPTER 4

Humanizers

Humanizers bridge the gap between the president and the people. They are particularly useful to those presidents who hold themselves apart from the mass, who keep their distance from us. Humanizers lend credence to the belief that if the president has a relative who is that much like the rest of us, he cannot be all knight, king, or saint. They have an air of wit or color about them. They are fun. They are idiosyncratic. They are apolitical. They bestow upon the president some of their own lively grace, and at their best they amuse as well as reassure.

We are talking here of the last of the three roles whose chief function it is to mediate between the president and the people, to sell, if you will, the president to the public. Decorations, we now know, need only to be seen to work their good effect. Extensions should be seen and heard, but only in the mirror image of their presidential kin. Humanizers are a different commodity altogether: they are valued precisely for traits that *distinguish* them from the president, and we expect that what they've got they'll flaunt. They are the least plastic of presidential relatives, and in the act of being themselves they market the Chief Executive.

Humanizers are fresh characters in their own right, possessed of a strong identity that makes them interesting to the public quite apart from the presidential connection. Look at the front chart. Rose Kennedy, Betty Ford, Lillian Carter, Billy Carter, and Ruth Carter Stapleton, the five Humanizers we have already met who are listed there, are all originals; all spark curiosity about their own lives; and all have contributed their own bons mots to the language of the presidential culture. In this last sense they are the opposite of Decorations. It is true that to work their maximum affect, Humanizers really ought to be seen. The trim, chic figure of Rose Kennedy and the lined, gray-framed face of Lillian Carter, for example, have strong visual impact. But what really sets this group apart is that we are interested in what it is they have to say. Make no mistake. Humanizers rarely address themselves to the problems of politics. But they have an opinion on just about everything else, and that opinion is frequently off-beat—coming as it is from the president's kin—and so we want to hear it. It was through *listening* to Lillian Carter that we first began to pay real attention to her. And her strong views and the unusual abandon with which she volunteered them did not exactly hurt the political fortunes of her elder son.

Which brings us to the main point. Humanizers are most useful—one might even claim necessary—in the case of presidents and especially candidates who are relatively unknown and who are not themselves exciting personalities. There is good evidence to suggest that Jimmy Carter, to take the most obvious recent example, benefited handsomely from having three relatives who were such colorful, earthy characters. Not only was the man himself quite unknown in 1975 and '76; the public image that he did have was altogether too pious, too mechanical, too removed from the rest of us. His clan came to the rescue: with siblings like Ruth and Billy and a mother like Miss Lillian, the man could not be all robot.

Perhaps the argument about the value of relatives like the Carters is driven home most effectively by comparisons. It is conjecture, of course, but who can say how much better the completely colorless George McGovern might have done in 1972 if he had been blessed with a few striking relatives? And what if Hubert Humphrey had had some real crowd pleasers in tow in that close call of '68? No one is claiming that the candidates' kin determine the outcomes of elections. But the publicity they gain for themselves and the vicarious benefits they thus bestow on the great man himself ought not to be discounted.

Rose Kennedy was an asset to Jack from the beginning, from the time when he first ran for Congress as a bachelor. Indeed, during those early years she, as the daughter of "Honey Fitz" Fitzgerald and the wife of the Ambassador to the Court of Saint James, was probably better known in the streets of Boston than was her son. Rose Kennedy was experienced. She was also at ease with the press, and could be depended on to speak articulately and interestingly whenever a suitable occasion arose. Of her contribution to Kennedy's run for the Senate in 1952, Victor Lasky writes:

> An unabashed effort was made to win the female vote. . . . Mrs. Joseph P. Kennedy . . . flew home from Paris to do her bit. An object of feminine fascination, both as the wife of a former Ambassador to Great Britain and as a Papal Countess, Rose Kennedy was everywhere—on television, at women's meetings across the state, and at the now famous teas. . . . She would change her garb to fit the kind of gathering. Seated in the back of her limousine, she would remove the jewels and furs which had delighted suburban matrons to change to a more simple dress when meeting with less pretentious ladies in the open wards. She was not the daughter of Honey Fitz Fitzgerald for nothing.[1]

She played the same kind of a role during the presidential campaign of 1960. The demand for Rose Kennedy was great, and as always, she obliged. For example, she spent eight days in Wisconsin to help out in the primary. Her standing rule was to never talk about the issues and always talk about the family. She became an expert in the art of presidential politics, and it was said of her that she was never stumped, that there was never a question that she did not manage to turn to her son's advantage.

Mrs. Kennedy herself remembers putting together a "rather rambling talk" for Jack in 1946 but recalls too that almost always the crowds were friendly. Soon she "gained the confidence that comes from practice and experience."[2] Her memories of 1960 confirm the enthusiastic tributes of others. They also indicate that her worth was never underestimated by those who manned the Kennedy machine.

> My schedule [in Wisconsin] began around 8:30 a.m. with a talk to a breakfast club, or a radio or TV appearance, and ended in mid-to-late evening, time enough for 7 or 8 hours sleep. . . . Everything was handled so efficiently that I was never exhausted in spite of a rather hectic schedule—a schedule that was made for me, without my advice but with my consent by Bobby and his campaign associates, who decided where and how and when I could help most efficiently."[3]

Mrs. Kennedy writes that she never missed a chance to ask any-

one to vote for Jack. "I talked with taxi drivers, elevator operators, waitresses, porters, manicurists and anyone with whom I
could strike up a conversation." And as a reward for her efforts,
when it was all over, her eldest surviving son gave her a map of
the United States which he had marked to show the places she
had visited. It was signed, "For Mother. With Thanks."

Lillian Carter, the other "First Mother" who has played the
role of Humanizer with zest, is cut from different cloth. (Author
Kandy Stroud, though, in an article in *McCall's,* finds a similarity between Rose Kennedy and Lillian Carter: she calls them
both "spunky, determined, witty and a dominating influence on
[their] sons"[4]). Rose Kennedy may have been a Papal Countess,
but Lillian Carter was available to talk to from a rocker on the
front porch in Plains. She was nothing if not earthy, this powerful Southern matriarch, but there was more to her than proximity
to the soil. The legend grew fast as a spring sprout. Miss Lillian,
the story soon had it, was a liberal. Before Jimmy was elected,
Time wrote of his mother that "she sat up through the night with
sick black children . . . and in an era of strict segregation, she
would greet black friends at the front door or in her parlor."[5] She
was also a healer. She was trained as a registered nurse, sat
through the night with all those children, and, at the age of sixty-
eight, joined the Peace Corps. (When asked why she joined, she
replied that she was "bored" and, "as a lark," decided to sign up.)
She was also a powerful influence on her son. Not only did she
bequeath him her pearly-toothed smile; it was said too that it was
her persistence, *her* endurance, and *her* inquisitiveness that
Jimmy had inherited. We also learned that the mother of the
Carter house always read at the dinner table, from which we were
to assume that if she wasn't exactly a model of manners, at least
she was a model of learning.

For once, the hype does not go beyond the recognizable. Lillian Carter is truly a candidate for "most unforgettable character." Recognizing this, the president has sent her on a variety of
goodwill missions ranging from inspecting drought conditions
in West African countries to heading the American delegation at
the funeral of Golda Meir. In addition, she toured the United
States on behalf of Democrats sympathetic to her son. These appearances were invariably full of surprises. No dialogue with
Jimmy Carter's mother is ordinary. The following exchanges all

took place during one brief campaign trip to Connecticut in October 1978:

- Squeezing the hand of William Ratchford, congressional candidate from the fifth district: "I only campaign for winners and that's why I'm here in Connecticut with Bill. I love politics and I think I do well everywhere I go."
- Quipping with reporters before a fund-raising party: Yes, she planned to be at the World Series later that week rooting for the Dodgers. Yes, her trip to Rome for the funeral of Pope John Paul was beautiful, impressive, and sad. "But Hussein's uncle held an umbrella for me when it started to rain."
- Continuing: "Don't believe all those rumors you hear about Billy Carter. He doesn't drink as much beer as they say; he would burst if he did. Billy's not running for anything, thank God."
- On the Equal Rights Amendment: "Don't ask me, I've been liberated all my life."
- On assuming that Connecticut's Governor Ella Grasso was Bella Abzug: "Are you the lady who wears the hats?"
- On her six-hour poker game with reporters on the return flight from Rome: "It's not true I wiped them out. I lost a quarter playing penny-ante, while Mayor Koch slept and Ella Grasso hooked a rug."
- On a visit to local senior centers: "I told them to get out of their rocking chairs and get going."[6]

Yes, Miss Lillian can be depended on to deliver. (She appeared on a Johnny Carson show in mid-1979 and volunteered such things as that Burt Reynolds was "the best movie actor on earth," and that audiences "have gotten to where they expect me" to be risqué." When she left the stage, Carson muttered in admiration, "There are votes out there."[7]) It must be said, however, that she is not merely an eccentric old woman. Indeed, she is almost certainly listened to with that peculiar mix of reverence and amusement precisely because it is known that she *has* led a life of substance. It seemed perfectly appropriate when she became the first woman to receive the Synagogue Council of America's Covenant of Peace prize (other recipients have included Martin Luther King, John Kennedy, and Earl Warren), and was cited for her contributions to the "furtherance of international

understanding, justice and peace." And we understood when
Edward Hoagland's review of a collection of Miss Lillian's letters to her family from India turned into no less than a muted
paean.

> The letters become urgent, telegraphic. . . . Over a period of weeks a
> leper woman starves to death before her eyes. . . . She herself lives
> on beans, cauliflower and sweet potatoes . . . and is soon going bare-
> foot. . . . Miss Lillian scrubs her hands until they're sore after her
> first job nursing a leper girl. She dislikes Voltaire, hates sym-
> phonies, but reads Anna Karenina and Huckleberry Finn for the
> 10th time. . . . Some days, [the doctor and] she and a male nurse
> named Raja examine 360, "besides the regular injections." She is
> so homesick that she has to say, "Get thee behind me, Satan." . . .
> She gives away her shawls and sweaters to the patients shivering
> from pneumonia. . . . "My little cross-eyed boy" dies of hunger,
> boils and mumps. She has tea with her new friends at cowdung
> tables on cowdung floors. . . .
>
> When Mrs. Carter reached Atlanta again, she looked so weak
> and worn her family had her taken off the plane in a wheelchair. . . .
>
> Of course, this is old-fashioned stuff. . . . I've probably made the
> book sound better than it is by quoting only the high points. But I
> haven't overplayed my affection for its author. It turns out that we
> do, after all, learn a little something about what the mother of a
> great president might be like.[8]

Ruth Carter Stapleton, favorite child of James Earl Carter,
Sr., has taken the dour out of religion for the Carter family. Her
commitment to Christianity appears to be total. But this is a faith
healer with a difference: Ruth Carter Stapleton is attractive, styl-
ishly dressed, and charming as well as convincing.

When Jimmy Carter became nationally known, her own fame
and fortunes multiplied. The advice she gave her brother after his
loss to Lester Maddox in the governor's race in 1966—"You've
got to commit yourself completely to Jesus. There's no halfway
position if you expect your religion to be of any value to you or to
anybody else, including the Lord"[9]—was now being spread all
across the land. Occasionally, she even had star converts (the
most notorious was *Hustler* publisher Larry Flynt), who effectively seconded the testimonial from Jimmy.

Soon enough, she, like the message she bore, was all over—
on television, in newspapers and magazines, at charismatic rallies. Most people didn't mind Mrs. Stapleton; in fact, she was

quite a drawing card. A meeting with her as headliner at the Meadowlands Stadium just outside New York City in May 1978, for example, drew a crowd of 54,000. But once in a while she touched a raw nerve. In her zeal to sell herself, she told of her evangelizing success with some Jews. Some other Jews, not surprisingly, were not too pleased with the boast, and protested. As a result, on at least one occasion Ruth Stapleton felt compelled to cancel an appearance before a religious group, stating, "I might have been used to convert, which is against my calling."[10] (She claimed, incidentally, that her brother the president did not pressure her into pulling out of the business of converting Jews.)

Now not everyone is excited by the idea of being turned on to Christ by the president's youngest sister. Nor was every single contributor to the Democratic party coffers who received a solicitation from "Ruth, Your Sister in Christ," moved to give to the "Ruth Carter Stapleton Ministries." But there is no doubt that Mrs. Stapleton has a wide appeal. She preaches a message that some want badly to hear. She is a sister of the President of the United States. And she is, in the words of Jules Witcover, "a striking blonde given to wearing eye shadow, gold rings in her pierced ears, and turtleneck sweaters; not your basic faith healer by any means."[11]

They are, then—Rose Kennedy, Lillian Carter, and Ruth Carter Stapleton—hardly your ordinary, humdrum types. Each of them is in the mind's eye as a strikingly individual character, and as such, each of them rendered a service to their presidential kin. They, like Betty Ford and Billy Carter, enlivened the man and allowed him thereby to pull more people in his wake.

Betty Ford

It was said of Gerald Ford, when he became our president in the odd month of August, that he was really a very nice guy. But who knew any more than that in the summer of '74? To be sure, the man had been around Washington for over two and a half decades. But he had never been elected by a national constituency to anything, and to most of the nation the new president was an unknown quantity.

The thing to remember is that we had never been in a situation quite like it. Richard Nixon had selected Gerald Ford to replace the disgraced Spiro Agnew as vice-president. Thus, when Nixon himself was forced from office, we found ourselves in the unique circumstance—no novelist would have gotten away with it—of having had our president chosen for us by the very man we had just deemed politically and morally unfit for public office.

Of course, many of us had supposed for some months prior to the deed that Nixon would be forced to resign. And of course we knew that when he did, Gerald Ford would become our thirty-eighth president. Still, when it actually happened, it seemed sudden. We felt ignorant about the new Chief Executive, and there was a rush to understand what the man was all about.

But try as we might, there was just not very much about Jerry Ford that grabbed the imagination. Even after the feverish digging into his past and present started, there was no pay dirt. The most exciting thing about Ford was that he took a swim every day and made his own breakfast. Beyond that, he seemed indeed to be as blond, bland, and benign as the early rumors had suggested. And so, desperate for something with a dash of color, we turned to those around him.

As the preceding chapter indicated, his four children were not terribly different from their father. Sure, they were younger, but late adolescence alone does not a Humanizer make. And if Gerald Ford did not exactly need someone to convince us that he was not all knight, king, or saint, it was clear early on that he stood to benefit mightily from someone who could bring him to vivid life. Enter Betty Ford.

Elizabeth Ann Bloomer Ford was, at first blush, hardly a likely candidate for the role of political star. True, she had been a Washington wife for a long time. Indeed, since 1965 her husband had been the House minority leader, and so the expectation certainly was that she would do her job as consort to the president and make a suitable First Lady. But what no one would have imagined was that Betty Ford, timid and unknown in 1974, would two years later be so popular in her own right that "Keep Betty's Husband in the White House" campaign buttons would be the thing to sport. Perhaps, though, we should have guessed when we witnessed the brouhaha triggered by Mrs. Ford immediately on her move into the White House. Her announcement that she and her husband would continue to share the same bedroom and sleep in their own bed after taking up residence at 1600 Pennsylvania Avenue was bound, any really proper First Lady would intuitively have known, to evoke some howls of protest. (Of that episode Mrs. Ford later wrote, "Well, people started saying I was disgraceful and immoral. I didn't care. I wanted to be a good First Lady. . . . I didn't believe I had to do every single thing some previous President's wife had done. . . . I was feeling slightly defensive."[12])

Apart from the bed brouhaha, which died away fast, the Betty Ford we got at first sell was not, in fact, terribly interesting. What came out the first month or so of the Ford presidency was all the sunny stuff, the kind of information that was intended to still our collective savage breast (after the trauma of Watergate) with assurances about the physical and mental health of the new First Family. We heard about a nice lady, who, using an archetypical suburban house in Alexandria, Virginia, as home base, raised four all-American children while her husband traveled 258 days a year to hawk the Republican party. It is macabre, perhaps, to assert that Betty Ford's first great claim to national attention and affection was when she had a radical mastectomy, but there's truth to the assertion nonetheless. Who knows what kind of a role she would have played had this drama not taken place? There is no doubt that it focused the nation's eyes on the new woman in the White House and created for her a wave of sympathy that would have been difficult to duplicate in another, less grim way. Less than two months after her husband assumed the presidency, Betty Ford was front-page news.

Two aspects of the story won our hearts. On the most basic level, we were saddened that the president's family had to face cancer, and moved by Mrs. Ford's courageous response to her illness. Specifically, we heard high tributes to the First Lady. President Ford said, "I just spent sometime with Betty [after the surgery]. Her spirits are excellent. She looks just great. . . . She's a great gal. And she's doing very well." Dr. William Lukash, the president's personal physician, then was quoted: "I might add from a personal note, that throughout this ordeal Mrs. Ford exhibited a . . . kind of inner strength that sustained the first family, her close staff and, I think, her doctors."[13] And *Newsweek* had a cover story on Mrs. Ford's surgery that concluded, "Betty Ford clearly has the gumption to make it through her ordeal. That was demonstrated, once again, only an hour before she went into the operating room [when she wisecracked to her family about her white hospital stockings]. It's hard to defeat a woman like that."[14]

On another level, it was clear that the Ford family's honesty about the First Lady's breast cancer was bringing a much-needed attention to a subject that had until recently been almost taboo. There was a spate of articles on the subject, with titles such as "How Women Face the Physical Effects of Breast Cancer Surgery" and "After Breast Cancer Surgery Exercise Becomes a Way of Life." And, through articles discussing the particulars of the Betty Ford (and later Happy Rockefeller) case, there was, for the first time, a broad distribution of information about how the disease might be detected and treated. To some, the cover story in *Newsweek*, for example, was no more than a personal tale told in excruciating detail, but others saw it as fulfilling a great opportunity to reach women with facts they should know.

The response to Betty Ford during this period was enormous. She received some 50,000 pieces of mail and enlisted 100 women volunteers in the cause of answering them. There was consolation, reassurance, and advice from men, women, and children, and there were donations of money in her name to the American Cancer Society. But the sense of community went both ways. Not only were people out there responding to Mrs. Ford, she herself felt for the first time the influence that was potentially hers. Later she wrote, "Lying in the hospital, thinking of all those women going for cancer checkups because of me, I'd come to recognize more clearly the power of the woman in the White House. Not *my* power, but the power of the position, a power which could be used to help."[15]

Betty Ford's recovery from surgery was traced with meticulous care by the media, and when it was all over, Washington had a heroine. There was no slipping back to the inconspicuousness that had enshrouded the woman before: by Christmas of 1974, it was clear that the First Lady was the Ford most likely to humanize the Ford administration. She came from nowhere to take a prominent place in the "most admired" polls (by early December she was seventh in a *Good Housekeeping* survey); she was given the credit for bestowing upon the White House a special ambiance marked by a blend of "warmth and easy hospitality with the traditional dignity of the home of the American president";[16] and around her persona there started to grow a special mystique. No less an authority on media communication than Marshall McLuhan was moved to comment, "She seems to have just what it takes to make people feel at home in the world again. Something about her makes us feel rooted and secure—a feeling we haven't had in a while. And her cancer has been a catharsis for everybody. . . ."[17]

By early 1975, Mrs. Ford began to establish a reputation as a lady who, despite her Midwestern, Republican credentials and her straight-arrow husband, was "with it." Slowly we found out that she was just off center from Middle America. For one thing she was a divorcee, only the second ever to occupy the White House. She also had a passion for the dance, a passion that rang truer than most because we learned that the woman had actually spent a bit of time when young under the tutelage of the high priestess of modern dance, Martha Graham. And, would you believe, this First Lady had paid regular visits to a psychiatrist? Finally, too, there were all those opinions on things: support for liberalized abortion laws, support for liberalized marijuana laws, support for the notion that trial marriages might be a good thing, support to the point of activism for the Equal Rights Amendment. On this last point there was some flack. The First Lady was criticized heavily by opponents of ERA, who went so far as to picket the White House. But she vowed to "stick to my guns" and keep lobbying. Which she did—so much so that in March 1975 *Time* wrote of her that she had "taken to the telephone with a zeal for public fray not seen in the White House since Eleanor Roosevelt."[18]

Mostly, people were delighted by this departure from Pat Nixon, for the way in which Betty Ford put across her newfangled ideas was wholly inoffensive. She never betrayed her middle American roots or veered too far from the mainstream typified by her husband. (At one point, for example, she reassured us that she was not the type to burn her bra.) Nor did she become a snob. She came across like the most ordinary of women; one observer commented that she was "like the sort you might find lined up with a loaded cart at a supermarket checkout counter." And she seemed fully aware of the accident of history that had thrust her into this position of potential power. At one early point she wryly noted, "I don't feel that because I'm First Lady, I'm any different from what I was before. It can happen to anyone. After all, it *has* happened to anyone."[19]

But in August of 1975 Betty Ford really shook us up, really pushed our tolerance for a "cool" First Lady to the limit. It happened during an interview for CBS's "60 Minutes" with correspondent Morley Safer. She volunteered that, in general, premarital relations with the right partner might lower the divorce rate. She said that she assumed that all her children had tried marijuana out of curiosity—and that she might have done the same herself had it been widely used when she was young. But worst of all, she said that she "would not be surprised" if her daughter, Susan, had a premarital affair: "I think she's a perfectly normal human being like all young girls. If she wanted to continue it, I would certainly counsel her and advise her on the subject. And I'd want to know pretty much about the young man that she was planning to have the affair with. . . . She's pretty young to have affairs." Then Safer asked, "But nevertheless, old enough?" To which the First Lady replied, "Oh yes, she's a big girl."

It was an absolute scandal. Or so some thought, anyway. (Including the president. In his book *A Time to Heal,* Gerald Ford cites the Safer interview as one of the three reasons for the 1976 primary challenge from within the Republican party!) The reaction to Mrs. Ford's statement—which was not, of course, anything much more than a First Lady making her public peace with already existing mores—was astonishment at her openness. Some were dismayed and astonished. Others were delighted and astonished. But no one saw her performance during that interview as anything other than a highly unusual departure from the behavior of her predecessors. To provide an idea of the debate that was sparked, consider this. The October 7 issue of *Senior Scholastic* made the question of just how open First Ladies should be the topic of its "Pro/Con" debate of the week. It was suggested that the nation's high schoolers be given a chance to respond to the following questions: "Can the First Lady speak out without being considered too outspoken?" and "How far is too far when it's the President's wife giving her views?"

By the time the dust had settled, it was clear that her outspokenness had won more friends for Mrs. Ford than it made enemies. Even the poll conducted by the tradition-conscious *Ladies' Home Journal* had 53% approving versus 30% disapproving Betty Ford's stance in the affair of the affair. But the following sample of angry excerpts demonstrates that a not inconsiderable segment of the society was outraged by Mrs. Ford's position, and even more outraged by the fact that a First Lady had elected to make such a position a matter of public record:

Letter to the editor of the *New York Times:*

> I am ashamed for my country, the President, responsible parents and all who hold the Judeo-Christian ethic sacred. What kind of hypocrisy was Mrs. Ford foisting on the American public last year as she held the Bible in her husband's oath-of-office ceremony? She obviously flouts the basic tenets it contains.

Phyllis Schlafly:

> By approving premarital sex for her daughter, the President's wife dealt a fatal blow to any remaining confidence in the moral standards of White House occupants. It is no defense to say that she is "honest." The Happy Hooker did not become virtuous when she honestly described her immorality. . . . To approve sin because other people are doing it, was the moral sickness of Watergate.

Harriet Van Horne in a column titled "Candor Overdone":

> [I] have been saddened by the unseemliness of it all, a First Lady forfeiting a certain privacy, some mystique that keeps the vital luster of the First Lady alive.

William F. Buckley:

> What she did was to use her high office as First Lady, achieved by a concentration of romantic and felonious coincidences, to rewrite the operative sexual code of Western civilization. It is very surprising, and very bad news, that Mrs. Ford abused her husband's position by speaking out in contravention of ethical values established, according to her husband, who not infrequently invokes His assistance, by an authority even higher than the Supreme Court.[20]

Some of the response to Betty Ford's naughty behavior was so extreme that her husband was moved to try to soften the blow. At first he tried to do so with a little humor. Just after the episode he authorized press secretary Ron Nessen to say that the president had long since ceased to be "perturbed or surprised by his wife's remarks." A few days later Gerald Ford wryly noted of the incident, "When I first heard it, I thought I'd lost 10 million votes. When I read it in the paper the next morning, I raised it to 20 million." Some weeks after that, he tried defending his wife's right to speak out: "I do not think I would be very popular at home if I tried to lay down the law. She does have very good judgment. Betty will probably speak very frankly as she always does." And on still another occasion, he tried to reinterpret what was said. He regretted that "there has been some misunderstanding" about his wife's remarks. "Betty meant we're deeply concerned about the moral standards. . . . There is a high moral standard in the family. . . ." Finally, during the campaign of '76 the man went all the way. He asserted in no uncertain terms that if *he* discovered that Susan was having an affair, he would "protest in a most vigorous way."[21]

By the end of 1975, her outspokenness notwithstanding, Betty Ford was one of the most popular women in America. *McCall's* said that "to a public used to canned and predictable First Lady comments, she is like champagne after *vin ordinaire*."[22] *Good Housekeeping's* poll found that she was now first on the list of "the most admired women", and a November Lou Harris poll reported that she as a "solid asset" to her husband;[23] and *Newsweek* devoted a smashing cover story to Betty Ford, the "Woman of the Year."[24] The *Newsweek* article epitomized what was then the prevailing wisdom. Some key points:

> "Not since Eleanor Roosevelt . . . has a First Lady spoken out more freely. . . . Her soft, hesitant voice seems to speak as much from her heart as her politics. . . . Says an admiring Nancy Kissinger: 'Betty is uniquely able to create an atmosphere of warmth and relaxation without losing the dignity of the occasion. . . .' Her outspokenness has added a new dimension of respect to an already strikingly affectionate marriage. . . . Certainly there was plenty of warning that a liberated woman lurked behind Betty Ford's amiable facade. When she divorced William Warren in 1947, Betty took an alimony settlement of only $1. . . ."

As the story goes, Mrs. Ford's participation in the 1976 presidential campaign came about gradually.

> . . . Jerry was President, but he was still running, and so was I. At first I'd said I would participate only as a wife, appearing with my husband when he wanted or needed me to. I didn't feel qualified to be a spokesman. But after New Hampshire it was decided that we could cover more ground by going our separate ways. . . . The decision made me anxious. I wasn't a good politician, I usually said what was on my mind, and that could cost my husband votes.* Still I

---

*Mrs. Ford's notoriety could make her very uneasy. For example, she wrote that the "furor after '60 Minutes' terrified me."[25]

agreed to try, and I was dispatched to Florida, where I worked for five days before Jerry came to join me.[26]

Before the jig was up that November, she had proven so successful an attraction that son Jack said of her that "we didn't want her in New Hampshire too much because it would look as though Father had ridden in on her coattail."

It is not at all clear, of course, how much impact any member of the candidate's family has on the vote, if any. What is certain is that professional politicians work on the assumption that captivating kin just might be an asset, and offensive ones just might be a liability—and they enlist or don't enlist them accordingly. During the primary contests between Ford and Ronald Reagan, for example, one observer noted, "It is not inconceivable that in a close, crucial primary in a state where abortion, the Equal Rights Amendment and concern over permissiveness toward children weigh heavily on conservative Republican voters, an honest outpouring of views by either Betty or Jack Ford, or maybe even Susan, might tip the balance to Reagan."[27] In this case, the assessment was that in some states with large conservative constituencies Betty Ford indeed might not be a help to the cause. Yet overall, she was seen as a valuable resource and used accordingly. During both the primary contests and the general campaign she made frequent public appearances—almost always to warmly affectionate crowds. A typical routine would consist of a motorcade down a busy street, a session with the local press, a ceremonial gesture such as ribbon cutting or plane christening, and a series of chats with small groups. Her mission as she saw it was to "see as many people as possible and tell them about the integrity, leadership and honesty of the President."[28]

And so she did, to not enough avail as it turned out. But when it was all over, her place in the political culture of this country was secure. It seemed perfectly appropriate that because Gerald Ford had a throat ailment, it was his wife—whom he designated as "the real spokesman for the family"—who read his concession statement to the cameras.

While Betty Ford was in the White House, we had no real idea that she had a dangerous dependency on drugs and alcohol. Sure, we knew she drank. Sure, we knew that she took tranquilizers. But the drinking we thought was purely social, and the tranquilizers and not too infrequent indispositions were, we were told, for an ailment variously described as a "pinched nerve," "chronic

arthritic condition," "ailment in the neck and back," and "fatigue." Very occasionally there were veiled hints in the press that
something more was going on. There was this sentence, for example, in an otherwise adoring article in *McCall's:* "In the most
formal situations, the open and natural Mrs. Ford is at her worst,
frozen stiffly into a pose that leads some observers to wonder if
she isn't dazed on tranquilizers."[29] And there was the quite unexplained quote by an anonymous friend in the "Woman of the
Year" story in *Newsweek:* "I've seen her so doped she didn't
know where she was."[30] Most suggestive of all was that story titled "The Strain on Betty" in *Newsweek* of August 18, 1975 (see
also Chapter 1); but even this collection of strong hints was never
really picked up by the rest of the press.

> . . . Betty Ford, standing limp and pale beside her husband on the
> last stop of his European summit trip, looked like an exceptionally
> weary tourist. . . . That afternoon Mrs. Ford kept a mechanical grip
> on her welcome bouquet. . . . At one point she seemed to waver, and
> the robust Mrs. Tito extended a steadying arm.
> Her shaky performance during the President's recent European
> tour renewed speculation about the state of Betty Ford's health. . . .

The truth about Betty Ford, to adopt a *True Confessions* cli-
ché, became known only some fourteen months after the Fords
left the White House. (She, it should be added, has claimed that
"I was fine when I was in the White House."[31]) In spring 1978
she voluntarily entered Long Beach Naval Hospital and announced publicly that she was addicted to both alcohol and prescription drugs. Needless to say, there was a renewed spate of
publicity for the former First Lady—and a renewed sympathy.
Once again, her candor was credited with bringing an ugly but
common problem out of the closet. Her subsequent honesty
about her cosmetic surgery, which followed some months later,
then became only the most recent corroboration of what the nation had come to think of as a truism: notwithstanding the cam-
ouflage of a problem of addiction that was almost certainly already in evidence during the White House years, Betty Ford was
the most self-revealing woman ever to play the role of First Lady.
Mrs. Ford once said of "Vote for Betty's Husband" buttons,
"I don't think it's bad or detrimental. . . . It humanizes the presidency." As the buttons humanized the presidency, the woman
humanized the president. She managed to be deferential to him
and to "do her own thing" all at the same time. As a result, she

appealed to a wide gamut—from feminists to all but the most rock-ribbed conservatives—and managed to bring some color and wit to an administration otherwise known for its post-Watergate caution. On one occasion the First Lady told an interviewer that she'd been asked about "everything but how often I sleep with my husband, and if they'd asked me that, I would have told them." The intrepid questioner quite naturally felt impelled to push on and ask, "What would you have said?" To which Mrs. Ford replied, "As often as possible." Can such a Humanizer help but be an asset?

Billy Carter

In the second half of 1977, they started to rob us of our innocence. They started to hint that all that beer made him vulgar, that all that attention made him greedy, that all that money made him corrupt. It was downhill from there on. By the beginning of 1979, Billy Carter's image was that of the repugnant alcoholic, probably also guilty of violating the banking laws and possibly even the federal election laws. By the end of 1980, he was an authentic bad guy—albeit a pathetic one—who had done no less than contribute to his brother's downfall (see Chapter 8).

But in the beginning, it was all great good fun: the pious struggling-to-be-known candidate from Georgia had a redneck for a brother. It had been many moons since a presidential relative had provided us with so many yuks. In fact, Billy was so perfect a Humanizer the first eighteen months or so of Carter-consciousness that he rapidly became a rousing part of American political lore. He never looked all that good. He never counseled. Indeed, he remained deliberately aloof from Washington. (It was May 1977 before he slept in the White House for the first time. And all he could say about the experience was "I got lost. It's too damned big.") He never let a serious word fall from his lips. But his political function was real, and for all the evidence at our disposal, brother Jimmy understood that very well. He who had the need for *Playboy* had the need for Billy. The president and Billy came out of the same womb, didn't they? Ergo, Jimmy could not be all good.

Jimmy Carter wrote, "I never even considered disobeying my

father.... He was a stern disciplinarian and punished me severely when I misbehaved."[32] But Earl Carter's attitude toward his youngest son was apparently much different. "When Billy came along as the child of his later life," his cousin Hugh Carter wrote, "he put away that old peach-switch thinking." Hugh Carter also volunteered that in his family there was a little joke that "according to uncle Earl, Jimmy could do no right and Billy could do no wrong."[33] As a result, perhaps, Billy takes after Earl Carter. Most who knew the Carters well agree, in fact, with Jimmy's assessment of the similarity between Billy and his father—"in appearance, habits and attitudes."[34] Jimmy, it was said, took after his mother, although years later all three of the other children remembered that Billy was also Miss Lillian's pet."[35]

Obviously, these particular family dynamics affected the relationship between Jimmy and Billy. It is certain, in any case, that because of the thirteen-year age difference between them, they were never very close during the growing-up years—at least not as peers. Such closeness as they did have was more like father and son. Jimmy at nineteen would take his six-year-old brother boating, for example. But when Jimmy returned home from the Navy after his Father had died to take over the family business, Billy was only sixteen and he was not, according to the testimony of his elder brother, "at all inclined to take orders" from him. Thus no one was surprised when, the day after graduating from high school in 1955, Billy left Plains to join the Marines.

Billy was a tough kid who seemed to spend his adolescence and early adulthood in resentment against the establishment. A youthful marriage to a local girl was the main source of stability during these early peripatetic years.

Billy returned to Plains in 1959 but two years later left again to enroll at Emory University. Three years after that he quit school to move to Macon, where for a while he sold paint. But in short order that too was left behind, and Billy came home again to Plains. By 1966 he had an interest in the family business, and with Jimmy now the candidate for governor, Billy's managerial responsibilities increased.

Whatever the exact nature of the financial transactions of the Carter farms and warehouse during the years of Jimmy's governorship and campaign for the presidency, one thing is clear: it was Billy who was mainly responsible for making Jimmy's political career financially possible. Even early on, no one denied that, and in May 1976 the *New York Times* observed:

> The strong bonds between the Carter family members and their willingness to work together has made them a potent factor in Mr. Carter's rise to become front runner for the Democratic Presidential nomination. . . . Billy Carter . . . said that figures now being prepared . . . indicated that 1975 was the best year in the history of the warehouse business and that it would result in substantial increases in Jimmy Carter's income and wealth. . . . The family business has other advantages. After his loss in 1966, with his brother on hand to take over and both of their wives involved in the business . . . Jimmy Carter was free to spend considerable time running for the 1970 Gubernatorial nomination. . . .[36]

And in his book *Why Not the Best?* Jimmy wrote of Billy, "Our friendship has grown steadily with the years, and I realize that his willingness to operate our farms and warehouse has made it possible for me to hold public office."[37] Only later did we wonder if there was an underside to all of this, if a price was paid by both Billy and Jimmy for the debt the latter felt he owed the former.

In the beginning, in fact, no one paid much attention to the financial affairs of the Carter family business, and people certainly did not connect brother Billy to anything as apparently remote as the banking or federal election laws. In 1976 and 1977 Billy Carter sold himself as a good ol' country boy, and we bought it whole—even at a steadily rising price. The man's clout, his hold on our curiosity as it were, grew out of the image he presented to the public during Jimmy Carter's presidential campaign. Shortly after the win, he began to shift on us; some said he began to bilk us. But it was too late to save ourselves from Billy. His spade work had been done and done well, and he was able to spend the better part of the next two years capitalizing on that early effort.

Ironically, it was our feeling about Billy that he was fundamentally stable and intelligent that allowed him to play the jester to such great effect. The early wisdom on Billy Carter was that he was really a straight arrow who just happened, on the side, to be a card. He had been married for twenty-one years, lovingly, to wife Sybil. He was a family man: "the beer hour never prevents him from sitting down to dinner with Sybil and their six children, who range in age from three months to 20 years."[38] He was a bang-up businessman who had raised the gross of the family peanut business from $800,000 to $4 million plus. Although a college drop-out, he was well read—four Georgia papers and the *Wall Street Journal* each day, as well as three books a week. (Faulkner was a favorite.) He was a closet liberal who financed a 1966 lawsuit against segregated private schools. He was hard-working and imaginative in his work, but also exuberant. Unlike brother Jimmy, it seemed he knew how to enjoy life, but he too, like Jimmy, had a sense of communal responsibility. It was said that he ran twice for mayor of Plains because he worried about its future now that over 2,000 tourists a day had started to lay siege. "The Real Brother Billy," as *Newsweek* said in a full-page article with that phrase as title, "is intelligent, intense and proud. He is nobody's fool."[39]

The other attribute that Billy was said to have, a trait that later came to be seen as a sin, was a strong streak of rebelliousness. Not for him the establishment niceties! He thumbed his nose at everything that Americans traditionally hold dear except, not insignificantly, family and money. He flaunted his failure in school: "I went to Emory for two and a half years, flunked out, I was a career freshman you might say. Never passed anything."[40] He boasted about his distance from the church: "I joined the church when I was twelve years old, and I've been back there three times since. Correction—five times."[41] He was a show-off about the amount of liquor he consumed, sporting a T-shirt that bore the inscription "CAST IRON," and running a gas station that he insisted was a "beer joint—we sell gas as a sideline." When he lost for mayor of Plains the second time around, instead of a funeral there was only the wake, a sudsy party at the Amoco station, where Billy blithely explained away his defeat by saying, "I lost because I drink beer on Sundays and because I am a Carter." It was, this performance of Billy's, both drama and real life. No doubt he really felt the need to distinguish himself from his model older brother, but when he ran around declaring that he wanted to be a "badass," he was, for show, gilding the lily.

We have seen that Humanizers become so popular not because of how they look or because of what they do, but rather because of what they say. Their words constitute a legend that envelops them. No wonder Billy Carter did so well. For he had a string of words for every occasion, words that could amuse as well as outrage, and that, in any case, never failed to provide a striking contrast to the image of his brother, the president. Indeed, Billy was quite unlike anything the White House had ever seen before.

The language could be shocking. The grammar was dismal, of course, but we could attribute it to local convention, or the soon familiar rebelliousness. The choice of words was something else again. "Damns" and "hells" floated through the air like so much dust. "Nigger" was acceptable, at least among friends. "Son of a bitch" was O.K., certainly when it was applied to politicians. And as for body functions, why as far back as February 1977 the man spoke out loud about "taking a leak." (It took about two more years for him to actually do it in public.) But even much more extreme than the dirty words or odd constructions was the sense of what he said. Almost unfailingly it was outrageous.

- On his brother's inauguration as President: "All I came up here for was to see that he got in. I promised Jimmy that I wouldn't get locked up."
- When asked if he lost 15 pounds by quitting drinking: "I've cut out eating."
- His opinion on what was then a hot political issue, the Panama Canal: "It's a good way to get from one ocean to another."
- On being a redneck: "Well, a good ole boy . . . is somebody that rides around in a pick-up truck—which I do—and drinks beer and puts 'em in a litter bag. A redneck's one that rides around in a truck and drinks beer and throws 'em out the window."
- On reporters: ". . . I've come to the conclusion that the only reason anybody's a television reporter is because they can't read and write at all."
- On religion: "Bunch of damned hypocrites down there at that Baptist church."
- On Plains: "I'm interested mainly in seeing Plains stay as much like it was as humanly possible. . . . Used to be at 10 o'clock on a Sunday morning you could walk out onto Main Street and take a leak and nobody would see you. Last Sunday there must have been 2,000 damned tourists here. I couldn't stand it. I went off to the bootlegger, bought me a fifth, drove around the rest of the day, and got good and drunk."

- On his brother: "Jimmy used to drink liquor. Now he's running for President and he drinks Scotch, and I've never trusted a Scotch drinker. . . . I think [Jimmy's] around too many people that kiss his ass all the time."[42]

Such bons mots from cracker country were in endless supply when Billy Carter was around, and millions giggled. In short order a book titled *Redneck Power: The Wit and Wisdom of Billy Carter* appeared in the stores and, as it happened, went through its first printing of 210,000 within the first week.

Rather quickly it became clear that Billy Carter was no passing fancy—or that at least he was a fancy that would linger long enough for several months of heavy fun and profit. In February 1977, Billy Carter signed on with Nashville talent agent Tandy Rice. According to Rice, one day after it had been announced that he would represent the president's brother, the number of requests received was "absolutely mind-boggling." They ranged from all those calls from "fans who just want to get in touch with good ol' Billy" to "significant offers for a personal appearance."[43]

It was the beginning of what would turn out to be a time of cashing in on that irresistible combination of overgrown rascal and brother to the pious president. Billy threw out the first ball of the baseball season. He hauled in $10,000 for appearing at a swamp-buggy race. He was approached to write his autobiography, and to appear in a network TV special and a movie. He endorsed a Billy Carter toy pickup truck, and his own brand of beer. He was on TV talk shows and was a part of a whole host of country-music shows. The more the crowds in Plains fenced him in, the more he took off for points yonder and the pots of gold they were now yielding with unfailing regularity. By the middle of 1977 Billy Carter was booked solid for two months ahead, with many of those appearances scheduled to net him a cool $5,000. His appeal had clearly extended beyond what *Time* on one occasion labeled "working class types who can identify with his beer-drinking, anti-Establishment ways," or there were, in fact, more of those sorts out there than anyone had an early right to expect.

It is interesting that for a while, even as Billy became more than ever the cartoon character, on another level he was able to maintain his reputation as solid and smart. That he had business acumen, in particular, was widely acknowledged as fact. At first no one even bothered too much about the high fees he was charging for his two-bit appearances, chalking it up to his well-known shrewdness with a buck. In any case, his fame as the one who had propelled "a small, family owned farm products enterprise into a thriving multimillion-dollar enterprise" remained intact, and the magazine *Nation's Business,* for one, held him up as a model to be emulated: "When he assumes the role of William Alton Carter III, businessman, a role seldom captured in television or newspaper accounts, he is a no-nonsense, hard-driving executive." In an article titled "Frustrations of the Small Businessman," Billy Carter was once again cast in the role of anti-hero against the establishment. But this time it was with a perfectly straight face, and the establishment was seen in terms of such systemic givens as the bureaucracy, unemployment compensation, and welfare. An example of Billy's "frustrations": "When unemployment was at the highest, I needed a man to run a peanut drying machine. It would have paid $250 to $300 a week. I couldn't hire a single person. They would rather draw $90 in unemployment benefits every week and pick up food stamps at the same time." *Nation's Business* was sympathetic. The magazine reported also that Miss Lillian said, "Billy is more popular with the farmers than Jimmy was," that Billy himself said, "Basically, I'm not a Democrat," that a Plains pal said, "Billy has insisted that all the profits be used for worthwhile civic projects," and that the president's younger brother was "usually at his office no later than six in the morning."[44]

It should probably be added that the anti-hero role was beefed up by Billy's early charge that he was being harassed by just those types of which his brother was one. In a lengthy interview with *U.S. News and World Report,*[45] he charged that federal regulators were singling him out for rough treatment, citing the fact that his taxes had just been audited for two years running, that his gas station had been cited for violations by the federal Occupational Safety and Health Administration, and that the state had come down on him for selling beer on Sunday. If all of this wasn't exactly Billy against his brother, it certainly was Billy against the world in which his brother played the leading part.

How to tell the precise moment at which the tide began to turn against Billy Carter? The first nasty crack by Johnny Carson? The first week without at least one appearance on a TV talk show? The first month without any mention in *People?* Hard to say for sure, but for starters we might take the essay by Joseph

Lelyveld in the *New York Times Magazine* of June 26, 1977, titled "The Prince of Plains." It was a thoughtful and bitchy attack. It was thoughtful because it wondered how far exactly the
phenomenon of exploiting public curiosity about presidents'
families could go—"But can the offers for Amy's memoirs on
growing up in the White House be many years or even months
away?"—and bitchy because it suggested, and demonstrated, that
even given the loony public hunger for kissin' kin from Plains,
this president's brother put on a mighty poor show. Sure as anything he wasn't worth the $5,000 Skeet Hewitt had paid him to
put in an afternoon's "guest appearance" at the Southeast Loui-
siana Cajun Music Festival.

> It was 96 degrees in the shade when Billy Carter—his only prop a
> can of Pabst Blue Ribbon in his hand—alighted from the lemon-
> colored Cadillac Hewitt borrowed in order to fulfill his contractual
> obligation to provide the First Brother with a suitable limousine.
> The Southeast Louisiana.Cajun Music Festival was already an un-
> mitigated disaster. . . . It's barely possible that there were 600 [peo-
> ple on hand] but many were actually there for the Cajun music.
> Milton Eisenhower, it seemed, would have drawn almost as well.
>   The "special guest's" performance behind the microphone
> lasted less than a minute and consisted of his taking a pull of Pabst
> and declaring it to be a "vicious lie" that he drinks beer. Then he
> got down to doing what he was paid to do. He had nothing to offer
> but his celebrity, but for several hours under the hot sun he made it
> available unstintingly—kissing any woman who proffered a cheek,
> posing for the Instamatics and signing whatever was shoved his
> way. Saying little, often wordlessly, he autographed photos, scraps
> of paper, sneakers and dollar bills.

The trouble with these things is, once someone starts badmouthing you, others think it's O.K. and start doing the same. By
August there was the interview with *U.S. News and World Report* mentioned above, which was titled "Billy Carter Talks
About All the Money He's Making," and in which some of the
questions he was asked were downright tough.

Q. How much do you charge for each appearance?
A. None of your business.
Q. Are you concerned that all these appearances may embarrass the
   President?
A. We never discuss it. I don't tell him how to be President and he
   doesn't tell me what to do.

Q. How do you handle accusations that you are profiteering from the Presidency?

A. I get those all the time. I tell them that while I was campaigning nobody said I was profiteering.[46]

And in *Time,* some six weeks later, Lance Morrow charged that there was something "decidedly wrong with the spectacle of Billy Carter. . . . [He] is hardly subverting the Republic by being tacky, but the psychodrama of his celebrity does not add much shine to the leader of the free world."[47] There were other sorts of unkind cuts too. For example, "Billy's Beer" was banned in Virginia because the state had a ban on selling liquor in containers with living persons on the label. And as if that wasn't enough, the chairman of the Virginia Alcoholic Beverage Control Commission said that Billy's brew was "downgrading to the office of the President of the country."[48]

The days of innocence were over. It can fairly be claimed that by the summer of 1977, many were weary and leery of brother Billy's act. He stood to make half a million dollars that year, it is true. It is also true that as late as November 1977 *Newsweek* had a cover story on the man that was more sympathetic than anything else. Although the article acknowledged that Billy's critics were getting increasingly vocal, that some said he was boring, others phony, and still others wondered whether he was devaluing the presidency, the author claimed that Billy was "seldom boring and never phony" and that the "loftier Presidential issue" doesn't "come up very often in south Georgia."[49] So the point is not that Billy Carter was all washed up with one great wave, but rather that, as a Humanizer, he was wearing thin. By October 1978, the symbolism was fully in place: the Falls City Brewing Company, which produced "Billy's Beer," announced that it was going out of business and that the President's brother's brew would disappear.

In the very beginning, all the way back in 1975, Jimmy Carter was unknown. One of the ways in which we first came to know him was through the large and varied Carter clan. As the candidate became more familiar, what we saw was a man largely lacking in excitement, wit, color, daring, or anything left in him of the little boy. That explains the part that Billy, as the other, if not better, half, came to play. He had what Jimmy lacked, and it was clear that in those early days he provided a much-needed and appreciated commodity.

The trouble began when he split off from the president to find his own media self. In less than a year's time the Humanizer grew so much so fast that he became something else altogether. He was not yet the liability that he would in fact soon become. But the jokes Jimmy now made about his brother were anxious ones touching on raw nerves. On one occasion the president assayed, "Billy's doing his share for the economy. He's put the beer industry back on its feet." And another time he told the audience at a Los Angeles fund-raiser, "I was hoping that you would raise enough money to have my brother Billy come out and speak next year." The impression conveyed was that the White House would just as soon that Billy would now disappear into the woodwork, but that they, that is the president, didn't have the nerve to tell him so.

The subsequent fate of this one-time Humanizer will be discussed later on. For now, only this closing caution: the loss of Billy as a Humanizer was a considerable deprivation to the Carter administration. Nothing had happened in Jimmy Carter's presidency to make the man any more appealing; he remained altogether incapable of humanizing his own self. There can be little doubt that this put him, along with all his other problems, at a severe disadvantage during the 1980 hunting season.

Person to Person

To humanize is to bring something that is hard to understand and remote down to the level of Everyman, to bring blood to something without color, and to establish a connection to a broad variety of persons where none existed before. It should come as no surprise, therefore, that Humanizers must, above all, have the ability to come on as "just folks." Every woman in America saw part of herself in Betty Ford, a housewife and mother who happened, through her husband's line of work, to live in the White House, but who—it was obvious in what she said—still shared the feelings and concerns of her more typical middle-aged and middle American peers. Billy Carter was not just *like* the rest of us, he *was* us, or at least that part of us that was sill a naughty child or rebellious adolescent, that had never fully accepted the conventions of being all grown up. Both he and Betty Ford could serve as intermediaries. They could acquaint us with the president and, by their own irresistible fallibility, bring him down to our level.

It was this quality of the flaw, plus being unpredictable, that made these two so unusual. In both cases they behaved in ways they were not really supposed to. Mainly they said things that had not been said before on subjects that had not been touched before. At times, Betty Ford and Billy Carter embarrassed their presidential kin. But precisely because for people with a close presidential connection they were so full of surprises and so unabashedly open and revealing about matters that had, heretofore, been considered unfit for public purview, they never failed to gain our attention. In their prime as Humanizers both were show-stoppers. As far as media and public were concerned, they could *say* no wrong.

Perhaps the reason Humanizers do so much for candidates and presidents is that they offer them such a perfect foil. Lyndon Johnson didn't really need a Humanizer: he was his own. But men such as Gerald Ford and Jimmy Carter, types who lack flair, benefit enormously from counterpoint—from having someone to do the things they cannot, someone to say the things they do not dare. Of course, the symbiotic tie works only as long as the Humanizer stays in line, on a fairly tight leash as it were. Betty Ford, for all her "radical" opinions, never let us feel for one moment that she would step so far out of line as to seriously hurt her husband. She was nothing if not a team player. The relationship between Jimmy and Billy Carter was more complicated. Their protestations to the contrary, the rivalries appeared to be as palpable as they were old, and when it came down to the nitty-gritty, it turned out that Billy Carter was working not for his brother, but for himself. The fact was that as soon as Billy's aims diverged from those of his brother, he could no longer be counted on. And within one year, what had once been a splendid asset soured.

CHAPTER 5

Helpmeets

Helpmeets derive their political impact from a good working relationship to the president. Although they are (here) either a spouse or a blood tie, the primary interaction is based on business. They become, in effect, trusted and respected junior business partners sharing the challenges which the enterprise of presidential politics presents. Their proficiency is respected and their willingness to help with the presidential burden mutually understood.

Joseph P. Kennedy was the father of President John Kennedy, and Lady Bird Johnson was the wife of President Lyndon Johnson. The Kennedys had, by all accounts, a good father-son relationship, and the Johnsons had, by all accounts, a good marriage. Indeed Helpmeets grow out of such bedrock; the most devoted among them derive their impetus from love. It does not, therefore, demean the quality of the relationship to say that by the time the office of the presidency entered the lives of these players, the interaction could most accurately have been described as a good *business partnership.*

Both Joseph Kennedy and Lady Bird Johnson had important functions in presidential politics. But unlike those we have just considered who took on the roles of Decorations, Extensions, and Humanizers, they derived their primary political impact not from an attraction or interest they had or came to have for the public, but rather from the nature and extent of the support they gave the president in private. "Support" is the key word here— support of a practical kind, the kind that translates into transfu-

sions of time, energy, and material resources. Again, that is not to
say that emotional sustenance is lacking. But in the present of
presidential politics, it is the practical matters that get most of the
attention: both parties invest all their resources first to gain the
presidency and then to occupy the office to maximum effect.

The president (or candidate) is the center of activity. The
good Helpmeet revolves around him as the earth revolves around
the sun. It is a partnership to be sure, but the president is the
senior partner, the determiner, even the taker. *His* needs are attended to. *His* long-range goals become the dream of both. Some
of this dedication gets rationalized through public service. That
is, the good of the country becomes entwined with the good of the
president so that, for a Helpmeet, serving the man is tantamount
to serving America. Still, it comes down to a situation in which
the Helpmeet puts himself or herself at the complete disposal of
the president.

What are the requirements for a Helpmeet? The first requisite
is a strong devotion to the president. Without it, the deprivations
that Helpmeets inevitably endure will leave a bitter aftertaste.
Second, there should be a well-seasoned interest in politics.
Among other things, this will help to assuage the president's
guilt because, although he gets the attention, at least he can point
to the shared passion for politics. Third, good Helpmeets must
have personal and political skills and resources. Presidential politics is the business here, and a partner, to be effective, must
bring into it some combination of knowledge, proficiency, and
perhaps even goods. Indeed, presidents ideally should have complete confidence in the abilities of their Helpmeets, especially
since they are often called on to do work on their own. A fourth
requisite is a situation that is relatively free of demands other
than those made by the president. During the time of service,
Helpmeets must be free to make presidential politics the center of
their own lives. Finally, Helpmeets must willingly subordinate
their own egos to those of their presidential kin. Wives, of course,
have traditionally stood aside. But even old Joe Kennedy—who
had been used to being director and star all in one—came to understand that if he was to lend his son full support, his own par-
tial withdrawal, in public and private, would be necessary. For
the satisfaction gained, of course, this muting of self was a small
price to pay.

The functions of Helpmeets are as varied as the people themselves. They range from giving money to giving counsel to giving affection. The Helpmeet's contribution is palpable, and manifest to anyone who troubles to look. It adds to the actual substance of a candidacy or administration; that is, Helpmeets do things that make a measurable difference in how presidents perform. On the other hand, bear their junior status in mind. As half of an unequal partnership, they serve more or less at the behest of the president. Their constant participation is by no means assured, and there may well be periods during which they serve by only standing and waiting. Of course, there will also be times when they make themselves no less than indispensable.

Of the three Helpmeets of former presidents listed in the front chart, only Pat Nixon falls very short of the ideal. Specifically, there is considerable question about the nature and degree of her devotion to her husband, and no question about her distaste for politics. (Indeed, some of the Nixons' marital problems almost certainly grew out of his insistence on pursuing a political career.) Yet she did play her role. She was, as Nixon called her, "a good trouper." With the great self-discipline that was her hallmark (as it had been the hallmark of Nixon's mother), Pat Nixon spent some three decades in a public performance appropriate to the role of the politician's wife. The smile, even if it did appear "fixed, unnatural, . . . artificial, something produced for an occasion,"[1] was almost always in evidence. On countless trips in scattered lands, in numberless public appearances in an infinite variety of settings, Pat Nixon could be counted on to do the right thing by her husband's side.

> Beside him his wife stood the three hours in high heels, her face chilled with smiles, her mouth puckering as the ninetieth child went by and had to be admired with a long-distance kiss. Her eyes are not like her husband's, here, there, and everywhere; they follow each person who moves by her . . . left to right, she keeps them each in focus; but for the split second when she turns back, right to left, to greet a new face, the eyes blur momentarily, blanking out all unnecessary sensation connected with this ordeal. . . . On her way to the school where these crowds waited for her, newsmen caught Mrs. Nixon and asked how she felt at the outset of another long campaign. She bravely answered, "I love it; one meets so many old friends again." But I watched her hands as she said it; the freckled hands were picking at each other, playing with gloves, trying to still each other's trembling.[2]

The private misery that was cloaked in the public performance was not in fact always so almost perfectly concealed. It was
said that the 1952 "fund crisis" permanently took the pleasure
out of politics for Mrs. Nixon, and there are a few accounts of
occasions on which she "chewed out" her husband in front of
others. Perhaps the most telling of these rare public displays occurred on the evening when Nixon told his wife, at a dinner
party, that he planned to run for governor of California—after she
had, some time earlier, extracted from him a written promise that
he would give up politics forever. The incident reveals both
Nixon's self-doubt and Mrs. Nixon's durable anger over his
choice of a political life.

Nevertheless, Pat Nixon was a Helpmeet to the extent that
she did use her political skills and resources to help her husband
win the presidency and to serve him as proper consort once he
was in office. Indeed, considering her aversion to politicking and
her passion for privacy, the sacrifice in her husband's interest
was especially great. But from what we know of the Nixon marriage and his performance in office, her service to his ambition
came at a great price. It was rendered out of duty rather than
devotion—either to the man or to his profession—and therefore
its benefit—to the man and to the office—was circumscribed.
Contrast this with our better specimens of Helpmeets, Joe Kennedy and Lady Bird Johnson.

Joseph P. Kennedy

Some would claim that for much of John Kennedy's political life
his father was less the Helpmeet and more the puppeteer who
pulled the strings that made Jack dance. The question "Who's in
charge?" was for many years an open one. Joseph P. Kennedy,
money maker, power wielder, and founding father par excellence,
was plainly used to calling the shots. John F. Kennedy, second
oldest, and second in just about everything else to brother Joe,
Jr., was plainly used to following his parent's directives.

I am talking here not only of Jack the young child but also of
Jack the young adult who, but most criteria that we would now
apply, would have to be considered "a Daddy's boy." He went to
Harvard rather than Princeton because his father insisted on it;
during what amounted to almost one-fourth of his total time in

college he was actually working with his father in Europe; he made sure to keep his father posted on even the details of his personal life; and his father influenced his choice of a senior thesis and then spent considerable energy on shaping and selling the final product, a book titled *Why England Slept*.

This picture-perfect image of long-lived compliance to father is given its final touch by the story of how John Kennedy actually got into politics. Legend has it that some few weeks after the wartime death of Joe, Jr., Joseph Kennedy announced to the next in line, Jack, who was twenty-seven at the time, that he would now have to pick up the banner. It would be no less than the duty of the second son to replace the fallen first. The father's dreams of political triumph in the Kennedy name were, very simply, reassigned.

During the fifties and before, both father and son gave credence to this story. The parent: "I got Jack into politics. I was the one. I told him Joe was dead and that it was therefore his responsibility to run for Congress. He didn't want to. . . . But I told him he had to." Or, two years later, "I thought everyone knows about that. Jack went into politics because young Joe died. . . . When he died, Jack took his place." The child: "It was like being drafted. My father wanted his eldest son in politics. 'Wanted' isn't the right word. He *demanded* it. You know my father. . . ." Or, in 1957, "My brother Joe was the logical one in the family to be in politics and if he had lived, I'd have kept on being a writer. . . . If I died, my brother Bob would want to be Senator and if anything happened to him, my brother Teddy would run for us. . . ." Later, when Jack's presidential candidacy was being taken seriously, there were apparently second thoughts about this vision of the son dancing to the tune of his father, and the legend was modified—at least to the extent that Jack was now pictured as entering politics for his own positive reasons. But even these newer versions did not bother to minimize the influence of the ambassador's urgent insistence.[3]

Do not assume that once Kennedy made the decision to enter Massachusetts politics, his father stepped aside. Quite the contrary. The evidence indicates that Jack's early efforts were orchestrated by his father. In 1946, the year of John Kennedy's first congressional campaign, he was hardly known in Boston. But if he had been abroad for the preceding years, and was too young and disinterested to have collected political contacts before then, the family name was nonetheless powerful and popular. Grandpa "Honey Fitz" Fitzgerald, the legendary mayor of Boston, was still around, and, even more important, John's own father, the ambassador, had brought his family to the point where they were considered the city's leading Irish clan. He had also brought them to a level of wealth where money was not much of an object. Some said that Kennedy spent more than a quarter of a million dollars on the first of Jack Kennedy's campaigns, and if the best later estimates fell short of that, it was still true that Kennedy far outspent any of his opponents. A small Boston advertising agency with a strong personal loyalty to the ambassador was hired to write speeches and direct public relations: billboards, posters, leaflets, and radio "spots" blanketed the district, and the luxury of opinion polling was used to calm Kennedy nerves (Jack Kennedy was always far ahead). But perhaps most crucial were the contacts that Joe Kennedy had, and his unabashed, even eager willingness to use them. His own testimony was that he "just called people. I got in touch with people I knew. I have a lot of contacts. I've been in politics in Massachusetts since I was ten."[4] But he was too modest. He apparently had a most unusually broad influence on his home turf, always knowing, despite his long absence from Boston "precisely whom to call to move the levers of local political power."[5] The recollections of Mark Dalton, then a young lawyer on whom was bestowed the ceremonial title of campaign manager, give the flavor of Joe Kennedy's involvement in this, Jack's first electoral effort:

> Certainly Mr. Kennedy's advice through the whole campaign was extremely valuable. . . . I think the essential campaign manager through all of these things was probably Mr. Kennedy. At least his advice was always available and he kept in close touch with the situation. . . . I can also remember once or twice when Mr. Kennedy made the rounds of the headquarters, of course, that was a real thrill for the workers to meet Mr. Kennedy. . . . He had been the ambassador to England and everybody was very eager to meet him. . . . Well, I'll tell you this, that Mr. Kennedy called me many many times, to know exactly what was happening. He was very very interested and he would talk at great length and wanted to know about every facet of the campaign in the first Congressional one and later at the start of the Senatorial one. As a matter of fact, that was one of my problems. He'd keep you on the phone for an hour and a half, two hours. . . .[6]

Interestingly, Dalton did not dare to hang up.

By the time Jack Kennedy was ready to run for the Senate, after having won three terms in the House, he was starting to make preliminary moves to separate from his father. It appears that the son, now thirty-five, was finally experiencing an internal need to differentiate himself from his ever-present parent, and also recognizing that such distance was mandatory if he expected to test his political strength on a larger stage. An example is in Jack's confrontations with the Jewish community which had harbored suspicions about his candidacy because of the alleged anti-Semitism of his father. On one occasion, after still sensing doubt in an audience of prominent Jews despite his efforts to convince them of his freedom from bias, he challenged, "What more do you want? Remember, I'm running for the Senate, not my father."[7]

Still, in the campaign itself, the father's role remained predominant. Joe Kennedy urged his son to take on the prominent Republican incumbent, Henry Cabot Lodge, and as soon as the duel got underway, he was the most fervent of seconds. Once again the ambassador milked his contacts. Once again he played the banker. Once again he hired and fired (a very green Bobby Kennedy eventually turned up as campaign manager—a happy choice since he could cope with his overbearing parent). And once again he tried to mastermind the whole. One campaign worker remembers that Joe Kennedy "dominated everything, even told everyone where to sit. They [were] just children in that house." Another campaign worker: "The father was a tremendous factor in the campaign. He remained out of public view. He didn't run things, but they happened according to his plans."[8] And Edward McCormack, member of another family prominent in Massachusetts politics, observed of the successful 1952 campaign, "Joe Kennedy at that time was very active, and he was really calling the shots for Jack Kennedy. . . . I am basing [this] upon conversations I've had with people Joe Kennedy called in to talk to and tell them what to do. . . ."[9] (There are dozens of stories of Kennedy's early manipulating of Jack. Lyndon Johnson relished telling how Joe would call him and plead with him to get his boy on the Senate Foreign Relations Committee.[10] And George Smathers, a senatorial colleague of Jack's in their salad days, remembers the time Joe Kennedy came to see him and said, "Someday I want to come down and talk to you about Jack's finances, because he has absolutely no understanding of it and won't stop and talk with me long enough to understand it. . . ."[11])

The first time that John Kennedy flouted the advice and will of his father was 1956: with all the energy and muscle that he and Bobby could muster, he unsuccessfully sought the vice-presidential nomination on the Democratic ticket with Adlai Stevenson. The ambassador had issued urgent warnings against the run in the interest of the contest four years hence. "I knew Adlai Stevenson was going to take a licking, and I was afraid Jack might be blamed because he was a Catholic. That would have made it much more difficult for another Catholic in the years to come."[12] And, of course, much more difficult for Jack as well. It is noteworthy that in the immediate aftermath of the failed effort, Jack flew to France to vacation with his father—this even though his wife was in the last months of a difficult pregnancy. (Shortly thereafter Jacqueline Kennedy lost the baby and Kennedy flew back to Newport to be with her.) The first need, obviously, was to make peace with his parent. But it is nonetheless true that the 1956 rupture was a turning point in the relationship. It was the first act of rebellion by the son against the father. Thereafter John Kennedy would gradually but steadily take control of his own affairs. Thereafter there would be some changes in roles and Joe Kennedy would come to play the Helpmeet and the image of the puppeteer would fade away.

The early signal of 1956 evolved into something of a *fait accompli* by 1958. Although he still led the cheering squad—in 1959 he quipped, "Now I know his religion won't keep him out of the White House. If an Irish Catholic can get elected as an Overseer at Harvard, he can get elected to anything"—and although he still invoked the collective "we," as in "our position" and "our worries," in this, Jack's second run for the Senate and, in a manner of speaking, dry run for the presidency, Joseph P. Kennedy stayed well in the background. That is not to say that he severed all connection with the campaign. His sons—the candidate and the campaign manager—still kept him informed, and one recollection has Joe Kennedy exploding at the exhausting schedule planned for Jack, "What are you trying to do to him? Kill him?"[13] But the remark also indicates how far he was from the actual planning. That his fortune was tapped is certain, but the man himself played, for the first time in any of John Kennedy's five Massachusetts campaigns, a secondary role. His biographer, Richard Whalen, describes him as going "into hiding."[14]

It was during John Kennedy's campaign for the presidency, in 1959 and 1960, that his father first engaged in intensive activity as a Helpmeet. That is to say, now the son was clearly in charge, now it was the father who did whatever it was the son wanted. Obviously the goal was shared: both ached for Jack to be president. But the way in which the end was to be gained was, as he reached forty-three, determined by Jack and by the coterie of young loyalists he personally had assembled over the preceding decade. If Joe Kennedy did not now exactly follow his sons' orders (Bobby, of course, was the campaign manager), at least he no longer gave them.

Consider Kennedy's qualifications to be a Helpmeet. He was, first of all, an intensely dedicated and devoted parent. To be sure, love and ambition were intermingled, but he was hardly the first father in history to want to use his sons to achieve immortality. Nor the last. Furthermore, he had had a lifelong interest and involvement in politics, and he could bring to Jack's political efforts a splendid array of personal and financial resources. Finally, he was at a point where he personally had little left to prove or gain, where his business could take care of itself (or at least function without his constant attendance), where the impulse to be generative—to support and nurture his children—came to predominate, and where his ego no longer required that he command from center stage. In 1960 Joe Kennedy became seventy-two. It was the season of his life when the role of Helpmeet would suit.

John Kennedy's campaign to win the presidency can conveniently be divided into two phases: before and after the Democratic nominating convention in Los Angeles. Joe Kennedy was Helpmeet during both. His first job was to—convincingly—vacate the premises. As it was, the candidate had his troubles, especially with the party's liberal wing, troubles which could in no small measure be traced to doubts about his father. Harry Truman, remembering well that Joe Kennedy did not support his own run in 1948, pointedly stated, "I am not against the Pope. I'm against the Pop."[15] Eleanor Roosevelt, a Stevenson diehard, warned that Joe Kennedy was "spending oodles of money all over the country" on his son's behalf.[16] As a result of the bad feeling reflected in remarks like these, the ambassador did indeed remain all but hidden from public view, exerting whatever impact he did have—and it was still very considerable—from well behind the scenes.

By 1960 father and son had a workable balance of power.

Most observers imply a tacit agreement of sorts: Joseph Kennedy
would take the back seat, but with the understanding that when
he did open his mouth, he would be listened to with respect.
Whalen alludes to several instances during this period when Jack
made sure that the public knew the difference between himself
and his conservative parent ("Dad is a financial genius all right,
but in politics, he is something else"), and he also could draw the
line in private: "We've heard the former Ambassador's views.
Now let's get on with our business."[17] But Whalen also points
out that Jack still paid attention and that during several of the
campaign's most critical episodes the father played an important
part. Those who actually worked on the campaign remember the
delicate balance between power and withdrawal in the same way.

> I think he [Joseph Kennedy] played a great role [in getting delegates
> in 1960]. . . . I think in the first place he gave the whole operation a
> certain solidarity that it might otherwise not have had. . . . He never
> involved himself directly, but everybody knew that Mr. Kennedy
> was there. . . . Then he did contribute a great deal because he knew
> so many of these people. . . . But I do remember one thing about the
> way he handled himself which really touched me. He worked as
> hard as anybody, but he had to make it obvious that he had separated
> himself from his son. . . . That probably was something that for
> somebody with his temperament was a difficult thing to do. . . .[18]

> I did detect what I thought was almost total respect [from Jack and
> Bobby toward their father]. They felt that he was a tremendous hu-
> man being, that they were very much involved with him, and they
> wanted to please him. But at the same time they had been . . . per-
> mitted the luxury of disagreeing with him.[19]

There were two areas in which Joe Kennedy's resources were
tapped without reserve: money and contacts. Although the financial outlays were never as enormous as Kennedy's opponents
suggested, they were certainly huge in comparison with those for
the other candidates, and they paid for such campaign amenities
as polling and publicity. Jack joked about charges that he was
trying to buy the West Virginia primary. "I got a wire from my
father: 'Dear Jack. Don't buy one more vote than necessary. I'll
be damned if I'll pay for a landslide.'"[20] (It was Joe Kennedy who
came up with the clever idea of using the name Roosevelt [FDR
was still revered in West Virginia] in that crucial primary. The
services of Franklin Roosevelt, Jr., were enlisted and he toured

the state saying, "My daddy and Jack Kennedy's daddy were just like that" — while holding up two fingers pressed tightly together. The ambassador also saw to it that letters praising Senator Kennedy and signed by Roosevelt were shipped to Hyde Park, New York, to be postmarked and mailed from there.[21]) As for the use of Joe Kennedy's contacts, here there was no holding back. Perhaps because much of this work could be done behind the scenes without risking public embarrassment, it was here that the elder Kennedy came into his own. With all the old vigor, he was in hot pursuit of delegates for his son.

> Bill Green [Democratic leader of Philadelphia] was dealing with [Joe Kennedy], and talking with Mr. Kennedy constantly, as was [Peter J.] Crotty up in New York. Now they might have been talking with Jack also, but I know that Mr. Kennedy was in constant touch with these people and doing whatever he could to line them up for his son.[22]

> Then as he got within a week and a half of the Convention . . . Hy Raskin one afternoon called the Governor [of California, Edmund Brown], then me, and said that Joseph P. Kennedy was up at Lake Tahoe, unknown to anybody, and would like to come down and have dinner that night with the Governor and me and Hy. . . . He drove down from Lake Tahoe. We had dinner at the Governor's mansion. It was quite interesting. The father made a very vigorous presentation on behalf of his son. . . . He was very effective. He didn't overdo it; he wasn't a table pounder or anything like that. . . . The old man was absolutely firm and to the point. . . . Unlike most politicians, the Ambassador wasn't going to imply things or double talk about this. . . .[23]

> Westchester, the Bronx, Queens County and Albany were left to father Joseph Kennedy's jurisdiction: and there he was working his old friendships. . . . Two Congressmen joined him as allies. By May [their combined] forces could safely count forty more votes. . . . New Jersey froze first. . . . Joseph P. Kennedy had, through the long spring of 1960, won the loyalties and votes of the North Jersey political leaders for his son. . . . Illinois broke first. Of Illinois' 69 votes, Mayor Richard Daley, boss of Cook County, controlled an estimated fifty-five. Once Daley had been a friend of Adlai Stevenson. . . . But all spring Daley had been under the persuasion of Joseph P. Kennedy, whose real estate interests in Chicago had given him a master's knowledge of Cook County politics. . . . Illinois caucused on Sunday afternoon in secret and when the door opened,

Mayor Daley announced that Illinois would vote 59½ for Kennedy, two for Adlai Stevenson, one uncommitted, the balance for Stuart Symington. First blood for Kennedy.[24]

The delegates that summer went for Jack, and all the family went to the convention hall in triumph to appear with the nominee—all, that is, except for the ambassador. The Kennedys, still afraid of what Dad's appearance alongside his son would imply, agreed that he had best stay in the shade.

But he did not rest. In fact, he did not even pause. It was the father who pushed hardest for Lyndon Johnson for the vice-presidential slot, and then telephoned the Senate majority leader urging him to accept. It was the father who packed his bag the moment the nomination was in hand to begin the second phase of the campaign, and that very night planned ahead: "Now here's what we have to do. . . ."[25] It wsa the father who, the Tuesday of convention week, rang up Henry Luce, editor-in-chief of Time, Inc., to arrange a dinner date, and then, on Friday in New York, asked for Luce's support.

> Right out of the blue . . . Joe Kennedy called me from Los Angeles and asked whether he could come to see me. . . . I think it went through my head that it was a little odd that he was getting back so fast. . . . By the time he got there we had the dinner about ready and, as I remember, two lobsters. He ate a very hearty meal and he was in great form. . . . Well, so we had this good dinner and it was over along about nine o'clock and, as I remember it, the television wasn't going on till ten. I thought that Joe hadn't come to see me just for chitchat about the convention, so I thought I better get down to cases. I said to him . . . Well, now, Joe, I suppose you are interested in the attitudes *Time* and *Life* and I might take about Jack's candidacy. . . .

Luce goes on to tell how he divided the matter into domestic and foreign affairs. When he suggested that Jack might be left of center in domestic policy, he quotes the elder Kennedy as bursting out with "How can you say that? How can you think that any son of mine would ever be a so-and-so liberal?" When Luce maintained that he would have to be against the Democratic nominee if he appeared to be soft on Communism, Joseph Kennedy insisted, "There's no chance of that; you know that." And when Luce objected to something in Kennedy's acceptance speech, which they watched together later that evening on television, the rejoinder was "Oh, well, now, don't mind that."[26]

When Kennedy left, he expressed his gratitude for all Luce had done for Jack. At Joseph Kennedy's request Luce had, many years earlier, written the foreword to *Why England Slept.* And both *Time* and *Life* had done covers and favorable stories on John Kennedy's young career. But in the heated contest that followed the evening with Joseph Kennedy, Luce was to wind up supporting Richard Nixon.

Although Joseph Kennedy still remained hidden from public view during most of the rest of the campaign, he did his work. He continued to serve as John Kennedy's Helpmeet in the best way he knew: now a judicious mix of power and discretion typified his style. Of the fact that he was one of the candidate's chief advisers there is no doubt. He was, for example, present at a critical five-hour strategy session at the beginning of October including only Kennedy's "inner circle."[27] He spoke frequently with both his sons between September and November, offering advice and good cheer. It is known that he was on the phone with Kennedy just before his first television debate with Nixon—and just after. In addition, there was abundant counsel in the area he knew best, the nation's economy, and there was the task of overseeing the pollsters. Justice William O. Douglas remembered, "Joe Kennedy was running his [Jack's] polls. . . . I talked to Joe three weeks before the election . . . and Joe's polls showed that Jack couldn't possibly lose more than 8 states."[28] And finally there was the strong-arming of old and powerful friends. Arthur Krock, the venerable columnist for the *New York Times,* was one of the chosen ones. Krock's conservatism kept bumping up against John Kennedy's new-fangled liberalism. Disagreements between the two, despite Krock's long-standing friendship with the elder Kennedy, found their way into print. "This must have been somewhat reflected in what I was writing because on several occasions Joe Kennedy, Sr. telephoned me and expressed some dissatisfaction with what I had written, saying, 'Why don't you give Jack a fair break?' and so forth." Later Krock got a letter: "I hope you still will be able before this is over to feel that you can come out for Jack."[29] Arthur Krock never did, and the tie between the two old men was irrevocably broken.

There is a wonderfully happy photo of the victorious Kennedy clan on the morning after the 1960 election. It is Joseph P. Kennedy, sprung overnight from his exile, who is at the immediate right of the president-elect. "After their long public separation, the press noted that father and son suddenly seemed to be together almost constantly. When a reporter asked whether this was just coincidental, Joe Kennedy's terse reply was epigrammatic. 'There are no accidents in politics,' he said. 'I can appear with him any time I want to now.'"[30]

But at this late date the role of Joseph P. Kennedy in the life of John Kennedy did not change anymore. He remained, until felled by a stroke in December 1961, a Helpmeet to the president. He was always available, and always looking for a way to be of service. (Not the least of his jobs was as resident cheerleader. During the debacle of the Bay of Pigs, Joe Kennedy was the only one to glimpse a silver lining. He maintained it was a good lesson to learn early in the administration and offered the President generous encouragement when his mood was lowest.) The elder Kennedy was also careful to be nonintrusive. In the years just before the election of 1960, the ambassador was circumspect because he wanted a Kennedy to be president. In the time just after the election of 1960, the ambassador was circumspect because he wanted to make things easy for his son. After the inauguration he called son-in-law and Kennedy aide Stephen Smith: "I want to help," he said, "but I don't want to be a nuisance. Can you tell me: do they want me or don't they want me?"[31] Rose Kennedy, wrote that "he did not set foot in the White House except once during the rest of that year [1961]. . . ."[32]

Still he was, as I said, always available. (Indeed, Mrs. Kennedy notes as much just after the above disclaimer: "In fact, there was a lively correspondence between the President and his father, and they talked by telephone several times a week and sometimes several times a day. . . . There was also, now and then, advice that Jack solicited, or his father felt was really worth offering about matters of state. . . ."[33]) Immediately after the election Joe Kennedy, through the intercession of his long-time friend Herbert Hoover, arranged for the president-elect to pay a courtesy call on Richard Nixon. And another long-time friend—another Hoover, J. Edgar, head of the FBI—also came into prompt play. "After the election, it was Ambassador Kennedy who advised the President-elect that if he were going to keep Hoover (and Allen Dulles, head of the CIA) he might as well make a virtue of it. [Along with one other family friend] they were President Kennedy's first appointments."[34]

Joe Kennedy also advised on the whole array of Cabinet appointments—although he had a particular interest in the post of attorney general. His choice for the job: Robert Kennedy. It is difficult to say whether Bobby would have become attorney general without the strong advocacy of his father. Probably not. He himself was reluctant, for a variety of reasons. The president-elect, although he knew he wanted his brother close by, was not certain that this was the right slot. And almost all their close advisers were against the idea. So it fell to Joseph Kennedy to play the decisive role. He argued forcibly "that Bobby obviously had to report directly to the President; if he were in a subordinate post, the position of the official who stood between himself and the President would be impossible."[35] In a less patient moment he steamed, "I don't know what's wrong with him. Jack needs all the good men he can get around him down there. There's none better than Bobby."[36] In the vacuum of indecision, the patriarch again prevailed. (The same vigor would be applied on behalf of his youngest son. It was the founding father who pushed all three of his sons into accepting the idea that Teddy should run for senator from Massachusetts—a scant three years out of law school and with not a lick of elective experience.)

Mainly, though, during his son's presidency, Joe Kennedy tried his damnedest to be on his best behavior. Of course, he didn't always succeed. A recollection of correspondent Peter Lisagor's illustrates:

> The two Kennedy brothers, John, the President, and the Attorney General, were sitting in the Kennedy compound up in Hyannis Port discussing the need to overhaul the State Department and the Foreign Service. Ambassador Kennedy, their father, was sitting in a corner presumably reading a newspaper or magazine and not paying much attention, but he was, in fact, eavesdropping. He heard the two boys say that they were really going to overhaul this thing, that they were going to get all of this tired dead wood out of there and going to put in some new lively young people, fresh, with a lot of get up and go about them. He listened until his patience ran thin, and then he said, "Sons, I want to tell you that I once went to see Franklin D. Roosevelt who made the same kind of talk that you're making now. He lamented the State Department. He talked about razing the whole thing (that is, burning it down) and starting from scratch. He didn't do a damn thing about it and neither are you.[37]

None of this is to say that the indispensable Helpmeet could bring no real grief. Questions about his associations, opinions, and luxurious life style persisted. And there was the Frank X. Morrisey affair. Morrisey was part of the "tight, protective circle of retainers, agents and hangers on" that had always surrounded Joe Kennedy.[38] For a while he was known as "the Ambassador's spy," and by the time of the Kennedy presidency he was already shepherding Edward to political meetings across Massachusetts to ready him for the senatorial run. According to the traditional Kennedy code, such loyalty was to be rewarded. Joseph Kennedy wanted Morrisey to get a federal district court judgeship.

The trouble was that Morrisey was totally unqualified for the job (he hadn't even gone to law school) and just about everyone knew it. Anthony Lewis wrote in the *July 3, 1961, New York Times*, "Though many lawyers have made critical statements privately, they have so far been unwilling to go on the record against Judge Morrisey for fear of damaging themselves. However, it is believed that one or more bar association officials will make public statements against the nomination if it is made." In fact, Robert Kennedy never did submit Morrisey's name. Years later he explained that he finally refrained from doing so because his efforts to raise the level of the bench would have been complicated if he himself had chosen someone so widely deemed unqualified. The educated guess, though, is that by this time the attorney general himself had the gravest doubts about whether Morrisey should get the judgeship, and that all the parrying was because of the conflict of interest between his father and his brother. Nicholas Katzenbach, who succeeded Byron R. White as deputy attorney general when White was appointed to the Supreme Court, put it this way: "Morrisey was a very nice guy. It was awfully difficult for Robert and John. It was for papa Joe. Bob knew what the problems were with Morrisey. . . . He tried to talk to me about it. It was difficult because the father did not impose himself on them and this was one of the few minor things which would have made a great difference to him."

Inevitably, Joseph Kennedy also became involved with the case of James Landis, who had failed to pay his taxes for five years. Landis had been an intimate of the Kennedy family for decades. The tie was with Joe, Sr. In 1934 Landis played a decisive role in making Kennedy chairman of the SEC; in 1937 Kennedy played a decisive role in making Landis dean of the Harvard Law School. The years that followed saw the same kind of mutual helping—so much so that by the spring of 1961, Dean James

Landis "was a virtual member of the immediate family." Landis'
problems—they proved to be psychological as well as legal—put
the Kennedys in a painful position.

> The code of the Kennedys was profoundly entangled with James
> Landis' fate. His tax delinquency was discovered because he was on
> the Kennedy White House staff. It was brought to old Joe's atten-
> tion because the District Director of the IRS shared the nation's
> image of the clannish, behind-the-scenes way the Kennedys do
> business. The case proceeded through channels partly because the
> Kennedys had officially disqualified themselves, partly because it
> was *not* part of the Kennedy way of doing business for Robert to tell
> his old University of Virginia tax professor, Mortimer Caplin, to get
> him off the hook at the expense of the integrity of the tax code,
> partly because Kennedy loyalists didn't want the Kennedy Admin-
> istration vulnerable to charges of fix. Landis pleaded guilty so as
> not to embarrass the Kennedys despite evidence that a not-guilty
> plea might have been sustained. He was sentenced to confinement,
> seldom the case in failure-to-file convictions, undoubtedly in part as
> a tribute to his importance as a member of Kennedy family.[39]

Perhaps, though, the thing that stands out most about the
Morrisey and Landis affairs is their uniqueness. The Morrisey
case is virtually the only instance in which we have clear-cut evidence that something that was pushed by Joseph Kennedy resulted in the public embarrassment of his sons. And the events
surrounding James Landis are virtually the only instance in
which one of Joe Kennedy's pals let down the side. Considering
the size of the human network that he called upon and the range
of influence it was able to exert, these two blots on the record are
relatively small.

The stroke that felled Joseph P. Kennedy during the
Christmas season at the end of his son's first year as president
was devastating. For all practical purposes he remained an in-
valid the rest of his life (although he outlived Jack). But there is a
description of a family dinner in the White House a half year or
so before the assassination that touchingly illustrates the central
place he still continued to hold, for all his desperate incapacity.
The witness is Ben Bradlee, publisher of the *Washington Post*
and, in the heydey of Camelot, a good friend to the president. He
describes the old man as "bent all out of shape, his right side
paralyzed from head to toe, unable to say anything but meaningless sounds and 'no, no, no, no' over and over again." But he

also recalls that the evening was "movingly gay," in good part "because his children involve him in their every thought and action. They talk to him all the time. They ask him 'Don't you think so, Dad?' or 'Isn't that right, Dad?' And before he has a chance to embarrass himself or the guests by not being able to answer, they are off on the next subject."[40]

An ironic, poignant end to the tale: the founding father, the power maker, broker, and wielder reduced to being a helpless child. No wonder, though, that even in this altered state, he retained his hold on his offspring. For he had created half of what they had become just as surely as he had created half of them. The remarkable thing was that he knew when to let go. John Kennedy was in large measure the invention of his father. And for years, for years longer than most would consider appropriate, his father called the shots. Yet when the time came for the would-be president to go it alone, Joe Kennedy felt it, and was able to act appropriately in response to Jack's increasing assertiveness. For one who had been used to helping his son but only on his terms, he evolved with considerable grace into a Helpmeet second to none.

Lady Bird Johnson

Once upon a time, a contented man could call his wife his help-meet (or helpmate). In fact, it was so common a label for a good woman that the term came to be almost synonymous with spouse. (Technically it could refer to the husband or wife, but for obvious reasons was almost always used when speaking of the lady of the house.) Now, the term is out of fashion. It is thought that for a husband to claim his wife as helpmeet is to imply that his needs, especially as they grow out of his work, come first, and that she exists mainly to service them; she, in other words, is the assist-ant, he the boss and, therefore, implicitly superior.

It is not recorded that Lyndon Johnson ever called Lady Bird Johnson "my helpmeet," but a rose by another name is still a you-know-what. It is surely the case that if the term has any meaning at all—however dated its ring in the "me" era, with its special focus on women's liberation—it must be applied to Mrs. Johnson as she lived her life during thirty-eight years of mar-riage. Her days were governed by her devotion to her role as Lyndon Johnson's mate. "She [was] the traditional countrywoman, the wife who by her very nature [turned] all her labor and all her love to harmonize with the ambitions of her husband. In the tradition of Southern plantation patriarchies, Lyndon Johnson [was] head of the family—period."[41] Not once, from either husband or wife, was there a word or deed that belied this statement. Not once did either deviate from what seemed to both to be the natural order of things. "What pleases him," she would say, "pleases me."

And so it happened that Lady Bird Johnson saw her duties as wife and First Lady as coincident with those we have defined as typical of the Helpmeet. Her love for Lyndon Johnson, her involvement with politics from day one of their marriage, her considerable political skills and high level of energy, her willingness to put her husband's needs even above those of their two daughters, and her stunning ability to *always* take second place to her mate made her nothing less than the living incarnation of the Helpmeet. Lyndon Johnson was a workaholic whose business was politics, and so, during the last phase of his public career, in the executive branch, the married pair became in effect two trusted and respected business partners sharing the challenges which the business of presidential politics presents.

Claudia Alta Taylor was born near Karnack, Texas, in 1912. The name Lady Bird was given her in childhood by a nursemaid who said she was "pretty as a Lady Bird." Some five and a half years after she was born, her mother was dead and she was left to be reared by her Aunt Effie, the younger sister of her mother, and Thomas Jefferson Taylor, the tall, broad, strong-willed father whom she adored. She denies any childhood unhappiness. "People always look back at it now and assume it was lonely. To me it definitely was not. I lived in a country of farm lands and pine forests and little country lanes. In the spring there were wild cherokee roses. . . . In the fall the roads are real bright with the sweet gum and hickory trees. . . . I spent a lot of time just walking and fishing and swimming."[42] Yet soon after she met another tall, strong-willed man whom she could adore, she left home. Not much more than two months after they met, Lady Bird became the wife of Lyndon Johnson.

It was clear at the outset that Lyndon wanted a capable, knowledgeable junior partner rather than a mere lackey. "The very first thing after we married, Lyndon asked me to learn the names of the county seats of those counties that his boss represented and, say, three or four of the outstanding men who were able to get things done in each county and the basis of the district's economy and working," Mrs. Johnson recalls. And when some three years after their marriage Lyndon Johnson decided to make his first run for Congress, it was his wife who made it possible. (Shades of Joseph Kennedy. As it turns out, both examples of Helpmeets played important roles as bankers.) Her father agreed to give her a $10,000 advance on her inheritance to defray the campaign costs. (His answer when she asked: "Well, honey, I can't get it to you before tomorrow morning at 9 when the bank opens.")[43]

But Lady Bird Johnson didn't really cut her teeth until her husband was removed from the scene. While he was in the South Pacific during World War II, his wife took over the management of his congressional office in Washington. She remembers it as one of the decisive experiences of her life. For the first time it was clear to her that she could function without a man to lean on (the two men in her life had been strong supports indeed), that she could make her own living, and that she too could cope with constituents in Texas and politicians in Washington. Still, when her husband returned to Washington, she retreated again, almost but not quite resuming her wifely duties as before. The main difference was in her management of the family's business affairs. During the war years, Mrs. Johnson purchased radio station KTBC in Austin, spending much time and energy in Texas on the effort (her husband remained mostly in Washington), and laying the groundwork for the wealth the family would accumulate over the succeeding decades. (The station's profits were used to make extraordinarily profitable investments in land and bank securities.)

In 1948 Lyndon Johnson made a second try for the Senate (he was defeated in 1942). To try to stave off another loss, although she was by now the mother of two babies, his wife campaigned on her own for the first time. She organized women, stood in reception lines, recruited volunteers, and trooped with her husband through city and town. One day before the election she was in a car accident. But she never told her husband, and on election day itself she was busy calling names from the Austin telephone book. His narrow victory meant the beginning of a new era for the

Johnsons. They had a permanent home now in Washington, and
Lyndon a rising career in the Senate. For the next decade Lady
Bird would hone her skills as the politician's perfect wife.

What exactly makes a "politician's perfect wife"? And how
does such a woman see herself? We have said that the traditional
helpmeet was the wife/assistant, on constant call to service her
husband's needs, which were implicitly deemed more important
than her own. Consider the case of Lady Bird Johnson. All the
evidence indicates that she perceived of herself as Lyndon Johnson's helpmeet in the old-fashioned sense of the word. The way
in which Mrs. Johnson carried out her responsibilities—in complete accord with how her husband's life structured them—and
the documentation of her own oral and written testimony indicate in no uncertain terms that she considered herself second to
his first. Independent she was not. But beware. None of this implies that she was, or thought of herself as, LBJ's doormat. To
the contrary. She became a Helpmeet. Recall that Helpmeets are
business partners. For them to do their job effectively, they must
have gained the full respect and confidence of the president.

In part, Mrs. Johnson played the traditional helpmeet because
she viewed herself as having been catapulted onto the world stage
through no special intelligence or skill of her own. Even after
one year as First Lady she was still standing two steps back: "But
the net of it is that I am a private person extended into public life
somewhat because of the opportunities and impelling call of my
husband's jobs through the years. The aspect of the role one
doesn't forget is that it all hinges upon the man you've married.*
My needs are groomed into helping him."[45] Her playing the traditional role also grew out of how she had been reared—in the
Southern patriarchal mode of the first part of this century in
which women were responsible for the care, feeding, and sooth-
ing of all the family. J. B. West, for long years chief usher at the
White House, was struck by Mrs. Johnson's early instructions to
him: "Anything that's done here, or needs to be done, remember
this: my husband comes first, the girls second and I will be satisfied with what's left."[46] West eventually concluded that the president was clearly the dominant one, noting that he was sometimes

*This theme repeats itself. In her *Diary,* Mrs. Johnson concludes at the end
of one day, "All in all, it was a day precious to me, afforded entirely by my role
here in the White House, and not earned by my knowledge or myself."[44]

"almost abusive" to his wife, shouting at her as he shouted at everyone else, and that even their two daughters seemed to dominate Mrs. Johnson's pliant personality. Finally, Lady Bird Johnson played the traditional helpmeet because she genuinely saw herself as less than equal to a husband who was—as many would agree—larger than life. Nowhere is this so clearly illustrated as in the interview she gave Henry Brandon for the *New York Times Magazine* almost four years after becoming First Lady. Despite Brandon's push, she would not be moved up from second place.

Q. How much help can you give in a [crisis] situation?

A. I can give none, really, except a peaceful setting right here in the house. The best thing I can do [for the president] is to try to create a pleasant little island where he can work—where you like the food and where you are not constantly bothered with questions about household and family and where you know you're coming back to somebody who, even if they don't always agree with what you're doing, are not going to—

Q. Are you not being too modest? Because you are a very alert, very intelligent woman, and you will understand the presidential dilemmas and, after all, you are his best friend, and its very difficult these days to have somebody one can trust 100%.

A. Perhaps there is this—I'm terribly average . . . and I think maybe my reaction would be the reaction of millions of people across the country. . . .

Q. Now, I presume that you really know something about Washington politics or national politics. Is this where the President takes your advice most?

A. Mr. Brandon, I think perhaps you think I've entered into it more substantially than I have. I have feelings about people and programs, but I think mostly it's been from the standpoint of the citizen. . . . No, sir, I don't think of myself as deeply versed. . . .[47]

But for those who trouble to wade through its almost 800 pages, the most revealing document about Lady Bird Johnson as First Lady is her own book on the subject, *A White House Diary*. We are talking here of how this woman saw herself, and although *Diary* is hardly a volume remarkable for its self-analysis and introspection, some truths do emerge.

Consider first the fact of the tome itself. That it exists at all attests to Mrs. Johnson's heightened sensitivity to her exceptional circumstance. That it exists in the form it does—it is a running account of her own wifely activities rather than a considered appraisal of the turbulent times of her husband's presidency, or of him, or of their relationship—is evidence of Mrs. Johnson's feeling that she was not really qualified to talk of weighty matters, and that, in any case, it was not her place to do so. So she recorded the news that she thought fit to print—for a politician's wife. The result: an overview with an accent on the positive. Incidentally, Lady Bird Johnson originally began the project for reasons of posterity and self-discipline—"I wanted to see if I could keep up this arduous task." By the time the family left the White House, she had self-disciplined herself to the point where the transcript totaled some 1,750,000 words! (The full diary is available in the Johnson Library in Austin.)

In line with all the other testimony, *Diary* also confirms that Mrs. Johnson felt most comfortable when dutiful, and felt most dutiful when exhausting herself in her three roles of wife, mother, and First Lady. If there is one thread that runs through this work, it is the notion that to do anything just for herself was almost decadent and certainly self-indulgent. "I got Lynda Bird off on her trip to Dallas and Luci Baines off to see the football game, and then I luxuriously and self-indulgently went back to sleep." "I slept late, self-indulgently. . . ." "I decided to treat myself to a visit to the National Art Gallery with Ida May today. Feeling delightfully truant. . . ." Conversely, most of the entries are of days that are heavily programmed from morning until night. The president's consort, the mother of two daughters, and the wife of Lyndon Johnson—all three jobs are attacked with the utmost seriousness and dedication. "This morning I tackled the mountain that is my desk, the tyrant that sits there and glowers at me." "If I am to win the battle to keep us all together, I'll need to apply equal time to the girls along with Lyndon's business, and my public duties and my own pursuits." "My personal request to the Lord is that I can somehow be tactful enough, and gay enough, and sometimes even mean enough, to get Lyndon home at a reasonable hour for dinner and bed. . . ." "I treasure a glorious night's sleep for Lyndon as I would a four-carat diamond on my finger."[48]

But of course it takes two. By the time the Johnsons got to the White House they had been married three decades, and so it is hardly surprising that the way Lyndon Baines saw Lady Bird was the mirror image of how she saw herself. The prevailing paradox is clearest from his vantage point. She was indispensable, but at

the same time she was curiously unappreciated. Or perhaps more
precisely, she was appreciated, but only as a good assistant would
be. Her services were taken for granted. There is no evidence that
when Johnson wanted his wife to do something for him, he
would ask. He did not exactly order her to do his bidding. It is
just that both knew that when he said, "Bird, let's ask Congress
over this afternoon," she would see to it that, if humanly possible, it would be done.

Of the fact that he trusted her implicitly there is no doubt. Yet
even here there is a reserve. The joke around the White House
was that the "only person Johnson trusts is Lady Bird; and then
only 90% of the time."[49] And it is remarkable that in his own long
book, *The Vantage Point,* the references to this woman who was
so close to him are precious few in number and circumspect in
their praise and affection. On a memo she wrote to him in 1964
gently urging him to run for the presidency that year, he writes:
"Through our years together I have come to value Lady Bird's
opinion of me, my virtues and flaws. I have found her judgment
generally excellent, but in this instance although I respected her
logic, I was not convinced."[50]

It is true that when he did get around to the subject of his
wife, Johnson had nothing but praise. There is no evidence that
he ever did less. But for most of his life it seems he did not fully
grasp the role she played in his career. The fact that she was
taken for granted made her somehow insignificant. A close reading of Doris Kearns on the subject illustrates the point. On page
83 of her book on Johnson[51] she writes, "To both mother and
wife Lyndon Johnson would always ascribe a scarcely credible
perfection." But one page later there is a tacit confession that
although Johnson may always have lauded his wife, or at least
done so when reminded of her contribution, it took him a lifetime
to properly appreciate her, to consciously acknowledge her efforts on his behalf:

> Without [her] devotion and forbearance, without a love steadily
> given and never withdrawn, the course of Lyndon Johnson's contin-
> uing ascent in the world of politics becomes inconceivable. During
> the final year of his life, he told me that he had come to understand
> that. . . .[52]

Incidentally, Kearns seems to fall into the same trap as her subject. In her full biography of Lyndon Johnson Lady Bird plays

only a tiny role. She is mentioned briefly on twelve of the book's
400 pages.

Kearns asserts in no uncertain terms that it was Lady Bird
Johnson's destiny to play second fiddle to Rebekah Johnson, the
president's mother, who died in 1958. "That Rebekah remained
the signal woman and influence on Lyndon's life there can be no
doubt," she writes.[53] No wonder that, faced with such casting and
a husband who was nevertheless (or should I say "therefore")
all-consuming and all-demanding, it was a tendency of Lady
Bird's to daydream, drift off eyes opened as it were. Kearns uses
the phrase "Her spirit took flight to some remote place," while
West describes what he actually seemed to see: "She had an es-
cape valve, some secret little room inside her mind that she could
adjourn to when things got tense. When the air got heavy with
personalities and pejoratives . . . she simply tuned it all out."[54]
But of course, as a Helpmeet, whenever the president would notice and call out, "Bird, are you with me?" she would snap back to
the present tense, alert and ready to serve.[55]

A word about Lady Bird Johnson as a mother. There were
times over the years when the needs of her children came into
conflict with the will of her husband. Most often Lyndon Johnson came first. But once again, in line with her training and natural proclivity (Lady Bird, say those who knew her from way back,
was *always* capable and disciplined), despite the myriad claims
on her time, Mrs. Johnson was a devoted and conscientious parent. The rearing of the children was left to her, and she attended
to their needs just as thoroughly and efficiently as she ran things
for her husband. It is hard, though, to say how really close she
was to her daughters. There have been suggestions that at least
in the case of her elder daughter, Lynda, the lines of communication were less than fully open. For instance, when Lynda awoke
her parents one night in August 1967 to tell them that she was in
love with Charles Robb and wanted to marry him, both parents
appeared to learn about the seriousness of the romance, and the
history of their daughter's intended, for the first time. Still, Mrs.
Johnson fills *Diary* with the doings of her children, however irrelevant to matters of state, and rhapsodizes about them with the
same gay vigor that she typically applies to only her greatest en-
thusiasms (e.g., beautification of the American countryside). (Actually, this touches on one of the problems with *Diary* as a book.
We are told that one of the reasons for this voluminous record is

to preserve history for posterity. Why, then, all the references to Lynda and Luci in matters of purely personal interest—their school marks, friends, romances, etc.?)

By the time Lady Bird Johnson became the First Lady, she was already highly trained as a manager. Johnson had always left so much in his wife's hands that when she was called upon to perform the duties of the president's wife from one day to the next, she was ready. Indeed, despite the suddenness of her initiation, it was said that she ran the White House like "no other First Lady . . . rather like the chairman of the board of a large corporation. . . . White House management was functioning more efficiently than ever before."[56] That comment, in fact, touches on the distinguishing characteristics of Lady Bird Johnson as First Lady and Helpmeet to the president. Hers was a tenure that was notable for many missions accomplished and a particularly dutiful devotion to the tasks at hand—as well as a fervent belief in both her husband and the country he so abruptly came to lead.

Laurance Rockefeller, a colleague in conservation efforts, once pointed out in introducing Mrs. Johnson to an audience that "the Constitution of the United States does not mention the First Lady of our land. Our statute books give the position no specific power or authority. Yet it can be a position of tremendous influence."[57] Although Lady Bird Johnson became First Lady from one moment to the next, she maximized that opportunity. But then Lyndon Johnson's wife, as we have seen, was hardly a novice! She herself has recalled that "after Lyndon was elected in 1964, and when we got back and settled here early in January of '65, I began to think of what I could do to be of help to him and his aims."[58] From all appearances, she concluded that the best way she could assist was to be the most dedicated and energetic First Lady in recent memory. As Liz Carpenter, Mrs. Johnson's dynamic press secretary whom J. B. West referred to as one of the First Lady's "generals," has written, "Most important, she wanted to be a working First Lady, not an ornamental one. Backed by the President's complete confidence in her ability— and his enthusiastic encouragement—she chose several projects which were ideally suited to her natural interest. . . . The President thought it was marvelous."[59]

The full list of her roles throughout her five years in the White House is almost too long. One wonders how any were filled well: hostess, manager, speaker, traveler, instigator, adviser, campaigner, celebrator, decorator, cheerleader, volunteer, publicist, planner, ideologue, intellectual, and resident woman, wife, and mother. But fill them well she did, all of them, even though many turned out to be demanding indeed. In everything Mrs. Johnson undertook there was effort and planning. Nothing was left to careless chance. When she traveled, she would study maps and the exhaustive briefing papers prepared by the Department of State for her husband. When she played hostess, "she wanted the experience of coming to the White House to be more than a perfunctory handshake for each visitor and she was willing to work long hours to this end."[60] When she gave weddings, they were the largest and most lavish in White House history. When she advised her own husband, the counsel was set out in carefully prepared written memos. When she propagandized for beautification, she logged 200,000 miles on forty different trips. And so on.

It is important to stress again that Mrs. Johnson was strong. Although she was the president's Helpmeet and apparently content to take second place to at least this particular man, she had—especially for the mid-sixties—a "raised consciousness" about the place of women in society. Much of her work was undertaken in the certain knowledge that she was a fully competent educated adult who had no more reason to fritter away her time around "the hearth" than any man would. To call attention to achieving women in America, she initiated a series of luncheons at the White House for "Women Doers." The idea may sound dated now, but then it was something rather new to even acknowledge that women in America were, in fact, doing. (It was at a Woman Doers luncheon in January 1968 that *l'affaire* Eartha Kitt took place. Ms. Kitt, although invited to lunch at the White House, refused to play the quiescent lady. The subject at hand was "Crime in the Streets," but Ms. Kitt was angry about the war in Vietnam. Mrs. Johnson sensed trouble but could not avoid calling on the singer, who kept her hand raised to signal that she wished to speak. When finally tapped, Ms. Kitt made the most of the chance: "We have forgotten the main reason we have juvenile delinquency. . . . There's a war going on and Americans don't know why. . . . Boys I know across the nation feel it doesn't pay to be a good guy. They figure with a record they don't have to go off to be [shot and maimed] in Vietnam. . . . No wonder kids rebel and take pot. And, Mrs. Johnson, in case you don't understand the lingo, that's marijuana." Needless to say, Mrs. Johnson and all the other Women Doers were stunned by Ms. Kitt's outburst. The luncheon, though, came to a reasonably civilized end as several women rose to defend the administration, and the First Lady answered the implied charges against her husband with relative equanimity. The general verdict was that Ms. Kitt had presented the opposition's case with force, and that Mrs. Johnson had defended the president with a grace under pressure that was typical.) Mrs. Johnson also lobbied with her husband to put a woman on the Supreme Court. Joseph Califano, then one of Johnson's key aides, recalls that during a discussion of the Supreme Court nominations, "Mrs. Johnson displayed a preference for appointing the first woman to the Supreme Court. . . . It was a typically straightforward argument. She thought it was important to put a woman on the court; it was time and there were several well qualified women."[61] (This conversation—which revealed that Mrs. Johnson could have an independent opinion on political matters—occurred, tellingly, in the privacy of the family bedroom. Incidentally, Johnson had already made up his mind to put the first black on the court.) Consider too this statement, delivered at a Georgetown preparatory school:

> Women must take their place in public life as well as home life. I believe the educated woman today has a role to play—of courage and conviction—unparalleled since frontier days when she was wife, teacher, physician, and, often, community leader. In a world of change and challenge, women can no longer afford to concern themselves only with the hearth, any more than men can afford to concern themselves only with their jobs.[62]

Mrs. Johnson's view on the competence of women was the counterpart of that other side that always put Lyndon first. And it was the source of her strongest initiatives. It took guts, for example, to be the first woman in history to undertake a campaign effort of the magnitude of the "Lady Bird Special," the whistle-stop train that covered some 1,700 Southern miles on behalf of Lyndon Johnson's 1964 presidential run. Wrote her former press secretary, "Not since the inimitable Dolly Madison dropped her Quaker primness and her neckline and held bi-partisan Congressional salons to help her husband with Congress, have the walls of the White House seen a First Lady involved in such political intrigue and planning of a major campaign effort."[63] Very simply, the trip was the president's effort to hold on to the South in the wake of the Civil Rights Bill of 1964. It was thought that Lady Bird, with her Southern drawl, charm, and genuine affection for the land (",'I want to make this trip because I am proud of the South and I am proud that I am part of the South. I am fond of the old customs. . . . I am even more proud of the new South . . .''), would be his most convincing spokesperson.

Typically, despite the intrepid nature of the enterprise, Mrs. Johnson was prone to wrap it in the cocoon of her husband's prominence. As always, her role would be played down: "The people want to know the man they're entrusting so much of their power to. . . . Well, the man can't be everywhere and meet every-body. An interpreter—somebody close to him, his wife or mem-bers of his family—can do something to explain him, his aims, his character, his hopes for the folks, and I was simply an exten-sion, an interpreter."[64] Still, despite the disclaimers, the consid-ered opinion of the journalists who covered the Lady Bird Spe-cial was that it was a "polished and professional performance." The First Lady's speeches were short and punchy; the advance men and political action groups delivered an audience; the press was carefully pandered to ("happy hour" in the free press buffet stretched out indefinitely); pretty "Ladies for Lyndon" were on board to welcome local dignitaries; and the supply of LBJ but-tons, balloons, and streamers and smiles from Lady Bird, Lynda, and Luci were endless.[65] The trip, it was agreed, was a triumph. Indeed, it evoked from Lyndon Johnson rare praise: "By any standard, the whistle stop tour had been a spectacular suc-cess. . . . The people who gathered around her railroad car praised her grace and warmth and poise. She had endured heck-lers with dignity; she had conquered thousands with love. I was terribly proud of her as I welcomed her that evening in New Or-leans."[66]

Mrs. Johnson's energy and robust ambition were as evident in the projects she undertook on her own behalf—for example in her campaign for beautification. The idea was a natural: the First Lady had always been a nature lover, and the conservationists' cause was just beginning to gather steam. Typically, she tackled the task with such skill and zeal that president-watcher Hugh Sidey wrote that "it may be, in fact, that the natural beauty pro-gram is the single most successful Great Society venture so far. And it is quite plain that Mrs. Johnson in the years ahead will be

identified with national beauty. . . ."[67] She did no less than begin
a mass movement in this country to beautify the countryside, a
mass movement that was notably free of partisan politics, steadily
drew some 200 letters a week to the White House, and elicited
donations large and small ranging from hundreds of thousands
from the Rockefellers to pennies from classes of schoolchildren.
There were countless meetings and ceremonies (e.g., tree plant-
ing), and there was the Highway Beautification Act that was supposed to rid the country of billboards and was finally passed in no
small part because of Mrs. Johnson's personal lobbying effort.
(Her success was illustrated by a cartoon showing a billboard
which read, "Impeach Lady Bird"). Most dramatically, there
were the trips: voyages across all the land to celebrate prairies
and rapids and mountains and oceans. The First Lady would
rhapsodize with the utmost sincerity at every stop and appear to
be—in her desire to see and extol more—indefatigable. From vet-
eran White House reporter Helen Thomas:

> I will never again be as rugged as I had to be covering Mrs. Johnson.
> It was adapt or die. Sheer survival impelled me. Climbing moun-
> tains pursued by gnats, riding Snake River rapids in Wyoming,
> watching from the beaches as she—not I—snorkeled in the Barra-
> cuda-filled Caribbean, bobbing in a flotilla of rubber rafts down the
> Rio Grande. . . . Lady Bird watchers had trouble keeping up with
> this woman who had the stamina of steel. We datelined copy from
> Moose, Wyoming, and Panther Junction, held our breath as the an-
> telopes were shooed off a dirt airstrip at Presidio, Texas, as we
> landed, sent out typewriter copy by Pony Express from the Big Bend
> in Texas which seemed as remote to us as the planet Mars. . . .[68]

Perhaps you had to be there, but by all reports when Lady Bird
Johnson would utter lines that might seem gushy in black and
white years later, the sentiment was catching. Her own manifest
joy "in the woodland [where] one can sense the great contrast
between the slow, steady life of the trees, with all their majesty
and solitude," made others converts.

As in any good partnership, both partners looked after their
side of the business. Lyndon Johnson was the boss and took responsibility for everything political. Lady Bird Johnson took responsibility for everything else. Generally, she gave political advice only when asked. Her daily activities, as *Diary* confirms,
rather than being intertwined with her husband's, ran parallel to
them. Mostly, the two went in separate directions; "the exigen-

Jacqueline Kennedy engages Robert Frost in conversation at the legendary spring, 1962 White House dinner for Western Hemisphere Nobel Prize winners. It was on this occasion that President Kennedy referred to his guests as "the most extraordinary collection of talent, of human knowledge, that has ever been gathered together at the White House, with the possible exception of when Thomas Jefferson dined alone." Courtesy of The John F. Kennedy Library.

Although slightly past the very cute, very little-girl stage, Amy Carter still makes a winning picture, together with "Grits," just after moving to the White House. They also made the cover of Time. Courtesy of The White House Photo Office.

Wearing a "Kennedy for President" button on his right lapel, Teddy Kennedy kicks off brother Jack's candidacy for the Democratic nomination for the presidency in West Virginia in January, 1960. He bore a striking resemblance—in looks, in speech, and in mannerisms—to his brother. Courtesy of United Press International.

Susan Ford, gamboling on the White House lawn with "Liberty." This picture was taken soon after the Fords rather hastily took up residence at 1600 Pennsylvania Avenue. Courtesy of The Gerald B. Ford Library.

The Fords scanning some of the volumes of "get well" mail delivered to Betty's hospital room after her mastectomy. By Mrs. Ford's testimony, "eventually fifty thousand pieces of mail were counted." Courtesy of The Gerald R. Ford Library.

(Left) *Billy Carter in Plains before his fall, beer can and beer belly in front of his Amoco filling station. In Billy's heyday, tourists would wait in line for thirty minutes just to be able to say they bought gas at Billy's place.* Courtesy of Tandy C. Rice, Jr.—Top Billing, Inc.

(Right) *President Kennedy kissing his father farewell after a Cape Cod weekend in the summer of 1963. Joseph Kennedy was disabled by a stroke in December, 1961.* Courtesy of The John F. Kennedy Library.

Lady Bird Johnson doing her bit to get votes for Lyndon during the 1964 presidential campaign. Mrs. Johnson broke new ground in her willingness to go out on the hustings alone. Courtesy of The Lyndon Baines Johnson Library.

That famous press conference in which Julie
Nixon Eisenhower, with husband David
alongside, took it upon herself to meet the
media on behalf of her Watergate-beleaguered
father. Courtesy of The National Archives,
Nixon Presidential Materials Project.

President Kennedy and his brother Robert.
Courtesy of The New York Times News
Service (George Tames).

Rosalynn Carter during the 1980 presidential campaign, doing what she had done all during the 1976 campaign: trying to win friends and influence voters without her husband alongside. Courtesy of The White House Photo Office.

The Kennedys in Rome in March, 1939 for the coronation of Pope Pius XII. From left to right: Kathleen, Eunice, Edward, Jean, Rosemary, Robert, John, Patricia, and Rose. Courtesy of The John F. Kennedy Library.

Sam Houston Johnson in the last year of the Johnson administration. Courtesy of
The Lyndon Baines Johnson Library.

*Edward, Richard, and Donald Nixon (left to right) midway through the President's
first term. Photographs of the three brothers together are rare.* Courtesy of The
National Archives, Nixon Presidential Materials Project.

Billy Carter after his fall (August, 1980), preparing to leave the Old Senate Caucus Room at the conclusion of Senate hearings on his ties with the Libyan government. Accompanying him is his attorney, Henry Ruth. Courtesy of Wide World Photos.

The Reagans (minus Maureen) as a happy family watching a telecast of GOP delegates casting their ballots at the Republican convention in Detroit. Courtesy of Wide World Photos.

cies of time—her frequent trips, his nonstop working habits—
kept them from spending a great deal of time together."[69] Indeed,
quiet moments alone were apparently so rare that Mrs. Johnson
would allude to them with some astonishment: "This morning
we had breakfast together and went for a walk—*just the two of us
...*" (italics mine). On another kind of morning she writes, "I
wait my turn to get a word in edgeways."[70]

But for all the busyness that enveloped them, they were also
close—in no small part, of course, because whenever Lyndon
needed Lady Bird, she was there. She provided him with a whole
host of services ranging from White House aide to in-house domestic: advice or lunch would be offered, as the occasion demanded. As a counselor, in fact, both because of her intelligence
and fidelity, she had no real equal. Jack Valenti wrote of her:

> Her political judgments were sound. She never spoke hurriedly
> about issues or problems. She thought seriously *when asked about
> her views* [italics mine]. She had definite opinions and she ex-
> pressed them lucidly, and in vivid phrases, with that edge of softness
> that dulls a critical response. . . . I would have to judge that in a
> crunch, the president valued her considered opinion more than any
> of his counselors because he knew that, alone among his entourage,
> she delivered her views without any self-interest or leashed ego. . . .
> She has lived with him and by him for over thirty years of rough
> political campaigning and though she was always a lady, she was
> also a sturdy political pro. . . . Years later I remarked to an audience
> that if anything had happened to Mrs. Johnson in LBJ's political
> career, he would have been severely crippled.[71]

Paradoxically the evidence indicates that Mrs. Johnson was
not "asked about her views" very often. But on the decisions to
run or not—for president in 1964 and then again in 1968—her
advice was critical. As early as May 1964 Lady Bird Johnson
wrote out a nine-page memo analyzing what she thought of her
husband's immediate situation. It included first of all, in case he
decided he wanted to use it, a suggested announcement that he
would not run: "I wish now to announce that I will not be a
candidate for reelection. I wish to spend the rest of my life in my
home state, in peace with my family. . . ." Then she set down the
alternatives. If he were to run, he would probably be elected.
During the ensuing four years, then, they would have to expect
frustration, criticism, and slander, and perhaps even an earlier
death for the president. (Johnson had had a near-fatal coronary in

1955, from which his wife and mother had nursed him back, and his health remained a concern.) But there would also "be times of achievement . . . which could provide satisfaction with no peer, I believe." On the other hand, if he did not run they would probably return to the ranch and the country they loved, but only at the price of a barrage of questions as to his real motives, and a widespread feeling, especially among Democrats, that he had let down the side. Also, how could "overseeing the cattle and maybe making a few lectures . . . contain him and consume his twenty-four hours a day in a constructive way"? The final part of the statement was prescient: "My final conclusion was that I thought he ought to run, facing clearly all the criticisms and hostilities . . . pacing himself . . . and then three years and nine months from now, February or March 1968, if the Lord lets him live that long, announce that he won't be a candidate for reelection. By that time, I think, the juices of life will be sufficiently stilled in him as he approaches sixty so that he can finish out the term and return to the Ranch, and we can live the rest of our days quietly." [72] She wrote all this out, put it in an envelope marked "Personal, please," and arranged for another to hand-deliver it to the president.

Lyndon Johnson's vacillation during mid-1964 was genuine. Gently but consistently, his wife would urge him to hang in. The culmination came in August, one day after the Democratic convention had actually opened. The president scrawled a withdrawal statement on a yellow pad. He showed it to his wife, who answered in no uncertain terms, but with the greatest love and support: "Beloved—you are as brave a man as Harry Truman—or FDR—or Lincoln. . . . To step out now would be *wrong* for your country, and I can see nothing but a lonely wasteland for your future. . . . I am not afraid of *Time* or lies or losing money or defeat. In the final analysis I can't carry any of the burdens you talked of—so I know it's only *your* choice. But I know you are as brave as any of the thirty-five. I love you always. Bird." [73] In his autobiography, Johnson would maintain that this note was responsible for his reversal: "She hit me on two most sensitive and compelling points, telling me what I planned to do would be wrong for my country and that it would show a lack of courage on my part." [74]

Mrs. Johnson's opinion on the 1968 decision held steady. From the spring of 1964 on (as expressed in the above-mentioned memo of May of that year), she did not want the president to run again. Husband and wife discussed often how to select the time and occasion to make the announcement, an announcement that firmed as the strains of Vietnam took their toll. A statement was drafted that Johnson gave his wife to read. Although she had, by his own account, always been "most deferential" in their conversations about 1968, she did pencil in one major change: the phrase "have no desire to accept" was altered to read "will not accept." The change stayed. A new statement was drawn up by Johnson's advisers; Lady Bird Johnson also drafted one of her own, at her husband's request. The final version was read to the nation in March 1968, much as Mrs. Johnson had foretold some four years earlier.

But Mrs. Johnson was still, of course, much more keeper than counselor. She writes of trying to "pry him loose" from his work to get some rest, talking with him in the blackness when sleep eluded, comforting him when his "dark countenance was dour and grim," telling him to stop when he spoke too long, facing him with a staunch smile when the polls were lowest, striving to keep the wolves at bay when there was loneliness in his voice. It was her nature to see the bright side, to avoid harsh realities if she could, particularly as these impinged on her husband. Thus it was as the president was increasingly beleaguered during his last two years in office that his wife's positive countenance and stiff upper lip served especially well.

Mrs. Johnson's contribution to her husband's life and work can hardly be overestimated. But perhaps the performance as president's Helpmeet can best be understood through evaluations of her as First Lady. Not then nor later was there a single gripe. Two tough critics could bestow no higher praise. Shana Alexander wrote for *Life*:

> What was handed to Mrs. Johnson was . . . a wrecked and blasted Camelot haunted by our own special vision of its dazzling martyred Queen. . . .
> Individually, [Mrs. Johnson's beautification] achievements seemed modest and rather colorless acts, like Lady Bird herself. . . . But in the aggregate, it was a heroic achievement. When you add in all the other quiet, half remembered things Mrs. Johnson has caused to happen, and caused not to happen . . . this quiet, plain, tough little woman looks more and more remarkable. Somewhere in that strange forest on that last day I began to sense how much more

Mrs. Johnson leaves behind her than daffodils coast-to-coast. Quite possibly she is the best First Lady we have ever had.[75]

And Alice Roosevelt Longworth, Teddy's daughter and long-time tart-tongued observer of the Washington aviary—it was she who said of Harding that he "was not a bad man. He was just a slob," and of Coolidge that he looked as if he'd "been weaned on a pickle," and of Franklin Roosevelt that he was "two-thirds mush, one-third Eleanor"—opined, "The plain fact is that there has never been a First Lady to equal Mrs. Johnson. No woman has ever accomplished the task with her combination of strength and grace. She has never put one foot wrong."[76]

"I Could Never Have Done It Without the Help of . . ."

Who can say whether Joseph P. Kennedy and Lady Bird Johnson were literally indispensable to the care and feeding of our thirty-fifth and thirty-sixth presidents respectively? Maybe Jack would have made it without Joe's money, contacts, advice, and support. Maybe Lyndon would have survived without Bird's money, advice, support, and labor. But this much is sure: the availability to Kennedy of his father, and to Johnson of his wife, contributes mightily to any conceivable explanation of their success.

The role of Helpmeet is a tricky one. Its political importance is derived from a good working relationship to the president. But when it works best, it grows out of something not at all political: a love of old vintage that no longer needs testing. The bond is assumed, and it enables both partners to experience the inequality of the exchange without guilt or pain. It is also true that although the junior-senior relationship between Helpmeet and president is a requisite for the role, the ability of Joe Kennedy and Lady Bird Johnson to mute their own identities for the sake of cause is not correlated to low self-esteem. No one would argue the size of the patriarch's ego, and as for the lady from Texas, one has only to look at the record of her accomplishments from a young age to understand that this was not exactly an insecure shrinking violet. Indeed, in what might appear to be a paradox, it was the extraordinary competence of these two that made them so effective in their roles.

Both Joseph Kennedy and Lady Bird Johnson acted their

parts perfectly. They had the necessary traits—a lifelong interest and skill in politics, personal and material resources, the freedom to devote their lives to their presidential kin, a vicarious ambition for success and power in public life, and a willingness to hide, if need be, their own light. All of these came, at one time or another, into play.

These Helpmeets were the great facilitators, paving and smoothing the way wherever they could. Neither Joe Kennedy nor Mrs. Johnson ever achieved any special status with the American people. In fact, a deliberate, and successful, attempt was made to keep Kennedy out of the public eye; and perhaps because Mrs. Johnson had an impossible act to follow in terms of broad appeal, she never even seemed to try much to win us over. No, the political import of these two came largely from what they did for the president. But in the act they transformed themselves into a resource that contributed so mightily to the achievement that the success itself must be labeled a team effort. Lucky indeed is the president who at will can tap a rich, clever, and doting relative who croons and means it, "Everything I have is yours. . . ."

CHAPTER 6

Moral Supports

Moral Supports have a special place in the heart of the president. They are politically relevant because they lend an essential support to the presidential ego, and because they extract, in turn, an intense emotional commitment. A child cannot qualify as a Moral Support. To be one it is necessary to be sufficiently intellectually mature to understand what it is the president is doing and, given that, to lend heartfelt encouragement and backing.

Although this book makes it a point to avoid psychological reductionism, this might be the place for the exception that proves the rule. Herewith the following hypothesis: Without Julie Nixon Eisenhower to provide the family's only public defense of him during the Watergate crisis of 1973 and '74, Richard Nixon would have suffered a complete mental breakdown.

There is, of course, no proving this claim. It is offered only to highlight the fact that the kind of support that Julie Eisenhower lent the president during the Watergate period was so critical to him that it was qualitatively different from what is more typically extended from the First Family to the president. Perhaps it should be made explicit that moral support is by no means a given. In just the period that we are covering, two First Ladies, Pat Nixon and Betty Ford, had strong reservations about their husbands running for and being president. Indeed, it is quite possible that the Moral Support comes to the fore only when the president is under particular siege, especially when one of his acts or policies is being questioned on ethical or moral grounds.

150

By that criterion, Mrs. Lyndon Johnson's most critical role during the last year or two of her husband's presidency may well have been as defender of his actions in Vietnam. But Lady Bird Johnson was, as we have seen, a relative of many parts who helped her husband in many ways. Julie Nixon was much less well equipped to be an all-around Helpmeet, and much more important as a voice for the defense when her father stood more or less entirely alone.

It is not the place of Moral Supports to question why. They accept, on blind faith if need be, the word of the president. Richard Nixon never had to prove anything to Julie Eisenhower. He never had to produce, for her benefit, any evidence that the charges against him stemming from the Watergate break-in were false. He said they were, and that was enough. His word was sufficient proof that he was innocent; and her belief provided the strength for him to hang in.

Before looking at this single case of a Moral Support, let us briefly consider the two words that define the role, taking them in reverse order.

A support is something that holds something up. Beyond that, support is sustenance, the provision of the means for sustaining life. Finally, to support can mean to go still another step further: to affirm, to confirm, to corroborate. Julie did all these things for her father, from the simple act of consoling him even after his own wife had become a recluse, to affirming his vision of history long after those who had once been his friends deserted him. As Watergate moved into high gear and edged ineluctably toward a denouement, it was Julie, and Julie alone, who was there for Richard Nixon. Both in private and in public, it was this younger daughter who held her father up, sustained him with her optimism, and believed him in full view of everyone else.

The moral aspect of the support concerns the matter of integrity. The Moral Support believes the president to be, even if wrong in certain particulars, fundamentally honest and well intentioned. Thus, hypothetically, Mrs. Johnson could have disputed her husband's policy in Vietnam and seen the issue as just one of honest disagreement.

With Richard Nixon, it was the moral component of Julie Eisenhower's faith that was perhaps the most critical, for it was precisely here that he was the most vulnerable. Watergate could not finally be defined in terms of honest disagreement; the charge was that the president had broken the law, that he had violated his oath under the Constitution, and that his actions constituted an impeachable offense. It was a question of law, and it was also a question of abusing the principles of right and proper conduct. More than most cases of presidential behavior, this was a matter of black and white, and here again Julie was unique. At a moment when the world, it seemed, was charging the president not only with wrongdoing in a legal sense but also with the veritable inability to understand the ethical consequences of his behavior, his daughter took it upon herself to defend him on a personal level. It was precisely on the subject of his goodness as a man, in fact, on which she was repeatedly the most vehement. When asked why she had taken on her role as his chief public defender, she responded, "I care very much about my father. He has always been a good father and a truly good person. Helping one another in our family has always been a two-way street, and now it's my turn to give him that little extra concern and attention in his hour of need."[1]

Julie was always something special in the Nixon family. Even outsiders thought so. In the sixties it was the "effervescent Julie who was the favorite of those who saw the Nixons from a distance."[2] And during the early halcyon days of the first administration, *Newsweek* described her as "the bubbler, the catalyst, the outgoing socializer and a politician like her father."[3] It was odd, in a way, that Julie should have turned into so political an animal, for as children, she and her older sister Tricia were always sheltered from their parents' political lives. Julie remembered that her parents didn't talk politics at home, that they would return from campaigning wanting to discuss what the children had been doing.[4]

In part, this early exclusion from real-life politics, with its peculiar mix of exultant triumph and devastating defeat, may have accounted for Julie's extreme reaction the first time she was exposed to what it was really like. She was twelve at the time, not exactly a little girl any more, but she recalls that "it was a shock in 1960 to learn that not everyone thought Daddy was perfect—it was shattering when someone tore him to pieces on TV."[5] In retrospect, in fact, the year 1960, the year of the bitter contest with John Kennedy, must be seen as a traumatic time for young

Julie Nixon, and she never, even many years later, came to terms with that electoral defeat. Nixon writes in his memoirs that when he discussed his decision to run in 1968 with his daughters, Julie answered "You have to do it for the country." Nixon adds that she "never really accepted the loss in 1960."[6] Later on, on another occasion, Nixon wrote in his diary, "I recall that in 1960, after the defeat, Julie was the one who . . . really never gave up. I remember going in to her bedroom . . . just to kiss her good night, and she would say. 'Daddy, can't we still win?' This was two weeks or so after the election."[7] And Julie herself, some eight years after the fact, would not, out loud at least, bow to the reality: "I still haven't conceded the 1960 election. I do believe Daddy won it. But my father said the presidency of the United States is never stolen and he wouldn't want a recount because he wouldn't want to win that way."[8] It was almost as if history could still be rewritten.

She apparently had a similar sort of reaction to Nixon's defeat in the run for governor of California in 1962. Of that event she said in 1968, "The 1962 California defeat was shattering. Right now I feel I never lived in California. Two years was such a short time and when we lost, we left. So you just blot California out of your mind."[9] This blocking out of unwanted, unpleasant information, this desire on some level to return to her world as a child when as far as she knew, Daddy was perfect, was a not unimportant factor in her ability to play the role of Moral Support during the onslaught of Watergate. The ability to deny which she had displayed as a youngster clearly stayed with her.

During the campaign of 1968, Pat, Tricia, Julie, and David Eisenhower worked "tirelessly," as Richard Nixon put it, for the Republican ticket. The Nixon women could, of course, always be counted on to put out for the head of the family, but now the very small band of loyalists had a new and very important member: the grandson of Nixon's onetime, sometime mentor, Dwight David Eisenhower. The match between Nixon's younger daughter and the only grandson of the former president was, as far as Nixon and also other Republican visionaries were concerned, made in heaven. As *Time* clucked, "G.O.P. strategists could hardly have cooked up such a promotional coup. The idea would have seemed too stagey or cloyingly obvious."[10]

Having David Eisenhower on board was important to Richard

Nixon on two levels, the personal and the political. Nixon had had a complicated relationship with Ike; psychohistorian Bruce Mazlish labeled it a "continuous crisis."

> Much of Nixon's mature life, until the present, has circled about Eisenhower: it was Eisenhower who picked him out of obscurity to be his running mate in 1952, almost dumped him in the Fund controversy that then erupted, allowed a "Dump Nixon" movement to spread in 1956, almost presented Nixon with the Presidency itself because of his heart attack in 1955 and stroke in 1957, and played an ambiguous role in Nixon's own campaign for President in 1960. . . . On the deepest personal level Eisenhower presented Nixon with a crisis of feeling, involving emotions about Ike as a beloved and admired father figure to whom death wishes as both father and President became attached. . . .[11]

Psychiatrist and Nixon biographer David Abrahamsen echoes the tune in a slightly different key:

> For years Nixon had sought to win Eisenhower's admiration and respect and had failed. . . . During his second vice-presidency, we observe a Nixon still preoccupied with himself and his status vis-à-vis Eisenhower. Apparently, he must have been so obsessed with placing himself in the best light in the President's mind, that everyone else had to be disregarded.[12]

In any case, the Eisenhowers were something special to the Nixons, and there must have been something especially sweet for Richard Nixon in his daughter's marriage to the only heir to the Eisenhower name. It was a vindication of sorts: finally it had come to pass that a Nixon could be father figure to an Eisenhower. It is said that when David broke his family's tradition by joining the Navy instead of the Army, as his father-in-law had done, Nixon advised him at the swearing-in ceremony, "I've got a couple of old uniforms you can use." And when campaigning with his future son-in-law in tow, Nixon would assert with a smile, "I always campaign better with an Eisenhower."

Young David Eisenhower did indeed play a central role in '68. All who saw him concurred: he inherited not only his grandfather's name but also his "magnificent grin"; and he and Julie became, for some anyway, America's sweethearts. Not everyone found them irresistibly cute, but to middle America they were a star attraction. David soon had his own groupies. Teenagers, flocking to greet him at the airport, would squeal, "I touched him! I actually touched him."[13] Moreover, he took over as national chairman of Youth for Nixon, a job that involved, by his own testimony, running around the country, opening up store fronts, inspecting the grass roots on behalf of the ticket, and publishing youth reports. Most of all, though, it was the image that he and Julie created of a wholesome, all-American couple, recalling the traditional values in a time when these were being bitterly contested, that was considered so valuable to the Nixon ticket. A visit to a small town in Virginia was described by the *New York Times* as going like this:

> Just about everyone in town apparently turned out to see the couple. [Julie was poised] and pretty in a pink and white summer suit. The applause grew even warmer when Mr. Eisenhower, introduced as "the grandson of just about the greatest American the country has ever known," smiled his thanks.[14]

On that same occasion, one spectator was quoted as saying about David that he "smiles just like his grandfather," and Julie, who would be twenty in a few days, said her birthday wish was "just to go on being with good Republicans and Nixon supporters like those of you here."

The last months of 1968 must have been among the best in Richard Nixon's life. There were two dramatic and wonderful events, and in both of these Julie played a central role. In November Nixon won the presidential election, and to the extent that he really shared that victory with anyone, it seemed he shared it with Julie. It was Julie who believed so hard in his victory that she spent many hours before election day even dawned laboring on a piece of crewelwork to hand to her father the moment the win had been secured. It was the Great Seal of the United States, which Julie had inscribed: "To RN—JN." As she handed it to her father, hugging him, she said, "Daddy, I never had any doubt you would win. I just wanted something to be ready right away to prove it."[15] The crewelwork became the symbol of Nixon's triumph. It was the centerpiece of the family victory photo on front pages of newspapers all across the land (the *New York Times* titled the shot "She Knew It All Along"), and it started a rage in the art of crewel, which until that moment had remained quietly obscure.

The second event to warm Mr. Nixon's heart was the marriage of his daughter. The ceremony was performed in New York by that guru of positive thinking Dr. Norman Vincent Peale. (He was Julie's personal choice.) For Nixon the best moment of the day came when, during the ceremony, at the altar, the bride turned impulsively around to kiss her father.

It was always Julie's perception that the Nixon family was very close. Once, commenting to her father on his desk photo of him, Pat, Tricia, and herself taken on the day they moved back to California after the 1960 defeat, Julie wrote him, "I like to think that the reason you kept it on your desk was that it symbolized the happiness that we felt as a family in the midst of a difficult defeat and a difficult new start for you in private life after serving so many years as congressman, senator, and Vice President."[16] And perhaps because of her understandable view of the Nixons as a kind of a team, during the turbulent years of her father's first administration Julie performed as the perfect team player. On the one hand, she was a typical young married: finishing college, keeping house in a cheap apartment just off campus, and having her parents to dinner on Daddy's birthday. On the other, she was the energetic and outspoken defender of the traditional virtues that her father's administration was presumably elected to defend, but that were nonetheless under constant attack—especially by the nation's young. Page 38 of the *New York Times* of April 22, 1969, strikingly illustrated the counterpoint. The two most important stories were headlined "75 High School Students Abandon Their Brief Sit-in at Columbia" and "Harvard Group Stages 'Mill-in' Forcing Evacuation of Building." Meanwhile, a small story at the bottom of the same page announced that Julie and David Eisenhower would be living in the White House during the coming summer.

The juxtaposition on that April day on a single page of the country's leading newspaper was symbolic. For the more turbulent the late sixties and early seventies became, the closer Julie Nixon edged to her father's side. Nixon, it was clear, played an active part in getting his daughters to assume the paragon's role. They were set forth as the embodiment of his own ideals, and he acknowledged, in fact, that he saw both Tricia and Julie "as front-line troops in the battle to reestablish the traditional virtues."

> They care about the world, the country, their generation, and each in her own way tries her best to help. It's a trait they've always had, and one that we've always tried to encourage. . . . In this time when

so many young people are in one form or another of rebellion, it's pretty satisfying for a father to have two daughters who are trying so hard to help and doing it so well.[17]

Tricia always lived at home, leading a quiet life suited to her temperament, protected by both the White House gates and the decorum of those who surrounded the president. And so it was Julie who, as she finished up at Smith, while David did the same at Amherst, bore the brunt of the dissidents' anger. And it was Julie who fought back. In December 1969 *Newsweek* labeled Julie "a semi-official defender of and spokesman for Mr. Nixon's Vietnam policy."[18] On dissent she said, "Every American has a right to express his views. My father said that he would much rather have kids doing something than not doing anything. But you have to draw the line when they prevent others from being heard."[19] On the women's movement, she charged that its leaders were "alienating a lot of women and most of the men." Even so, she said, she did not think that her father had appointed enough women to top jobs in government; still, she did not press him on it "because I know all of the problems [he has]."[20] And on the night Nixon announced to the nation that he had taken the decision to expand the war into Cambodia, he found this note on his pillow:

Dear Daddy:

I was very proud of you tonight. You explained the situation in Vietnam perfectly—I am sure the American people will realize why you made your decision. I especially want to tell you how effective—and heartfelt—your final message to the people of South and North Vietnam, the Soviet Union, and the United States was. I feel that the strongest message which resulted from your speech was: We cannot abandon 17 million people to a living death, and we cannot jeopardize the chances for future world peace by an unqualified pullout of Vietnam.

I know you are right and, again, I am so proud.

Love,

Julie[21]

It could not have been an easy time to be the president's daughter, especially if you were the one who was, in Nixon's words, the "extrovert, warm, very outgoing and gregarious, who is doing something all the time."[22] (On the same occasion Nixon described Tricia as "more of an introvert," and himself as "somewhat an unusual man to be in political life because I tend to be less gregarious, frankly, than the average person in this position in public life."[23]) The ultraliberal I. F. Stone was the speaker at the Amherst graduation in 1970, but David did not attend to receive his degree, and when his name was read from the roster of the graduating class, it was greeted with a lusty mix of cheers and hisses. Julie herself was glad to get out of Smith. In retrospect she recalled that there was "a very oppressive atmosphere" in her senior year there, and that there "really was belligerence" against those who didn't want to be involved in a strike, or in a fast for peace.[24]

Still, both she and David remained staunch defenders, and David was said to be close to his father-in-law. Pat felt that it was inevitable that the young man would someday enter politics. "He's crazy about politics," she said. "He calls Dick and Dick calls him all the time to talk things over."[25]

In 1972, it was Richard Nixon's strategy to minimize his own campaigning while his family traversed the country making the requisite public appearances. Once again it was Julie who did the most. By July 1972 she had put in thirty-five appearances in thirteen states in contrast to her sister's sixteen appearances and her mother's twenty-five. In an article titled "With Julie on the Campaign Trail," *U.S. News and World Report* commented on her special position in Nixon's life and on her own political role.

Seasoned politicians are keeping a weather eye on the comings and goings of Julie Nixon Eisenhower. . . . At 23, she has been sharing the platforms—and the speechmaking—with Governors, Congressmen, mayors and federal officials. . . . Julie plans to continue her efforts on behalf of presidential programs. . . . "I really like to get involved in programs of my father's I really believe in. . . . He's done so much. . . . It shows we do care. . . . I think some of his programs are so terrific, I'd like to see them publicized more. . . ." David usually ducks arguments on the Vietnam war . . . While Julie is too much the political and family cheerleader to resist sticking up for Daddy. She claimed to notice an "overwhelming reaction" to the President's November 3 speech on Vietnam, for example. "I'm not saying he changed 10,000 minds on the college campuses, but he really did influence quite a few.[26]

In one of his diary's earliest references to Watergate, Richard Nixon writes about Julie's concern. The entry was on October 8, 1972.

> Julie was worried about the story in the paper to the effect that [Bill] Timmons, [Robert] Odle, and one other White House aide had had access to the reports on Watergate. She said that if any of them are really guilty that we really ought to get rid of them. I told her not to be concerned about it, that the reports were false. It does show how sensitive she, and probably others like her in the campaign, are about this issue. . . .[27]

Nixon's focus on Julie in this early private reference to what must slowly have been becoming a difficult subject was prescient. For it was Julie who would, over the next twenty-two months, be her father's principal ally.

By the spring of 1973, it was clear that Nixon would need all the help he could get. In order to be near her parents, Julie Eisenhower, along with husband David, moved into a Maryland home owned by Bebe Rebozo and worth some $125,000. (The Eisenhowers paid Rebozo an undisclosed rental fee. After a year, presumably in response to inquiries into the Nixon-Rebozo relationship, Julie and David moved out of Rebozo's home and into a $409-per-month Washington apartment.) It was during the summer of '73 and fall that Julie fully assumed the role of Moral Support. Before too long she was the chief spokesperson for the entire Nixon family on the hot topic of Watergate. She was capable of putting in as many as six appearances in different parts of the country in one week. And she had guts. On one occasion she specifically asked to go to the annual Radio and Television Correspondents' dinner—well known for its sharp-tongued after-dinner humor—just to prove that the Nixons were not ashamed to attend such events. The jokes were tough on her father and on his administration, but she stuck it out. She was also enterprising. In July she traveled to England to take Nixon's case abroad. On a BBC television interview she was subjected to questions ranging from why President Nixon did not lay the full Watergate case before the public to how the affair had affected the Eisenhowers' social life. Throughout the difficult interview she maintained her composure and insisted on her father's innocence; and when asked whether she wished he had carried out his 1962 vow to retire from politics, she replied, "I can't wish that when I've seen my father end the war in Vietnam."[28]

In his *Memoirs* Nixon writes that he did not want Julie to take the brunt of the Watergate questioning but that "she could not bear the fact that there did not seem to be anyone else who would speak out for me. Whenever I suggested that she not become so involved, she always replied, 'But Daddy, we have to fight.' "[29]

One of Julie's special strengths was translating the state of her family to the outside world. No one else was going to provide a by now insatiably curious nation with any information, and so Julie was the conduit. Of her father she would say that he was the strongest one in the family these days. "He's the one who's always calling us and saying, 'Now don't read the papers tomorrow because it's going to be bad, and I don't want you to worry about it.' " Of her mother she said, "She just has great inner strength, I don't know how she does it. She's an inspiration to the rest of us, and she's a great help to my dad. I don't think people realize how really great she is." Of the condition of her family on the weekend of the famous/infamous "Saturday night massacre" (which led to the firing of Watergate special prosecutor Archibald Cox and the resignations of Attorney General Elliot Richardson, and his deputy, William Ruckleshaus), she said, "Well it was a busy weekend for my dad, but in the evening we did relax and Friday night turned out to be a kind of a [family] party"—with a lively dinner and a showing of *The Sting*! And of herself she said that when her father reversed himself on the Watergate tapes, she felt "disappointment. He was standing with a constitutional principle, and he wanted to preserve this for future presidents [but] he thought it had reached the point where there was no public understanding for his position."[30]

As a by-product of Julie's defense of her father, both she and David became media superstars. Thus they were asked not only about Richard Nixon but also for their opinions on a wide range of other topics. To many, they were representative of what the younger generation could be if only it would shape up. *U.S. News and World Report*, for example, devoted seven pages of its October 8, 1973, issue to a "candid conversation," a "unique and far-ranging interview," with David and Julie Eisenhower. The discussion included the immediate events of the Nixon presidency, but it also covered Vietnam, the student revolts, values, the military, the press, and women's liberation.

But despite the Eisenhowers' effort to diversify, the main hunger for them stemmed, of course, from their proximity to the principals of Watergate. And a great hunger this was. Try as they might, they could not appease the curiosity. During 1973 Julie Eisenhower made over 150 personal appearances, and *gave more interviews to reporters than all the other members of the First Family combined.* Her style was to "tough it out," and one way of doing this was to block out the possibility, out loud at least, of disaster. In early 1974 Julie said that she did not think her father "would ever leave office before the end of his term because he really believes that some of his programs are needed, and he wants to fight for them. . . .When the going gets rough, I don't think he'd ever bug out. . . . That would indicate an admission of wrongdoing, and he hasn't done anything wrong. . . ."[31]

Not surprisingly, all of this insisting in the face of increasingly poor odds took its toll on Julie and David alike. David wrote to his father-in-law on one occasion mentioning his "low spirits this past week. In a nutshell, nothing in my life prepared me for the thunder clap of criminal charges pressed against people I know and respect and essentially on grounds growing out of dedication to your case. . . ." And Julie, for a spell, grew daily "quieter and more inward." One time, even she could not contain her unhappiness and said quietly to her father, "Everything is so dreary." But, Nixon writes, "the next day she had bounced back, and within a week she and David decided to hold a press conference in response to the storm of criticism of the transcripts and the calls for my resignation that were now coming from friends and enemies alike."[32]

According to Woodward and Bernstein, it was around May 1974 that, for all practical purposes, Pat Nixon and Julie Nixon Eisenhower traded roles. That is, Julie by that time was more the strong, supportive adult, while Pat retreated into the guise of the helpless child. It does not take a psychologically trained eye to see that Julie's role as Moral Support developed, in good part, because of her mother's withdrawal—both from Richard Nixon and from the objective events. By the spring of 1974, Pat Nixon's reclusive behavior was becoming noticeable. She made occasional appearances at a few requisite events—generally affairs of some sort for women—but even these were kept short and to the ceremonial point. Mostly she stayed in her room, reading, writing, some say drinking too much, and avoiding her family as well as the public. It was a circumstance that seemed to worsen as the final months of Watergate dragged on. One of Betty Ford's staffers claimed that at the end Pat Nixon subsisted on popcorn and television, and got to the point where she would allow few — not even the servants to clean — into her private quarters.[33]

And so in the May days after the release of the transcripts, when the White House was being more heavily bombarded with requests for interviews than ever, it was again Julie who was left to cope. At least one reporter addressed the oddity of the situation directly at a Saturday morning press conference with Julie and David in the East Garden of the White House.

> "Do either of you foresee any point at which the President would resign?"
>
> "Absolutely not, no," David replied.
>
> "He is stronger now than he ever has been in his determination to see this through," Julie added.
>
> The next question came from Robert Pierpoint of CBS: "Mrs. Eisenhower, may I say first of all that I feel I have to apologize for addressing these questions to you, since in our system we do not hold the sins of the fathers against the following generations, and we don't have a monarchy in which you are going to inherit the power, I am not quite sure why you are here to answer these questions."
>
> Julie was visibly agitated. "Mr. Pierpoint, I am going to try to control myself in answering the question, because it really does wound me. . . . I have seen what my father has gone through, and I am so proud of him that I would never be afraid to come out here and talk to any members of the press . . . even though it goes against my grain because I know he does not want me out here because he does not want anyone to construe that I am trying to answer questions for him. . . . I am just trying to pray for enough courage to meet his courage. Really."[34]

By the summer, though, when both Pat and Tricia had become more or less invisible, the press and the nation had acclimated itself to the unusual circumstance. The president and Julie had spoken together almost every day for months, and so by now she had the double advantage of being both the most accessible and the most knowledgeable Nixon insider. Julie also had the invaluable asset of being the most appealing member of the Nixon family. She and David were so earnest and energetic in their support of the president that even diehard Nixon haters found it hard to extend their distaste to his most ardent ally. And as for the rest, well, they almost wanted to be convinced: after that difficult appearance in the East Garden, the White House was flooded with calls praising Julie's performance.

As the time edged near when Nixon would feel impelled to resign, Julie began to play the supportive wife not only in public but in private. There is a description of her behavior toward her father on the presidential yacht *Sequoia* one lovely summer night that tells all:

> Julie hovered around her father. "Do you feel okay, Daddy?" she asked. "Is the sun in your eyes?" "Do you want another drink?"
>
> He seemed to recede deeper into his own thoughts, acknowledging the questions only perfunctorily. . . .
>
> The President walked to the head of the table and pointed to his left. "Julie here," he said. . . .
>
> The stewards served steaks. The President was lost in his own thoughts, staring into his plate.
>
> "Daddy, eat your steak," Julie said.
>
> He took a bite.
>
> "Isn't this a good steak?" she asked . . . .
>
> A steward asked what they wanted for dessert.
>
> Julie turned to her father. "Have some apple pie."
>
> He shook his head no.
>
> "Have some ice cream, Daddy."
>
> No.
>
> She turned to the steward and said that the President would have some ice cream with chocolate sauce.
>
> Acquiescing, the President ate it.
>
> "Wasn't the food good?" she asked.
>
> "It was okay," he said. "Not as good as last time."[35]

Inevitably, the attention Julie gave her father, and her blind faith in the correctness of his every action, put a strain on her marriage to David. As the president turned increasingly to Julie for love and support, her denial of what David deemed likely explanations and outcomes made it difficult for the two to communicate. She considered damaging evidence mere technicalities and would tell David not to bore her with the facts.

By the end of July David was convinced that his father-in-law had been involved in a coverup, and he advised the president to "admit his participation" by acknowledging misjudgment—but not criminal conduct. Julie's response was one of anger. An admission of any kind was still out of the question. The mere suggestion of it was tantamount to disloyalty.

Julie claimed to the end that there was family solidarity on the matter of resignation, but she was wrong. Pat Nixon and Tricia remained more or less out of the discussions; their views were neither offered nor solicited. Ed Cox, Tricia's husband, seconded the president in his decision on August 3 to hang in for the time being, but his more basic orientation was to be as objective, as realistic, as possible. And David had felt for some time that resignation was the only way. He tried his best to make it a viable option to the president.

At the very end, though, that is, during the days just before the resignation, most of the family, in one fashion or another, put pressure on Nixon not to resign. The evidence indicates that Mrs. Nixon's silence persisted, as did David's ambivalence. Tricia and Ed Cox, however, joined Julie now in strongly urging the president to "hang in." This last-ditch crusade was led, of course, by Julie, the only one who had consistently believed that her father should tough it out. According to the diary kept during that time by Tricia, Julie was the first to hear from Nixon that he intended to leave office. Julie subsequently informed Tricia (who had flown to Washington to be with her parents during this time); the First Lady was the last of the family to find out. As the countdown continued, Julie's resistance to the president's resignation intensified. She felt that if he quit, his life would inevitably be ruined. But if he stayed on to fight, his enemies could be made aware of what they had done, "so in future years they'll see they were wrong, and that will make them not do it again."[36] On the night that Nixon stayed up late agonizing over his resignation speech (August 6–7), when he got to his bedroom in the dark hours of the morning he found the following note on his pillow:

Dear Daddy:

I love you. Whatever you do I will support. I am very proud of you.

Please wait a week or even ten days before you make this decision. Go through the fire just a little bit longer. You are so strong! I love you.

Julie

Millions support you.

Nixon writes that "if anything could have changed my mind at this point, this would have done it."[37]

One is reminded of Julie's response to her father's loss in 1960. "Can't we still win?" she asked then, weeks after the fact. Her behavior here reflected the same resistance to reality. She orchestrated the final days so that they might be as painless as possible, and that meant that wherever she could, she put the accent on the positive. One day, just before the end, when the family was scheduled for a sail on the *Sequoia,* Julie arranged to have a group of about fifty female staffers on hand to cheer her father as he left the White House. "We still love you," they shouted. And there was some applause, and they all tried to act as if nothing at all was wrong.

The question arises as to how really useful this exaggerated will to win was. One Nixon aide suggested that it had a disadvantage: "Julie was the fighter. She was so much like her father — a real, tough, little battler — that at times that week I think she lost touch with reality. And that just fed her father's illusions."[38] It is not surprising in any case that when it was all over, when the family stood in a row together to pose for pictures just after it had been announced to them that Nixon was now finally poised to resign, it was Julie who broke ranks, burst into tears, threw her arms around her father, and sobbed, "I love you."

After Nixon left office, especially during the first year, it was still Julie and David Eisenhower who talked the most about the family. David Eisenhower appeared on the "Today" show to say that the former president's spirits were "not great," and there were rumors that Eisenhower rushed along the pardon of Nixon by telling Gerald Ford that he was deeply concerned about his father-in-law. Another story had it that Ford was convinced to pardon Nixon by General Alexander Haig, who had been warned by Nixon's daughters that they feared for him were a pardon not granted. At the same time, though, Julie was assuring the press that her father was O.K.: "Of course, he's not on top of the world. But under the circumstances, I think he's handling it very well. . . . As for his mind wandering, that's just crazy."[39] And by the time a full year had passed, David could remember how very generous Mr. Nixon was with the office of the president. "I got to know Mr. Nixon better than I did my grandfather when he was in the White House. Mr. Nixon had a trait of being almost boyish about the presidency. . . . He was so excited about it that he shared it with me, almost carelessly."[40]

The evidence indicates that one of the few strong, good relationships of Nixon's life has been with his daughter Julie. From his point of view, it probably was, at one point anyway, the best one of them all. By default if you will, because there really was no one else who was on intimate terms with him (with the possible exception of Rebozo), Julie's place alongside Nixon's public and private self was central. David Abrahamsen claims that the famous picture of Nixon and Julie embracing tightly on that next to the last night in the White House reveals how extremely close the two of them were. He asserts that there is a "great deal of emotional similarity in their makeup."[41]

But whatever the psychoanalytic explanations of why the alignments and allegiances in the Nixon family fell as they did, there can be no doubt that in the seventh and perhaps final crisis of Richard Nixon's life, his younger daughter was the mainstay. Julie's support never flagged, and her absolute belief in the goodness and rightness of his position remained constant to the end. She was, in a real way, the mirror image of her father, and there is no saying how events would have played themselves out if she had not been there to reflect, and to echo out loud, his feelings about himself. It is, though, safe to assume that there would have been a difference: her role as Moral Support in the drama of Watergate was a starring one. And by the end of 1974, Julie Eisenhower had placed fourth in *Good Housekeeping's* poll on the "most admired" women.

CHAPTER 7

Alter Egos

Alter egos are those rarest of relatives: people to whom we are so close, on so many levels, that they and we are one. The interaction is in every area. It is constant. I would claim that when a president has an Alter Ego, he or she is the second most powerful political figure in America. And the benefit to a president lucky enough to have one is considerable.

John Kennedy's relationship to his brother Robert has been described as almost mystical. Ordinary conversation, for example, was said to be unnecessary.

> [When the Kennedy brothers talked], there was such a *total* intermeshing of the minds that there didn't have to be a long exposition. Their sentences were very short and covered an immense amount of ground very quickly. . . .[1]

> Between them was built a bond of confidence and affection that is rare even among brothers. They communicated instantly, almost telepathically. Even the President observed that their communication was "rather cryptic."[2]

And Jimmy Carter's wife, Rosalynn, has been referred to as the Mom of the Mom and Pop presidency. In both cases, what comes to mind is two halves of one integral, inseparable unit, second selves, Alter Egos.

Alter Egos are unique in the equality of their relationship to the president. Here there is no senior or junior partner, nor any of the other limitations that characterize the more ordinary presidential interactions. When a president, or candidate, is so fortunate as to have an Alter Ego, he has steady access to someone who is always close by, literally and figuratively, and who is emotionally and intellectually equipped to share whatever it is that occupies the president himself.

One effect of this unusually close tie is that Alter Egos have considerable power. Both Robert Kennedy and Rosalynn Carter have been called "the second most powerful person in America," and with good reason. Since Alter Egos have exceptional access to the president, they have exceptional access to information—and, consequently, exceptional possibilities for influencing and representing the president. There is, of course, a fundamental difference between Bobby Kennedy and Rosalynn Carter: he held an official post as a member of the president's Cabinet, while her duties were supposedly limited to the informally prescribed ones of First Lady. And on the basis of this difference an argument could be made for the proposition that Mr. Kennedy was more powerful and influential than Mrs. Carter. But such things are not to be measured precisely and any attempt to do so would sorely miss the point. Long-time president-watcher Hugh Sidey put it simply when he labeled Rosalynn the president's "most trusted, wise, durable and important adviser in virtually every phase of his stewardship."[3]

What makes an Alter Ego? What produces such a special relationship? First, it appears that an Alter Ego can only be a spouse or a sibling, for the *equality that defines the interaction* would be difficult if not impossible to achieve with a parent or child. Moreover, a similar background and being part of the same generation are important, if not essential. John and Robert Kennedy were male offspring of Joe and Rose, and by the time Jimmy Carter became president, he and Rosalynn had shared three decades at the head of their nuclear family—as well as their young years in the church and schools of Plains, Georgia. A bond such as the one between a president and his Alter Ego is not forged overnight. Alter Ego relationships can take root only in a long history, and then only if that history is richly entwined and, largely, untroubled.

A second prerequisite for an Alter Ego relationship is a fully shared *work life*. Broadly speaking, of course, that work is politics (although the Carters labored together in the peanut business too), and *always it predates presidential politics.* Bobby managed Jack's campaigns for the Senate in 1952 and 1958, and also his try for the vice-presidential nomination in 1956. Rosalynn worked alongside Jimmy when he was governor of Georgia, and had helped him even before that in his run for the Georgia State Senate. By the time John Kennedy and Jimmy Carter were ready to test their fortunes on the presidential level, Bobby and Rosalynn were in place, prepared to play an equal part in the pursuit of the presidency. As it turned out, both campaigns would have been inconceivable without the extraordinary dedication of the candidates' Alter Egos. (Both Bobby Kennedy and Rosalynn Carter illustrate the recent ascendance in presidential politics of the personal organization over the traditional party organization. For more on this, see Chapter 1.)

Finally, the special nature of the Alter Ego's relationship to the president must be explained by a *unique compatibility.* The two are, above all, best friends. It is a fragile, mysterious commodity, such a relationship, an alloy that is next to impossible to define — although surely it contains the following components: love, trust, loyalty, shared values and goals, intellectual compatibility, mutual respect, and personal and emotional congeniality. The result, in any case, is a bond in which the Alter Ego becomes nothing less than the president's second skin.

Unelected and not necessarily appointed to anything, Alter Egos nevertheless assume for themselves all the president's burdens. They are so intimate with the man, and so inextricably wound up with his successes and failures, that they quite literally come to share his office. Recall the original definition: An Alter Ego is that rarest of relatives — someone to whom the president is so close, on so many levels, that the two of them are one.

Robert Kennedy

Robert Kennedy was born in 1925, some eight years after his next oldest brother John, and eleven years after the eldest son, Joe, Jr. So it was natural that during the growing-up years Jack and Bobby did not have much to do with each other. The two eldest were something of a twosome, companions and competitors. Bobby, the seventh child and the slightest of the boys (even, in time, shorter and lighter than his younger brother Ted, seven years his junior), was and remained, in the words of his biographer, Arthur Schlesinger, Jr., "the gentlest and shyest in the roaring family, the least articulate orally and the least coordinated physically, the most conscientious and the most dutiful."[4]

Bobby became the second oldest male child after Joe, Jr., died. But there is no evidence that the shift in status made him a replacement for the dead brother in Jack's life. The two continued to have little in common, and even less to do with each other. Jack had matured (in good part by his experiences in the war) into a cool, somewhat detached young adult; Bobby still seemed so much younger and so untested. Indeed, when John first decided to run for the House of Representatives in 1946, the thought of Robert helping him seemed foreign and even a little silly. To Paul Fay, a Navy friend who had come to pitch in, he said, "It's damn nice of Bobby wanting to help, but I can't see that sober, silent face breathing new vigor into the ranks. . . . One picture of the two brothers together will show that we're all in this for Jack. Then you take Bobby out to the movies or whatever you two want to do."[5] Still, Bobby hung around for part of the campaign; indeed, he was eventually assigned three Italian wards in East Cambridge. (The wards were lost on primary day, but by a smaller margin than expected.) It was a minor task, gamely executed. It did not, however, draw anyone's attention to him, least of all Jack's.

Rose Kennedy wrote, referring to the relationship between John and Robert, that "in maturity the differences [between brothers of different ages] lessen, and soon they discover one another as equals and contemporaries with the same interests. And so it was with Jack and Bobby."[6] Almost everyone who has known the Kennedys long and well traces the beginning of the brothers' extraordinary relationship to the time of Jack's first campaign for the Senate in 1952. As the story goes, Bobby became involved only reluctantly. He was fresh out of the University of Virginia Law School, contentedly ensconced in his first job at the Department of Justice, and quite removed from his brother's fight to unseat Republican Senator Henry Cabot Lodge, Jr. But things were not going well in Massachusetts, and there were those who felt strongly that unless Bobby came up to take over and take charge, Jack would probably lose.

It was Kenneth O'Donnell, an old football friend of Bobby's from Harvard (O'Donnell had joined Jack's campaign at Bobby's request), who sent the most urgent pleas. He begged Bobby to come up and take over. Later, he wrote, "[Jack's 1952] campaign began as an absolute disaster. His father had come up and associated himself with elder statesmen who knew nothing about the politics of that day and age. . . . But he was such a strong personality that nobody could, nobody *dared* fight back. . . . So we were headed for disaster. . . . [After Bobby] got to Massachusetts, he put it together. . . . He was tough enough to handle his father, and he was tough enough to handle the organization."[7]

It was not an easy task. There was a generational conflict in the Kennedy ranks: the father, Joseph Kennedy, businessman, ambassador, and Massachusetts political figure extraordinaire, had his personal cronies and his own way of doing things, while Jack and the younger men around him were struggling to bring a new look to the traditional Irish-American way of politicking. Resentment flourished on both sides. The old-timers railed against the intrusion of the cocky youngsters, while the cocky youngsters were exasperated by the now archaic tactics of their predecessors. A typical incident occurred when a local politician, best known for singing "Danny Boy" from a sound truck, burst into an incredulous string of profanity when he discovered that Robert Kennedy had never heard of him. Kennedy, in turn, offended by the swearing in the presence of women, threw him out. As Rose Kennedy wrote, the men of the older generation were unhappy with Bobby's appearance on the scene. They considered him no more than "a politically innocent boy who had been sent to do a man's job."[8]

Theodore Sorensen, Kennedy's closest aide besides his brother during the presidential years, has observed that in Jack's 1952 run for the Senate Bobby was the logical choice for campaign manager. Who could be trusted more implicitly, say no more emphatically, and speak for the candidate more authoritatively? One wonders, though. In 1960, to be sure, Bobby was an experienced and proven politician, a natural as campaign manager. But in 1952 he was still a young kid with no political experience or credentials that would hold up to any employer other than family. Indeed, there is precious little evidence that John Kennedy was especially anxious to have him. Schlesinger confirms that it was mainly at O'Donnell's urging that Bobby came to Massachusetts to help out in '52; he produces no evidence that Jack voiced a similarly urgent request.

Of course, as far as Jack was concerned, Bobby was still the younger brother with whom he shared the same family but not the same generation or even necessarily the same interests, values, or goals. There simply had never been, up to the summer and fall of '52, much occasion for them to be together. Within the family the father was paramount, and outside it they had gone their separate ways. It apparently did not even occur to Jack that Bobby was tailor-made to fill this particular job.

Bobby was. It was a job that involved both politics and family, for the task was not only to win the election against Lodge, but to do so in a way that would not hurt Joe Kennedy—who still saw himself as overseer—and his old-time politics and pols unnecessarily. In this delicate task, Bobby met his first unqualified success, albeit not by treading gingerly. To the contrary: Schlesinger suggests that the "ruthless Bobby" idea was born in 1952. He was tough, and even brusque and rude when the occasion seemed to demand it; but he also knew better than anyone how to handle his father, and he proved himself a winner. There is a connection between all these. Precisely *because* he was smart and tough and a winner, he was able to handle his father, who in later years took pleasure in boasting, "Bobby is like me."

But even more importantly, his 1952 triumph also marked the first time that Jack took him seriously. In that long-ago Senate race the brothers discovered for the first time that they shared a passion: politics. It was through their joint political work that each learned to take notice of, and gradually appreciate, the brilliant skills of the other. A friend of both puts it succinctly: Bobby "became one hell of a good campaigner. These mutual *political* experiences, along with the natural brotherly love that already existed, brought them together."[9] Sister Eunice puts it less sentimentally: "All this business about Jack and Bobby being blood brothers has been exaggerated. . . . They had different tastes in men, different tastes in women. They didn't really become close until 1952, and it was politics that brought them together."[10]

Of Bobby's effort in 1952 Jack would later say that it was "an exceptional job." He acknowledged at the same time that "it was the first time I ever saw Bobby operate."[11] But after the family victory celebration in Hyannis Port, Jack was a senator and Bobby was unemployed. Typically, it was Joe Kennedy who took the bull by the horns, reminding Bobby that he could hardly expect to sit on his tail end all his life, that he had better go out and get a job. With the ambassador's help, he landed a position as assistant counsel to Joseph McCarthy's Permanant Subcommittee on Investigations of the Senate Government Operations Committee.

For the next several years Robert and John both worked in Washington. But although Jack had also been assigned to the Government Operations Committee, he was not on the Investigations Subcommittee; thus the brothers saw each other mainly in the evenings. The relationship between them was good now—the spirit of '52 had endured—but their work and personal interests (Jack was becoming interested in foreign policy and Bobby in the exposure of corruption) took them in different directions.

It was 1956 before there was another task in common. Once again it involved pushing Jack's career in electoral politics. Adlai Stevenson was the Democratic nominee for president, but with Stevenson's own preferences unclear, the vice-presidential nomination was up for grabs. Names were being bandied about: Estes Kefauver of Tennessee, Hubert Humphrey of Minnesota, and John Kennedy of Massachusetts. Kennedy himself had been vacillating about whether, and how hard, to try for the slot. His father cautioned strongly against it, convinced that if John were picked, it would only be because he was a Catholic, that Stevenson was bound to lose anyway, and that for his son to be associated with such a defeat would be a "devastating blow" to his prestige.

But the Kennedy brothers ignored the advice and, in the last minute, plunged ahead. O'Donnell, who had once again been enlisted by Bobby to help out, remembers that although Bobby was ostensibly in charge, neither Bobby nor he "knew two people in the place," and that they spent most of their time running around the convention floor "like a couple of nuts." The effort was ambivalent, belated, and amateurish. It was bound to fail, and fail it did—but not without teaching the principal characters some valuable lessons. It was the brothers' first appearance at a national convention, and one suspects they felt instinctively that it would not be their last. As Schlesinger notes, Bobby "was learning: the importance of communications at a convention; the importance of an accurate delegate count; the importance of the rules . . . the importance of friendship . . . the unimportance of celebrated senators; the importance of uncelebrated party professionals—all points filed away in that retentive mind"[12]—a mind that had a lifelong habit of hating to lose.

But that was not all Bobby got out of 1956. After the convention Stevenson asked him to join his campaign as a signal to certain groups—Catholics, conservatives, and old Kennedy allies, for example—that ecumenicism would be the hallmark of the Democratic platform. Thus it was that Bobby had a front seat for the full show—from nomination to defeat. He did not waste it. His own recollection was that "nobody asked me anything, nobody wanted me to do anything, nobody consulted me. So I had time to watch everything—I filled complete notebooks with notes on how a presidential campaign should be run."[13]

When John Kennedy ran for the Senate in 1958, Robert had no real role. The election was a shoo-in and he preferred to stay in Washington, where his work on the Subcommittee on Investigations continued apace. These were the years of his involvement with Jimmy Hoffa, the Rackets Committee, and his book *The Enemy Within.* But the brothers stayed close: Bobby had proven himself in '52 and learned lessons in '56, and he was, after all, implicitly trustworthy and loyal. When the time came to select a campaign manager for Jack's wholly unambivalent run for the presidency in 1960, Bobby was indeed the "first and only choice."

The first task was to win the nomination. It was Bobby who set the pace, and it was during this period too that he set the pattern for his relationship to Jack during their remaining years together. Bobby came to the campaign at the very end of 1959, impatient to push on, irritated that more had not yet been accomplished. "A day lost now can't be picked up on the other end," he admonished, quickly developing a reputation for being the Kennedy to contend with. That "gentlest and shyest" of the family took it on himself to be the bad Kennedy, the naysayer, the tough guy with no heart, and he thereby spared his brother the most vitriolic of the anti-Kennedy attacks. Almost everything that people despised about the Kennedys—particularly the impression they gave that ideas counted for little and winning was everything—could be pinned with seemingly delicious accuracy on Bobby. It was almost as if he had made a conscious decision to draw all the hostility on himself so that he might protect his brother along with the cause.

> Anyone, in those simplistic days, who opposed Jack was a bad guy likely to be roughly treated. . . . A lifetime of intelligent and dedicated service to certain principles meant nothing if the person was somehow blocking . . . Jack Kennedy's presidential ambitions.[14]

[Bobby] directed his brother's 1960 Presidential drive with a single-minded intensity. Delegates and rivals were threatened, and Kennedy seemed indifferent to substantive issues of policy. The tactics used to win the West Virginia primary were ugly and foul. At one meeting of campaign workers Kennedy said, "It doesn't matter if I hurt your feelings. It doesn't matter if you hurt mine. The important thing is to get the job done."[15]

The job *was* done. The Democratic nomination was handed to John Kennedy on the first ballot. Bobby's labor and shrewdness and temper had paid off. He went on to direct the second stage of the campaign, against Richard Nixon, without missing a beat. T. H. White on the subject:

Young as he was, he knew as a privileged witness, not only the inner personality of his brother Jack . . . but also the mechanics of American electioneering. . . . To this knowledge he brought, moreover, the force of his singular personality. . . . Almost all the key decisions that dominated the Kennedy campaign in the next 10 weeks were taken in Hyannisport in early August; and in the execution of these decisions . . . one must always recognize Robert Kennedy as the chief propelling force.[16]

As "the chief propelling force" Bobby paid a price. On a purely personal level, he drove himself to exhaustion, like a man possessed. As *Time* noted in the fall of '60, "His nerves are frayed, deep circles rim his eyes, his slight shoulders are stooped with fatigue. . . . Says Jack: 'He's living on nerves.' "[17] On another level, his reputation for ruthlessness grew, and became entrenched. In 1952, stories about Bobby's insensitivity started to spread. They multiplied during the intervening years through his activities as a so-called remorseless prosecutor. The 1960 campaign appeared to close the case. It had been confirmed before the American people: Bobby was clever all right, but he was a son of a bitch. In the words of columnist Stewart Alsop, here was a "sweet and sour brother act, Jack uses his charm and waves the carrot and then Bobby wades in with the big stick."[18]

The campaign of 1960, every aspect of which the brothers conducted as partners, sealed the bond between John and Robert Kennedy. Jack recognized Bobby's unique contribution to his own success and defended his tactics: "Every politician in Massachusetts was mad at Bobby after 1952 but we had the best organization in history."[19] It was not that they agreed on everything, but rather that when one of them decided to pursue a particular course, the other defended it, and often even came to see it as correct. Bobby, for example, was not convinced that the vice-presidency should have been offered to Lyndon Johnson. But when he heard that his brother intended to do just that, he took the news calmly. Anything that Jack wanted to do usually seemed acceptable to Bobby. As Kennedy intimate Dave Powers remarked some time later, "Even if Jack wanted to give the Vice Presidency to Eleanor Roosevelt, Bobby would probably have said all right."[20]

By the time John Kennedy took over the office of the presidency, the relationship with his brother had matured to the point where he was closer to him than to anyone else in the world. Thus he was simply not willing, now, to be in politics without his brother alongside. It was remarkable how they complemented each other.

> Jack Kennedy was a much more eighteenth-century character; he was cool, he was so self-disciplined; he certainly wasn't a cold man ... but he was a man who mistrusted passion. Bob trusted passion more. ... Jack was always standing off looking at himself; Bob never used to do that. ...
>
> Bob much more than Jack had this drive to the direct approach. Jack was much more resigned to the restraints of institutions, of what human life was all about; I'm not sure that Bob ever accepted that there were limitations. ...[21]

And it was remarkable how each came to value the other's special skills and traits. Bobby, it was said, was "more appreciative of his brother's greatness than anyone else," and was observed to have a "rather protective attitude. ... One had the feeling that he was looking after his older brother. ... He seemed to look at every aspect of a given situation, asking himself, 'Now, how can this affect Jack? How can it hurt Jack?' "[22] The president, for his part, never hesitated when asked about Bobby, and why he should be appointed attorney general: "Well, an Attorney General doesn't have to be a lawyer, he doesn't have to ever be in court. An Attorney General is supposed to run a department of some 30,000 people, and it needs a hell of a manager, and my brother is the best manager I've ever had and the best one that I know of. ..."[23] Some time later, after Robert had already taken over as head of the Department of Justice, the president's good friend Ben Bradlee asked him why he thought Bobby was great. The president answered:

> First, his high moral standards, strict personal ethics. He's a puritan, absolutely incorruptible. Then he has this terrific executive energy. We've got more guys around here with ideas. The problem is how to get things done. Bobby is the best organizer I've ever seen. Even in touch football, four or five guys on a team, it was always Bobby's team that won, because he had it organized the best, the best plays. He's got compassion, a real sense of compassion . . . . His loyalty comes next. It wasn't the easiest thing for him to go to [Joe] McCarthy's funeral. . . .[24]

It was Joseph Kennedy who kept insisting that Bobby should be in the Cabinet, and by that he meant attorney general. He asserted that Jack was going to have a lot of problems and would need all the help and support he could get, that Bobby's work on organized crime and labor corruption was superb training for the post, and that a Cabinet officer's main job was as administrator and organizer—both Bobby's specialties. Jack was listening.

But to name Bobby attorney general would not be without political cost, and Kennedy was worried about public reaction. Moreover, Bobby himself was ambivalent about taking the post, although he had no other alternative in mind. Working on the White House staff was ruled out because that would almost certainly mean taking direct orders from his older brother. (Bobby shrewdly perceived that part of the explanation for why he and Jack got on so well was that they had always had their own areas: "He never involved himself in what I was doing . . . and I was not directly associated with what he was doing. . . ."[25]) Bobby would refuse an appointment to the vacant Massachusetts Senate seat, and he was not particularly attracted to the idea of becoming attorney general. The only option that had any appeal was the idea of going back to Massachusetts and running for governor in 1962.

All the reservations notwithstanding, when the president-elect's other choices for attorney general did not for one reason or another work out, he became convinced that Robert Kennedy should take the job. Bobby's misgivings were set aside one morning over bacon and eggs with Jack, who by now had become vehement on the subject. He intoned that if he could ask men like Adlai Stevenson, Robert McNamara, and Dean Rusk to make all kinds of sacrifices to be in his Cabinet, he should be able to expect his own brother to give him "the same kind of contribution." He urged Bobby, "I need you in this government."

Later on, Bobby explained his decision to accept this way: "I began to realize what a lonely job the Presidency is, and I realized then what an advantage it would be to him to have someone [in the government] he could talk to."[26] But the press was less than pleased at the outcome of the brothers' negotiations. Editorial comments such as this one from the *New York Times* were not unusual: "It is simply not good enough to name a bright young political manager, no matter how bright or how young or how personally loyal, to a major post in government that by right (if not by precedent) ought to be kept completely out of the political arena."[27]

As a result of the Bay of Pigs fiasco some four months into the Kennedy presidency, the brothers' relationship became even more interdependent. The debacle convinced the president that he could not necessarily trust the competence or loyalty of his expert advisers, and Robert saw for himself how even a watchful president could be ill served. At an early point in the proceedings, when the bad news started to filter in from the Cuban beaches, the president observed grimly, "I should have had Bobby in on this from the start."[28]

Indeed, Bobby had not been involved with the decision to have 1,200 anti-Castro rebels invade Cuba; the plan was hatched by the CIA and approved by the Joint Chiefs of Staff. He found out about it only some four or five days prior to its execution, when, at the president's instructions, he was personally informed by a CIA official. Yet as soon as John Kennedy realized there would be trouble, he rang Bobby and asked him to rush to the White House.

The disaster that the operation became (the United States eventually rescued some thirty men) had a devastating effect on John Kennedy. His feelings about the presidency were never again quite the same. Early on, Kennedy learned the hard way that if the U.S. government made a mistake, he would be held accountable, and that for solid advice he had to turn not only to the "experts" but also to those whose *main qualification was personal loyalty*. And it was during and just after the Bay of Pigs that Jack Kennedy acquired the habit of coming to depend on Bobby

even in those areas in which he had absolutely no expertise—
such as foreign relations. He assigned his brother, along with
General Maxwell Taylor, CIA chief Allen Dulles, and Admiral
Arleigh Burke, to a board of inquiry whose mandate was to discover why the Cuban operation had failed. Schlesinger notes that
the transcript of the inquiry showed that the attorney general
took the lead in examining the witnesses and probing them with
"unsparing questions."[29] It was Robert's debut in his role as pro-
tector of his brother's presidency.

Several observers have commented on how the older brother/
younger brother relationship appeared to be turned around in the
case of John and Robert Kennedy. To the extent that this is true,
much of the impetus came from the Bay of Pigs trauma. During
the campaign Bobby would play the mean guy to deflect ill will;
during this early Cuban crisis he added the role of the nurturing
sibling to that of business adviser.

Perhaps the role reversal took place because Bobby saw the
effect the Bay of Pigs was having on his brother. A family friend
has said of Jack's reaction: "He was a happy man who enjoyed
himself in everything he did, but if he ever had any illusions . . .
that the presidency could be something more diverting than
breaking your back, the Bay of Pigs dispelled them. . . . He was
totally different after Cuba. . . ."[30]

Bobby himself noted in a memorandum composed six weeks
after the event, "[The Bay of Pigs] even had a great physical effect on Jack. I noticed him particularly a week from the following
Saturday when we had a talk for a half hour before [a] meeting
began and even during the meeting he kept shaking his head,
rubbing his hands over his eyes." Later on, Bobby added, "We'd
been through a lot of things together, and he was more upset this
time than he was any other."[31] Not too surprisingly, then,
Bobby's reaction to the fiasco was "emotional and belligerent,"
and when he saw that the president was badly served by almost
everyone around him, he was outraged "and vowed never again to
let it happen."[32]

It is not clear how much John Kennedy imagined he personally would consult with his brother when he first decided to appoint him attorney general. Probably he thought Bobby would be
fully occupied running the Justice Department, and useful only
for occasional advice and support. The Bay of Pigs changed that.
Thereafter the president wanted Bobby at every crucial meeting.

He was "in on so many urgent problems in the State and Defense departments and in the CIA that he had to delegate many of his Attorney General duties to his deputies in the Justice Department."[33] After April 1961 there was not a single critical international decision that was made without Bobby present to lend advice and consent.

> After the Bay of Pigs, Robert became his brother's eyes and ears around the national security establishment. "If you wanted to get a dissenting idea into the White House," Michael Forrestal told David Halberstam, ". . . the best channel—almost the only channel—was Bobby Kennedy." Kennedy ambassadors, frustrated by State Department orthodoxies, made the Attorney General's office a port of call on home leave. "Where I had need to bring pressure on the State Department," said John Kenneth Galbraith (India), ". . . I found a very good ally in Bob." He was . . . "the most attentive listener in town." The national security community soon recognized him as a major countervailing force on international decisions. "He seemed to have a damn good intelligence apparatus . . . that kept him very well informed of what was brewing." "Kennedy, a student of guerrilla warfare," observed Patrick Anderson, "was applying its techniques to intergovernmental relations."[34]

Bobby became his brother's "eyes and ears" not only at home but also abroad. For example, he was dispatched on a variety of Third World missions such as a 1961 trip to Africa, an early 1962 voyage to Asia, and a late 1962 journey to Latin America. All of this activity in an arena which was new to him did not particularly endear him to old-line professionals. One officer of the United States Information Agency felt that Bobby was seen "as a headstrong, unreliable upstart in the field of foreign affairs. . . . He was regarded as quite a menace by most of the people in the State Department. . . ."[35] But if any of this badmouthing affected the president, there is no evidence of it. As his term wore on, he came to depend on Bobby more in this area, not less.

There was, of course, a Department of Justice to be run too. Here Robert was more separate from his brother, who left it to him to run things at Justice pretty much his own way. The general consensus on Bobby's performance as attorney general is that despite his many responsibilities to the president, he did well. He was tough with his staff, but not inconsiderate. He strove for excellence, but not at the expense of those under him. Of course, as the president's brother, Robert Kennedy had a unique opportunity to push his Cabinet post to its limits. Victor Navasky, in his book *Kennedy Justice,* makes it clear that Bobby's bloodline to the White House was a not insignificant factor in how he discharged the duties of his office. Navasky also points out that the bloodline flowed both ways. Not only was it an advantage to Bobby to be the president's kin, it was an advantage to Jack to have a brother at Justice, which "served as a 32,000-man addition to the White House staff for random Presidential business."[36] There was, in other words, a kind of symbiotic interaction between the White House and Justice during this time, an interaction that derived its strength from the tie between the brothers.

> It would be silly to deny that Robert Kennedy had more clout than the average Attorney General, partly because he also had a brother in the White House. But it would be misleading not to emphasize that Robert Kennedy's ability to make things happen was more than the arithmetic sum of JFK power plus RFK power, an equation that doesn't account for the Kennedy network, the Kennedy style, the Kennedy values. . . . Robert and John alike drew their sense of identity from membership in the Kennedy family. . . . They were more like an extended family, an informal organization, a network. . . . It was one of Robert Kennedy's major achievements as an administrator that he found ways of converting selected bureaucrats into on-the-job Kennedys.[37]

Robert Kennedy saw his own performance at Justice as contributing to the success of his brother's administration. Moreover, those who dealt with Kennedy as attorney general, fueled by the similarity in the brothers' appearance, speech, and confident manner, and by the knowledge of the exceptional rapport between them, felt almost as if they were talking to the president. Thus, through the men at the top, the missions of Justice and the White House were merged.

It is impossible to quantify contributions, and Bobby did so much for Jack that comparisons are ridiculous. But if one had to choose, it could fairly be claimed that the Cuban missile crisis is the occasion on which Robert Kennedy best served his brother. Not a single member of the Executive Committee of the National Security Council (ExCom)—that group of some seventeen men whom the president appointed to handle the threat of Russian surface-to-surface missiles 90 miles off shore—has disagreed with

the assertion that the presence of the attorney general among
them deeply affected the outcome of their discussions.

Once again, to look at the record of these two weeks is to have
the feeling that Robert Kennedy's main mission in life was to
save his brother from committing a disastrous mistake. Not only
was he a dove from the start—at one point he scribbled an unhappy note to Sorensen, "I now know how Tojo felt when he was
planning Pearl Harbor"—but he served also in a variety of roles
during these thirteen days of crisis that made him no less than
John Kennedy's indispensable partner in the eyeball-to-eyeball
ploy against Khrushchev. He was his brother's conscience and
stand-in during the meetings of ExCom, going for days without
sleep to be available as necessary. But he also conducted a series
of important secret negotiations with Anatoly Dobrynin, the Soviet Ambassador to Washington, in which, because of the fraternal connection, he was perceived to be speaking for the president
in every detail. And he played a substantive role in drafting the
final all-important reply to the Khrushchev letters, a reply that,
by deliberately taking a moderate tone, ignored the Russian
leader's more vituperative messages.

To read the story of the Cuban missile crisis is to be convinced as never before that the president with a loyal relative
close by is twice blessed. There were moments indeed when it
seemed as if the two brothers were quite alone, with trusted allies
to be sure, but finally solitary together against the Russian bear.
Both Kennedys themselves seem to have had this sensation at
moments; Bobby certainly did, as is evident from this reconstruc-
tion of a moment on the eighth day:

> I think these few minutes were the time of gravest concern for the
> President. Was the world on the brink of a holocaust? Was it our
> error? A mistake? Was there something further that should have
> been done? Or not done? His hand went up to his face and covered
> his mouth. He opened and closed his fist. His face seemed drawn,
> his eyes pained, almost gray. We stared at each other across the ta-
> ble. For a few fleeting seconds, it was almost as if no one else was
> there and he was no longer the president.
>
> Inexplicably, I thought of when he was ill and almost died;
> when he lost his child; when we learned that our oldest brother had
> been killed; of personal times of strain and hurt. The voices droned
> on, but I didn't seem to hear anything until I heard the President
> say: "Isn't there some way we can avoid having our first exchange
> with a Russian submarine—almost anything but that?"[38]

In the early ExCom meetings Robert Kennedy said little, preferring to listen, to press others to offer their thoughts, to push them to produce the maximum possible number of alternatives. But as the days wore on, he became more active. He played the mediator, acting repeatedly to keep members of the group from exploding at each other; and he contributed substantively by opposing the use of military action to take out the missiles, by supporting the quarantine, and by preparing the conciliatory response to Khrushchev's communications. Eventually, it was his argument for moderation that became the focal point of the discussions.

McGeorge Bundy's memory is of Bobby sometimes deliberately sitting in one of the smaller chairs. But his memory too is of the tactic making absolutely no difference, "because, in a generic way, wherever he sat was one of the most important places in the room, and everybody knew that. . . . RFK was really the senior person whenever he was there . . . because he was the president's brother . . . he *was* the Attorney General, and he *was* the person closest to the president in human terms."[39] Bobby's tie to his brother permeated the response of all who dealt with him. Psychologically, his every sentence carried special weight because of who he was. George Ball, one of the members of ExCom, remembers that at one point Bobby said, "My brother's got to be able to live with himself if we [go with the air strike]. I don't think America could, and I don't think my brother could." Ball goes on to say, "That had, of course, a major effect. It was one thing for me to say; it was something else for the President's brother to say."[40]

The president, who was not in the habit of displaying any open praise or affection for his brother, was enough moved by his contribution on the occasion of the Cuban missile crisis to make an exception. To Dave Powers, perhaps his closest friend outside the family, he spoke on the black Sunday of October 27, 1962, of Bobby's determined stand against those who supported an air attack, of how Bobby had brought several members of ExCom around to supporting the blockade, of his repeated meetings with Dobrynin, and of how he had drafted that ingenious reply to Khrushchev. As Powers recalls it, the president then "paused thoughtfully for a moment, and said, 'Thank God for Bobby.' "[41]

Robert Kennedy took on so much during his brother's presidency, his own thirty-fifth to thirty-eighth years, that the unrelenting pressure was etching lines in his face, and his hair became flecked with gray. In an article titled "What Drives Bobby Kennedy?" Anthony Lewis suggested the range of his contribution.

> In the last fifteen months, in addition to presiding over the regular business of the Justice Department, Robert Kennedy has debated with Japanese Communists, helped to settle the Dutch-Indonesian dispute over West New Guinea, played a vital role in his brother's Presidency over steel prices, the University of Mississippi and Soviet missiles in Cuba, made a flying trip to Brazil to discuss her economic crisis with President João Goulart, took a critical part behind the scenes in the Cuban prisoner ransom, and—most recently—directed the Administration's planning on youth unemployment and delinquency, culminating in the proposal for a domestic peace corps.[42]

All this meant that Bobby was being assessed not only as attorney general but also in his unofficial capacity as the president's closest adviser. Here too, overall, his marks were good. Those who worked with him on the inside came to value Bobby's contribution as a liberal. "Gradually the New Frontiersmen came to see him as their particular champion, knowing that he was often free to say and do things which the President, in the nature of things, could not say or do. . . . He was also increasingly the voice of New Frontier idealism to young people at home and abroad. . . ."[43] The public at large was impressed by his quick learning and managerial skills. In a national television interview, none other than Richard Nixon revealed that even he was convinced of Bobby's excellence: "In looking at Robert Kennedy, you have here a man who, except for the lack of experience, which he is now gaining, has many of the qualifications that would make him a very effective leader in the field of foreign policy. He's tough minded, he's quick, he's intelligent. He is one who has a tremendous will to win."[44]

The quality of Bobby's relationship to Jack made a deep, lasting impression on all who witnessed it. Not that the brothers never disagreed. To the contrary. The president was quick to find flaws in Bobby's proposals, and Bobby came to feel that the president would do well to pay more attention to the Cabinet. In a 1963 memo to the president he observed pointedly, "I think you could get a good deal more out of what is available in Government than you are at the present time."[45] Moreover, not every aspect of policy came under the rubric of the fraternal partnership, and the president also made certain to "draw a line between trusting Bobby's judgment and depending on him to handle a problem, and the further step of allowing Bobby, or anybody else, to make a Presidential decision."[46]

But recollections such as these, from witnesses to the relationship, tell the important story:

> John Kennedy used Robert in part as Franklin Roosevelt used Eleanor—as a lightning rod, as a scout on far frontiers, as a more militant and somewhat discountable alter ego, expressing the President's own idealistic side while leaving the President room to maneuver and to mediate. At the same time, the Attorney General was John Kennedy's Harry Hopkins, Lord Root of the Matter, the man on whom the President relied for penetrating questions, for follow-up, for the protection of the presidential interests and objectives.[47]

> Robert Kennedy recognized that his greatest contribution to the President would be to speak candidly, to contradict him if he felt he was wrong and to move him to the right course if he felt he was not on that course. The President never hesitated to turn down Bobby's advice, but many, many times he took it when, initially, he, the President, was in favor of an opposite course. They had an *extraordinarily* close relationship: affection, respect, admiration.[48]

It is simply not possible to think about the last four years of John Kennedy's life without thinking at the same time of his brother Robert. When the president was assassinated, Bobby lost not only a beloved brother, but the man around whom he had built his life. The effect was devastating. One friend had the feeling that Robert Kennedy was experiencing something like physical pain, "almost as if he were on the rack or that he had a toothache or that he had a heart attack." Pierre Salinger recalls that after the death of the president, Bobby "was the most shattered man I had ever seen in my life."[49]

We know that he recovered, to the extent anyway that one ever recovers from a trauma of this sort, and that he went on to take up where his brother had left off. It was in the natural order of things in the Kennedy universe that he should, of course. As a senator, Jack had once observed that he went into politics when Joe, Jr., died, and that "if anything happened to me tomorrow, my brother Bobby would run for my seat." But it would never be the same for him. Among other things, his only surviving brother was already ensconced in a Senate seat and could not play Bobby to Bobby. And so the great gap, despite legions of old and new friends, remained. Indeed, as the following exchange—which took place on the last evening of the Cuban missile crisis—suggests, the bond between John and Robert was no less than unique. The immediate threat had been avoided when the president said to Bobby, making reference to Abraham Lincoln, "This is the night I should go to the theater." To which his brother replied, "If you go, I want to go with you."[50]

Rosalynn Carter

The Carters and the Smiths had been neighbors in Plains, Georgia, for generations. To be sure, the Carters had more money than the Smiths. The head of the Smith household, Wilburn Edgar, a garage mechanic, had been struck down by leukemia when Rosalynn, the eldest, was only thirteen years old, and to the extent that there were class differences in Plains, the Carters ranked higher. But what is more important to understand about Jimmy and Rosalynn Carter is how much they had in common before they ever even met. Both spent all their early life in the same small Georgia town at the same moment in time. In fact, the two families knew each other. Miss Lillian, Jimmy's mother, a registered nurse, tended to Mr. Smith as he lay dying, and Rosalynn first met Jimmy through her friendship with Ruth Carter, Jimmy's younger sister. Rosalynn Carter's long-time shyness and reticence—a trait that has ebbed only in the last decade and a half or so—is often explained by the fact that she came from more modest circumstances than her husband. But it is also true that this difference was the exception rather than the rule—that they shared a background so similar that it was almost bound to inculcate similar values in them as adults.

When Rosalynn's father died, she became, at fourteen, a mother surrogate to her one younger sister and two younger brothers. Mrs. Smith was forced to support the family by working as a postal clerk and seamstress, and so Rosalynn was left to do many of the chores at home as well as augment the family income by working part time as a shampooer in the local beauty parlor. At the same time she managed to graduate Plains High School as both valedictorian and May Queen. It was her father's deathbed wish that all his children should work to go to college, and so, promptly after finishing high school, she enrolled in Georgia Southwestern College in nearby Americus. Rosalynn thought she might be a teacher, or perhaps an interior decorator.

At about this same time Jimmy Carter, who had been away from Plains for the past three years, was home on summer leave from Annapolis. One day, while "cruising around in a rumble-seated Ford with a friend," he spotted his sister Ruth sitting in the churchyard with another girl. A double date ensued and, according to Jimmy, the rest followed quickly.

> I returned home later that night and told my mother that Rosalynn had gone to the movies with me. Mother asked if I liked her, and I was already sure of my answer when I replied, "She's the girl I want to marry." Rosalynn has never had any competition for my love.
>
> The next Christmas we saw each other every night. I asked Rosalynn if she would marry me, but she said NO. Later, at Annapolis on Washington's birthday holiday, she finally accepted my proposal. We set a date for our July wedding.[51]

The response to the marriage was mixed: "Her mother was pleased. His mother was dubious."[52]

The young couple moved to Norfolk, Virginia, where Jimmy was assigned his first ship. They were separated much of the time—apart all during the week and together only part of two weekends out of three. Apparently the separations caused no problems. Rosalynn remembers their time in the Navy as among the happiest periods of her life, and Jimmy wrote that the being apart was "interspersed with ecstatic reunions and the melding of ourselves over the years into a closer relationship of love, understanding, and mutual respect."[53] In short order two sons were born. The blessing of children to be enjoyed on a long-term assignment to the Hawaiian Islands made the young Carters' life complete.

Or so it appeared. But Jimmy's decision to return to Plains after his father died to make a success of the family business suggests that all along, on some level, he planned to go home again. There is no evidence that Jimmy was coerced by anyone into returning to Georgia (there is no record of Lillian Carter's feeling on the subject), but there is evidence that Rosalynn was. Jimmy's strong impulse to go back, and her equally strong wish to continue their life in the Navy, resulted in their first marital strife.

Although Jimmy prevailed, there is no doubt that it was at a cost. Understandably, Rosalynn was upset.

> She had feared the loss of the autonomy she had found and nurtured in her life as an officer's wife. . . . She was in many ways . . . her own person. Jimmy was gone so much, she was forced into the role of decision-maker for the family. She paid the bills, she managed all the finances, she took care of the car, she handled the children's medical appointments and arrangements for kindergarten—and she made the major choices for the use of her time.
>
> In Plains, she knew it would be different. There, she would be subject to the restraints and interferences she thought she had escaped once and for all.[54]

Jimmy and Rosalynn never let on as much, but it seems clear from family tales told by others that one of the main reasons Rosalynn Carter was so reluctant to return to Plains was the strong presence there of her mother-in-law, Miss Lillian. For most of her son's marriage Lillian Carter had merely tolerated his wife. A cousin of Jimmy's remembers that "Rosalynn could never feel completely at home with her mother-in-law. She always felt somehow on probation, as if she were being judged worthy or unworthy of the privilege of being a member of Miz Lillian's family."[55]

Rosalynn's response was understandable. Although strong-willed, she was retiring. Miss Lillian, to the contrary, was one of the more formidable women of Plains and tended to be the dominating force in almost any company. Thus when Rosalynn returned to Plains, she was bound and determined to hold on to the independence she had won during her years away. It became clear almost immediately that although she labored to be the perfect housewife, that would not be enough to keep her satisfied and independent. In the Carters' second year back home, Rosalynn started stopping by at the office one day each week to help with the books and the preparation of invoices. As time went on, she began to spend half of each work day there; sometime after that she began working at the warehouse full time. Rosalynn tackled her job with typical thoroughness. Her newly acquired skills as a bookkeeper and her hard work soon made her an integral part of the Carter family's financial fortunes.

It was a new phase in the marriage. While Jimmy was in the Navy, Rosalynn's independence had been forged apart from her husband; now she experienced it in partnership with him. They

had a common goal—making a success of the business—and
they gradually learned to talk about reaching it in a way that en-
riched their marriage as a whole.

> They discovered in themselves a capacity for reasoned dialogue and
> debate. Their previous pattern had been simply to argue—with no
> really beneficial conclusion. They quickly found that as real part-
> ners they were able to disagree, discuss without arguing and reach
> mutually acceptable decisions. The business was making it possible
> for them to deal with each other more candidly, more openly than at
> any time since their marriage, and in the process, each of them was
> finding in the other a variety of admirable traits that had escaped
> notice before.[56]

It was the difficulty of resurrecting the family peanut business that made it necessary for husband and wife to work together. Times were hard at the beginning. In their first growing
season (1954) they endured one of the worst droughts in the history of Georgia; they were refused loans; their employees totaled
one (Carter himself); and after twelve months of labor the business showed a profit of exactly $184.

In time, of course, the Carters' peanut farm and warehouse
would support the entire family. This financial success, and the
fact that Jimmy soon put other members of the clan on the payroll
(Billy's help was invaluable), enabled him to enter politics full
time less than a decade after his return to Plains. He writes that
"*we* decided to enter politics" (italics mine), adding that Rosalynn helped him "from every standpoint" and that the shared decision was a typical one: "We have been full partners in every
major decision since we first married."[57]

By the time Jimmy Carter first ran for governor in 1966, Rosalynn was politicking by his side. She was not a natural speaker,
and shy by habit. But once the campaign was in full swing, she
was making small talk with voters, delivering short speeches, and
spending sixteen to eighteen hours a day spreading the gospel
according to Jimmy. Between the two of them, Carter once estimated, they came into personal contact with at least 300,000
Georgia voters.

But they lost the race in 1966, and Jimmy Carter sank into a
depression. He was deep in debt, down 22 pounds, and feeling
sorry that he had neglected, for much too long, so much that was
dear to him. Rosalynn was more upbeat. She reminded her husband of all the people they had met, of the many who had actually

worked for him and voted for him, and she reminded him of the long lists of names she had compiled during the campaign—lists that would be valuable in their political future. As Jimmy remembers it, it was not long before he called to mind an aphorism often quoted by his professed hero, Hyman Rickover: "You show me a good loser and I'll show you a loser." Within a month he was running for governor again—although the election was still almost four years away.

The interim years were good ones for Jimmy and Rosalynn Carter. To their delight, especially Jimmy's, Amy was born. Moreover, their three sons were healthy, they had plenty of money, and their marriage—cemented anew by the shared experience of the 1966 campaign—was stronger than ever. Rosalynn enthusiastically supported her husband's second candidacy, "although she dreaded the Kennedy-style campaigning—with everybody in the family out on the hustings—that he insisted on. She dreaded spending all that time away from home again, meeting people she didn't know, making speeches that frightened her and kept her awake all through the preceding night, but if Jimmy wanted to run for governor, he would have her complete endorsement and cooperation."[58] It turned out to be an exhausting effort for both. They shook some 600,000 hands, and during the last months of the campaign each of them would meet at least three factory shifts each day. Jimmy Carter writes:

> We shook hands with entire crowds who came to high school football games, livestock and tobacco sale barns, rodeos, college athletic events, and horse shows. Between these we would visit every barber shop, beauty parlor, restaurant, store, and service station in a town, and then move on to the next one. We stood for hours in front of swinging doors at major shopping centers, meeting every customer who entered the most heavily patronized business places. When it was too early in the morning for people to be at work, we met them at downtown bus terminals, or went to assembly points for municipal policemen, firemen, maintenance crews, or garbage collectors.[59]

Quite clearly, the governorship of Georgia was won together.

There is a Carter family yarn about a last showdown of sorts between Rosalynn and Miss Lillian; it is said to have taken place just after the Carters moved into the governor's mansion. As the story goes, Miss Lillian simply went along too, announcing her intention to act as Georgia's First Lady because Rosalynn, she

thought, was not sophisticated enough to handle the job. Rosalynn's response was to tell her mother-in-law that she fully intended to run her own household, but that Miss Lillian should of
course feel free to visit whenever she wanted. The spat resolved
any lingering doubts about who was the central figure in Jimmy's
adult life. And as Georgia's undisputed First Lady, Rosalynn was
a competent hostess, interested in her own special projects such
as mental health and the education of retarded children, and,
more than ever, a close working companion to her husband.

Given their history—the time in the Navy when Rosalynn
started to manage their domestic affairs, the early years back in
Plains when husband and wife worked together as partners in
business, the venture into state politics in which Jimmy's electoral victories were sought by both with equal determination—it
was only natural that when Jimmy Carter first began to contem-
plate a run for the presidency in 1976, he contemplated it in con-
junction with his wife. Before Jimmy talked to anyone else about
his White House dream, he talked about it with Rosalynn. It was
almost as if only with her, this partner now of some twenty-six
years, could he allow himself such a grand fantasy. As he has
said:

> It was hard for us to talk about the prospect at first. It was all very
> tentative and somewhat embarrassing. We never used the word
> "President" for the first three or four months, because it was kind of
> presumptuous. . . . We tried to assess the inventory, everything that
> existed in the way of an asset or a problem. . . .We enumerated all
> those problems and tried to figure how we could either minimize
> the problem or make an asset out of it.[60]

But once the Carters had committed themselves, they made yet
another all-out joint effort. Rosalynn wanted to win the nomination and the election every bit as much as Jimmy. Her campaign
efforts on his behalf were Herculean.

By now Rosalynn Carter, having survived two races for governor of Georgia, was something of a skilled campaigner. Above
all, she was no longer terrified at the thought of making a speech.
She was ready, willing, and able, for example, to venture into the
Florida panhandle one year before the presidential primary there
was even scheduled to take place, and follow Jimmy's instructions: make friends in George Wallace territory, and show them
there is an alternative. Rosalynn and friend Edna Langford

. . . set out on a lonely trek through the small towns of the Florida
panhandle, the most conservative, the most redneck, the most Ala-
bama-like Wallace country in Florida. Quincy. Marianna, Bonifay.
Chipley. They would hit the town and walk in unannounced to the
local newspaper office and the local radio station and try to get Mrs.
Carter interviewed and get her picture taken. . . . And often they
would, and then it would lots of times wind up on the front page.
[Langford recalls that] "We'd always have Rosalynn holding a
Jimmy Carter bumper sticker so people would get to know his name
even if they didn't read the story. And at the radio stations, if the boy
didn't know what to ask, sometimes we'd write down the questions
for him."[61]

And so it was that during most of 1975 and 1976 Rosalynn
Carter stumped the length and breadth of this country for her
husband—but only very rarely with him. According to a scale
drawn up by Hamilton Jordan, Carter's chief campaign strategist,
one day of campaigning by Mrs. Carter was worth 4 points—in
contrast to Jimmy's 7, Walter Mondale's 5, and Joan Mondale's 3.
The Carters correctly estimated that they could cover more
ground more efficiently if they were not in the same place at the
same time.

In an Iowa auditorium, Rosalynn Carter went into the bal-
cony handing out oversized Carter buttons to people in the front
rows, an easy target for television cameras. (Rosalynn was not the
only Carter in Iowa. Witcover writes that Carter's sons and sister
Ruth all also "worked Iowa like some foreign mission whose na-
tives had not found salvation, but only needed to hear the
word."[62]) Before the primary she traversed the state of Florida for
weeks. She dined alone with Jimmy for a quiet three hours just
before his first debate with President Gerald Ford and advised
him on campaign strategy—recommending, for example, that he
schedule extra trips to Rhode Island and South Dakota. She
counseled him, too, on how to handle some of the trickier questions, and suggested on one occasion that on the issue of home
mortgages and tax reform he avoid confusing his audiences by
telling them only, "I'm not going to raise your taxes."[63] She even
kept her cool when almost everyone else around Carter lost it
over the controversial *Playboy* interview in which Jimmy admitted to having "committed adultery in my heart many times". Rosalynn defended him in public in response to reporters' questions, appeared by his side in an attempt to boost his relatively

low standing among women voters, and smiled gamely when five reporters, to the tune of "Heart of My Heart," serenaded the couple (in honor of Jimmy's fifty-second birthday) with a ditty that went something like this:

Lust in my heart, how I love adultery;
Lust in my heart, that's my theology.
When I was young, at the Plains First Baptist Church,
I would preach and sermonize—
But oh how I would fantasize. . . .[1]

No less a person than her own husband was impressed with how well Rosalynn Carter had learned to cope with her insecurities. Gone were the days when he needed to give her little boosts and lectures and hints and tips on how not to freeze in public. When Jimmy saw with his own eyes how far she had come, he was moved. The first time he heard Rosalynn stumping for him during the presidential campaign was when they shared the same platform in Trenton, New Jersey. To his surprise, he was genuinely touched by her account of how they had "scrimped and saved to make the peanut business a success," and tears came to his eyes when she said, "There has never been any hint of scandal in Jimmy's business life and Jimmy has never had any hint of scandal in his personal life." When she finished, he rushed to her side, kissed her, and shouted to the audience, "How many of you would like to have this woman as First Lady?" When the crowd clapped its approval, Jimmy answered them back, "I agree with you!"[65]

Mrs. Carter was every bit a match for her tireless husband. On her campaign forays she averaged thirteen-hour days, with a typical three-day swing going something like this: visits to eight cities, seven news conferences, speeches before fourteen audiences, a dozen newspaper and magazine interviews, and at least ten television appearances. In addition, there were meetings with Democratic and labor leaders and the usual ceremonial appearances. It was true that she had her own campaign themes—especially, increased financial aid for the elderly and the mentally afflicted—but much more than most wives she echoed the dominant notes of her husband's campaign: Jimmy Carter's ability to restore trust in government and his skills as a fiscal conservative. Small wonder that the Carter camp was sufficiently convinced of Mrs. Carter's effectiveness to charter, from its limited funds, two six-seater jets to keep her show on the road practically all the time.[66]

It took America some six months or so to figure out that Rosalynn Carter would be an unusual First Lady. It was in May of Carter's first year in office that we received a signal from Washington that this First Lady would not be relegated to mere hostessing. The president took the unprecedented step of sending his wife on a twelve-day tour of the Caribbean and Latin America. The intention was to make the trip more than just a goodwill tour, and in that spirit the White House indicated that Mrs. Carter would conduct "substantive" talks on issues of bilateral, regional, and global importance. No claim was made to the effect that Mrs. Carter would herself be a negotiator, but she was to impress on all the countries she visited "the sincerity of the Carter administration's commitment to human rights and to social and economic progress, complementing the message with a new awareness that what happens in the world is not determined by Washington alone."[67]

To prepare for the trip, Rosalynn received thirteen two-hour briefings in the preceding month. But she made no bones about the fact that her most important preparation lay in her unique relationship to the president. When asked by an American television reporter during the trip what it was exactly that made her think that she was fit to discuss serious matters with heads of state, she replied tersely, "I think I am the person closest to the President of the United States, and if I can help him understand the countries of the world, then that's what I intend to do."[68]

More than just a few wondered if such a venture would produce results. After all, some stops promised to be less than wholly benign — Jamaica, for example, whose prime minister was pushing Washington for financial assistance lest it feel compelled to turn to Cuba for help; or Brazil, which had a recent history of strained relations with the United States. And there were the macho misgivings of those governments that would have preferred to do business with the First or even the Second Man. One Latin American diplomat found it "not exactly a compliment that Carter sent his Vice President to Africa and left South America to his wife."[69]

But despite all, Rosalynn Carter's trip was finally judged by no less an observer than the *New York Times* "a striking success." She was praised by her hosts: the Foreign Minister of Peru remarked that Mrs. Carter showed "full knowledge of Latin American problems" and was "highly competent" (similar comments were made by the President of Venezuela); a writer in Ecuador called her a "lively spokesman of the greatest goodwill"; and the President of Costa Rica said in a farewell statement that it was "the first time since President Kennedy that a United States administration brings us a message that kindles hope, love and attachment."[70] She also received virtually unanimous good marks from the press back at home. The *Times* went on to say that Mrs. Carter won acclaim for being "simpatica"; *Time's* correspondent reported that "Rosalynn Carter has shown herself to be intelligent, tough and understanding, and her trip clearly has been worthwhile"; *Newsweek* claimed that her notices were "mostly glowing"; and *The New Republic* wrote that "throughout the trip, Mrs. Carter impressed Latin American officials with her mild style, which often softened the impact of some decisive policy statements, especially in the field of human rights."[71]

President Carter was so flushed with pride at Rosalynn Carter's Latin American tour, her first major performance as First Lady, that he gave *Newsweek* a special interview on the subject of his wife.

> There's very seldom a decision that I make that I don't discuss with her—either to tell her after the fact what I've done, or, very frequently, to tell her my opinions and seek her advice.
>
> We have an absolutely unconstrained relationship, an ability to express our doubts and concerns to each other. When different members of my staff try unsuccessfully to get me to change my mind about something, they'll go to Rosalynn. . . .I consider that to be the ultimate approach to my consciousness. . . .
>
> She's got superb political judgment. She probably knows the human aspect of the American people and the relationship to the people better than me. And she's approachable. . . .[People] can talk to Rosalynn. . . .She's always surprised people. When we go out of the White House, she will have left behind a good legacy of quiet achievement.[72]

But successful as the trip was, it was perhaps even more notable for drawing the nation's attention for the first time to the extraordinary relationship between the president and First Lady. Their self-proclaimed partnership took on obvious meaning. We learned that Rosalynn sometimes attended Cabinet meetings, that she received briefings from National Security Council Chairman Zbigniew Brzezinski, that she went over her husband's energy speech of spring 1977 line by line because she thought, self-effacingly, that "if I could understand it, then everybody could understand it," and that she played such a central role in his decision making that when the president was asked if he had, as rumored, decided to retain Federal Reserve Chairman Arthur Burns, he answered in exasperation, "I haven't talked to Bert [Lance], Charlie [Schultze], or Mike [Blumenthal]. I haven't even talked to Rosalynn." The White House couple went so far as to institute a once-a-week "working lunch." It was a custom Jimmy Carter had begun with his vice-president, and thought to duplicate with his colleague-in-residence.

By the end of Jimmy Carter's first year in office, Rosalynn Carter's credentials as one of her husband's counselors were fully established. Hugh Sidey noted that Mrs. Carter was a "critical element in the Carter assessment of his counterparts," going on to add that when the "champagne has been drained and the music has died, Jimmy and Rosalynn sit down together and add it all up. Rosalynn has diminished Prime Ministers with one cool sentence or helped, as with Japan's Takeo Fukuda, elevate them to higher esteem."[73] And she continued to be regarded by Democrats as a considerable campaign asset; in the fall, for example, she was sent to New Jersey to help reelect Governor Brendan Byrne (whom she dutifully described as compassionate and courageous).

Around Christmas of 1977, Mrs. Carter was interviewed at length for ABC-TV by Barbara Walters. The interview was an unusual one for a First Lady. Although there were brief comments on personal matters such as family, the rest was all business. References were made to the energy bill, the social security bill, Carter's drop in the polls, the problems of the cities, unemployment and inflation, and Carter's mistakes and his toughest decisions. And on her own pet projects, Rosalynn referred to pertinent discussions with Arthur Burns and HUD Secretary Patricia Harris to underscore the seriousness of her effort. At one point during the interview, Walters pointedly observed that whenever Mrs. Carter talked about what the administration thought, or was doing, she said "we."

It was abundantly clear by then that Mrs. Carter had become an influential national leader in her own right. Eleanor

Roosevelt may once have been the same, but somehow she got by with only three aides—an administrative secretary, a social secretary, and a messenger. Times were different now: Jimmy Carter, despite his wife's protest, felt obliged to reduce her personal staff from twenty-two to eighteen full-time employees. (The salaries even of the eighteen totaled some $465,000 a year, a sum not specifically authorized by law but tacitly allowed by Congress as part of the White House budget. The cutback was part of a larger effort to reduce the size of the White House staff. The intention was for Mrs. Carter to rely more heavily on temporary detailees and unpaid volunteers.) Her staff had plenty to do. Key assistants included a press secretary, a social secretary, an appointments secretary, a personal assistant, and a director of projects; all had a hand in managing Mrs. Carter's busy and complex schedule. A partial list of the First Lady's official activities during 1977 looks like this: traveled a total of seventy-one days, visited sixteen nations and twenty-one U.S. cities, attended fifty public and 177 private meetings, worked 250 hours on mental health, held twenty-one press conferences, supervised thirty-nine receptions, twenty congressional leadership breakfasts, fifteen luncheons, eight state dinners, and eight picnics, took part in nineteen arrival ceremonies for visiting heads of state, attended seventy-one hours of briefings on foreign affairs and various domestic issues, handled 8,000 requests for appearances and 28,000 requests for pictures and autographs, received approximately 130,000 letters, and spent 210 hours learning Spanish and ten hours learning speed reading.

This list is especially long, and not all of it is ceremonial stuff, the elemental matter in any contemporary First Lady's daily routine. Rosalynn Carter was not content with just ceremony. From the start, she indicated that she would be a proper First Lady to be sure, but she also intended to be something more, something of substance.

During Jimmy Carter's second year in office, Mrs. Carter's balancing act continued: she dispensed tea and cookies, but she also contributed ideas to the president's State of the Union speech and worked for the Equal Rights Amendment. She discussed the plight of the inner cities with Henry Reuss, chairman of the House Committee on Banking, Finance, and Urban Affairs, and urged the president to stand by Bert Lance during the investigation of his banking practices. She lobbied successfully for changes in White House staff and changes in federal funding (for example, she persuaded the director of the Office of Management and Budget, James McIntyre, to tack on $23.4 million more to the budget for the National Institute of Mental Health, $12 million more to the drug-abuse budget, and $4.8 million more to the alcoholism budget); and she continued to sit in on meetings of the Cabinet and White House staff.

It was largely at Rosalynn Carter's instigation that Gerald Rafshoon, the Atlanta advertising man who had produced the Carter campaign commercials, was hired in mid-1978 to bolster the sagging Carter image. In other words, it was the president's wife who spearheaded the effort to defend him. She sounded the theme loud during a July 1978 luncheon meeting with reporters and editors of the *New York Times:* "[The public] thinks he's incompetent—he is not incompetent. They think he's indecisive—he's not indecisive. He's very strong, he's very determined, he knows what he wants and he doesn't back down, but he knows that in politics you have to compromise."[74] She placed the blame for her husband's poor image on a press that focused unnecessarily on negative or irrelevant details, an "open administration" that aired its differences in public, a post-Watergate mood that nourished distrust of anyone in power, and a White House staff that failed to convey the president's accomplishments.

The determination with which the First Lady undertook the campaign to boost Jimmy Carter's image, and to push old Georgia hand Rafshoon for the job, is illuminating in two respects. It suggests first of all that her primary goal was, in fact, a rather traditional one: to help her husband in *his* chosen career. This is not to say that Mrs. Carter was reluctant to take credit for what she had accomplished, or too shy to claim influence. It is merely to make explicit that Jimmy's professional life was always the center of both the Carters' attention. Second, her determination reflects the fact that Rosalynn Carter had a singular knack for positive thinking under adverse circumstances. In an interview in August 1978, she was asked whether she really expected things to turn around for the president and the administration "by 1980, specifically." John Osborne of *The New Republic* reports on her response:

> The interviewer suddenly understood why she was called the Steel
> Magnolia in Georgia and has been called the Iron Lady in Wash-

ington. . . . She stiffened, seemed almost to freeze. Her eyes—brown, hazel, blue-green depending on mood and dress—narrowed and hardened. Her voice, southern and soft and low, dropped to a whisper. She repeated the question as if she couldn't believe it had been asked. *"Turn around?"* she murmured. *"Of course!"* she said. . . .

Rosalynn speaking: "The polls have stabilized since last April and I think we're starting up. And the only reason we went down was because there were so many problems that were just here and somebody had to be courageous enough to tackle them. You make enemies doing that. But Jimmy has never, that has never bothered him. He couldn't care less. . . . What Jimmy's doing takes time. But it's going to start. . . . Things are going to start happening and I think people are going to see it. Jimmy is a (pause) VERY (pause) STRONG (pause) person. . . ."[75]

First Ladies are in position to exercise two kinds of clout: the first is through the impact of their own personality and the attention they bestow on areas they particularly choose to influence; the second lies in the nature of their relationship to their husband. Which was the greater clout for Rosalynn Carter?

With regard to her public impact, Mrs. Carter made a difference mainly in the field of mental health. She was honorary chairman of a special Presidential Commission on Mental Health, and spent many laborious hours devoted to improving the care of mental patients by studying and refining the commission's report. Yet even after the report was issued, her visibility in the mental health field remained rather low. Certainly as far as the public was concerned, there was little in the way of increased attention. She was diligent in her work, but she lacked flair.

A similar problem plagued her in another one of her projects: spurring voluntarism in the cities. Mrs. Carter had a large hand in organizing and conducting a seminar in Washington in the summer of '78 that was attended by some 300 representatives of local organizations engaged in training disadvantaged people for jobs. She also participated in a variety of other forums that pushed the cause of community self-help. On the whole, though, the public remained oblivious (as it did to her propagandizing for the Equal Rights Amendment). Her good intentions failed to strike a spark.

Thus it must be said that the impact of Mrs. Carter's person-

ality on the American public was small. There is no evidence
that she was particularly beloved, and there is none to suggest
that her causes found special favor. Why, then, was she described
as the most powerful First Lady in recent history? And from
where did she derive this power?

It was Christmastime again when Rosalynn Carter next sat
with Barbara Walters before the television cameras. It was 1978
now, and this time Jimmy was in tow. Ms. Walters reminded Mrs.
Carter that the president always called her his equal partner, that
she did things like sit in on Cabinet meetings, and that she was
said to discuss with her husband all sorts of political, economic,
and foreign-policy questions. Ms. Walters went on to describe the
First Lady's situation as "somewhat unique," and she encouraged her, on the strength of this, to argue with the president for
the benefit of the viewers. Politely, the invitation was declined; a
little later in the interview we heard why: "I feel compelled to
disagree with him at times [but] I never have publicly disagreed
with him and I have a very good reason for doing that. . . . I know
Jimmy well and I think that if I made our disagreements public, I
would lose all my effectiveness with him. I don't think it would
help in any way to change his mind about anything."[76]

There it is, in a nutshell. The power that Rosalynn Carter
wielded was derived from the so-called second kind of clout: the
nature of her finely tuned relationship to her husband. She had
developed, over the course of a highly successful thirty-year marriage, a way of dealing with Jimmy Carter, of influencing him to
see things her way, that was unrivaled by anyone else. Indeed, no
one else even came close. The thirty-ninth president was a loner.
He did not socialize easily, either with old pals from Plains or
with new ones from Washington. He was most comfortable with
family, and when he was not called on to do otherwise, he shared
his hours mainly with Rosalynn. She was his wife and the
mother of his children; but she was also his best friend and closest, most constant counselor, and it was through this connection
that she gained exceptional political power.

Rosalynn Carter said that the reference to her as "the second
most powerful person" was "an exaggeration." She was careful
to deny undue influence, calling herself merely "a sounding
board." Questioned once about whether there were any policies
or changes that she felt reflected her advice to the president, Mrs.
Carter replied, "I don't know whether . . . I consider myself a

force in his decisions, but he does let me in on things that he's doing." On another occasion, she elaborated further:

> People have written that I'm Jimmy's greatest adviser, and so forth. I'm not. But I talk to him about all the things he's trying to do. If there's something that involves the elderly, women's issues, the mentally ill, things that I know about, that I feel I can advise him on, I do it. And he trusts my opinion because he knows that I've worked on these things for a long time. I don't even try to advise him on a lot of things. But I can talk to him about what I feel ought to be done. He talks to me about welfare, tax reform, and I tell him what I think about it. I don't say, do this or do that, I've never done that. And (laughing) I'm not saying that he always does what I want him to do. But he always listens.[77]

Her husband, to the contrary, continued to insist that his wife was a "perfect extension of me." He regularly repeated that "she is a full partner with me in every sense of the word," and embellished the assertion with living proof. He would remark that "she is even involved in foreign affairs" (it has been said that Mrs. Carter was closely involved in the strategy, albeit not in the substantive details, of her husband's Mideast shuttle diplomacy[78]), and he would comment with pride on, for example, "the arrival statement that Rosalynn had made" at the funeral of Pope John Paul (she was the head of the United States delegation to the Vatican for Pope John Paul's funeral). And he would confide sotto voce to a staffer that "I've never won an argument with her, and the only times I thought I had, I found out the argument wasn't over yet." In an interview that took place halfway through his term, he expounded on the subject:

> She's a quiet, soft, female who has grace and confidence and who is very tough in an emergency. She doesn't get rattled. When I come home very discouraged, she listens to only just a few words of it and she looks around at me and says that I've got a problem with this or that. She knows enough about the background of that problem that I don't have to sit for two hours and explain it to her.*
>
> She says, "Well, what are you going to do about it?" And I say, "Well, I have three or four options." She says, "Jimmy, what are you going to do about it?" And I say, "I don't know. Well, I don't know yet."

---

*This shorthand way of communicating is reminiscent of the communication between the Kennedy brothers that JFK described as "rather cryptic."

And so I'll discuss the options with her and she'll say, "I think we should do this or that."

I try to be a quiet-spoken person. But there is an aura that surrounds any President that makes me less accessible to people than I was before. Sometimes I have a visitor come into the Oval Office . . . and he's so overwhelmed with where he is that he can't even tell me what he wants. Later, he'll leave my office and maybe call Rosalynn on the phone and say, "Well, what I wanted to tell the President was this. . . ."[79]

Especially early on, several observers harbored doubts about how much influence Rosalynn Carter really had. Everyone agreed that she was no intellectual, and some concluded that her main function was simply to raise questions from an intuitive, common-sense perspective. Others cast aspersions on her objectivity, saying she was excessively opinionated. A couple of White House insiders backed her own claim that "I don't advise [Jimmy] on things I don't know anything about." They added that she never really offered any specific policy advice: "She would not be so presumptuous, and [the president] would cut her off at the knees if she were."[80]

As Carter's term progressed, however, this became more and more a minority view. By the third year of the Carter presidency there was consensus that Rosalynn Carter was, in the traditional use of the term, the president's alter ego:

- A White House insider: "If you want Jimmy to do something, you'd better get Rosalynn on your side first."
- Tim Kraft, presidential aide: "Jimmy places the greatest stock in her judgments of people. Her word is gospel."
- Hamilton Jordan, then de facto chief of staff: "She just has a very good mind and political sense and doesn't hesitate to tell the President what she thinks. Whenever I think the President is pursuing an unwise course of action and I strike out with him, I try to get her on my side."
- Jody Powell, press secretary: "People will tell her things that they're reluctant to talk to the President about. If we've got a particular problem that's one among many that a President has to deal with, she can be a particular asset in getting him to focus."
- Patrick Caddell, Carter pollster: "I think her political perceptions and judgments are very good. She's extremely shrewd, her instincts on people are generally good and dur-

ing the campaign I found her to be a tremendous help, particularly on problems that needed to be brought to Jimmy's
attention. When we were trying to get him to decide something that was very tough, she played an important role. I
know that [remains true in the Carter White House]."

- A mental health official: "My impression is that we don't
test whether she has clout or not. So, by definition, she
does have it."
- Charles Kirbo, Atlanta lawyer and presidential confidant,
speaking of her "real input" when it came to choosing presidential appointees: "She knows so many people, and she
has good judgment about who will be responsible and
loyal. If I know what she thinks of the candidates, I can
often predict who'll get the job."
- Robert Strauss, the Democrats' man for all seasons: "I've
been in and out of Washington ever since the Roosevelt
era. There's just never been a First Lady with any more
impact than Rosalynn."
- Senator Jennings Randolph to Mrs. Carter after her appearance before Congress on behalf of the mental health program: "I vividly remember Eleanor Roosevelt when she
came up here. She had a shrill voice and you have a soft
voice. But you both have the same quality."[81]

Mrs. Carter, her cautious modesty notwithstanding, was not
reluctant to press her position. Demurely, she said of being First
Lady, "I feel awed. But I also feel a responsibility. The opportunities are here. Am I taking advantage of them as I should?" No
one can deny that she tried. With her drive for self-improvement,
her energy, her lifelong habit of hard work, and her determination to make the role of First Lady a substantive one, she arrived
at the forefront of Carter administration politics. Reports of fric-
tion between her staff and the president's staff subsided, largely
because "the West Wing" (Jordan, Powell, and company) came to
feel more obliged to utilize Mrs. Carter's talents, and "the East
Wing" (the First Lady's staff) came to feel more comfortable
about asserting its autonomy. It was almost as if there was no
longer any need to prove—to themselves, the press, the public, or
the world at large—Rosalynn Carter's importance. Her position
alongside the president came to be taken for granted.

The evidence of 1979 substantiated the feeling. In January,

Bella Abzug was fired as cochair of the National Advisory Committee for Women. Her presence in the job, it turned out, was most strongly opposed by Rosalynn Carter, who stated in a May appearance on the "Phil Donahue Show," that Bella was not the right person at that time: "We need someone to work in a quieter way." In February, Mrs. Carter became the first president's wife since Eleanor Roosevelt to appear before a congressional committee. The subject was mental health, a pet project and hardly a hot issue, but no matter. The Senate Resources Committee's Subcommittee on Health and Scientific Research, chaired by Senator Edward M. Kennedy, was all ears. Later, the committee chairman said the First Lady's appeal for the mentally ill was "passionate and eloquent."[82] In April, Rosalynn Carter made her strongest appeal yet for passage of the Equal Rights Amendment, in a speech with strong feminist overtones to a group of women "communicators." To a responsive audience she quoted the dismal statistics on the number of women in the legislative and judicial branches, adding, however, that her husband had done far better than his predecessors in bringing women into the executive branch. Noting at one point that she herself was "a relatively traditional person," she went on to say that "I am not threatened by the Equal Rights Amendment. I feel *freed* by it."[83] (On another occasion she called the ERA's failure to pass thus far her "biggest disappointment.") The First Lady also took on Senator John Glenn and his reservations about the SALT treaty. On the occasion of the launching of the first of the Trident nuclear submarines, she said to the senator's face, "It is my feeling, and Senator Glenn understands this, that premature public debate on issues such as this can be very damaging."[84] (The senior senator from Ohio was not pleased.) And in May the First Lady made an unusual joint appearance with her husband in the White House press room when he announced that he was sending Congress legislation to revamp mental health care in the United States that would cost $99.1 million in the first year.

But it was during July 1979, during the summer of Carter's discontent, that Rosalynn's impact was greatest. It was she who, when shown a draft of the president's originally scheduled energy speech said, "Don't deliver it. What's new? It's just more programs and proposals. I don't think anyone is going to listen." It was she who, prompted in part by an April memorandum from Carter's pollster, Patrick J. Caddell, urged her husband to press for a new sense of control and direction. It was she who sat by Jimmy Carter's side during the twelve days of meetings at Camp David during which the president talked to leaders from across the country about what was nagging the body politic. It was she who was privy to every single thing Jimmy Carter read and every single thing he heard during this unsettled time. (At the smaller staff meetings especially, she allowed herself to be outspoken, offering unsentimental assessments of programs and personalities. Said top aide Mary Finch Hoyt, "She has been very heavily involved in all aspects of the whole Camp David evaluation. . . .") It was Rosalynn—referred to during this period as the first among the powerful few—who encouraged the president to act quickly when the time came to make Cabinet changes that resulted in five men losing their jobs. (As she explained on a subsequent 5,500-mile political swing, "I just—uh, we—uh, Jimmy thought, and I agreed, that it was better to do it fast, and then we could go forward. The nation has so many problems that Jimmy had to have a good, tight Cabinet to work together. He accomplished that in the best possible way, cleanly and quickly.") And it was she who was then commissioned to explain the turmoil in Washington to such politically important groups as the National Urban League. When the dust had settled, *New York Times* columnist Tom Wicker summed up the reaction of all who had watched Rosalynn Carter's most recent performance: "She may be the most powerful First Lady since Edith Bolling Wilson virtually took over for a stricken President."[85]

Ever since Rosalynn Carter first hit the presidential campaign trail, she let us know what we would get if her husband triumphed. From 1975 on she proclaimed, "I talk issues." But she was and will continue to be much more than Jimmy Carter's adviser for all seasons. She has been compared to a "guardian lioness" in her steely zeal to protect him from assaults ranging from political attacks to crippling fatigue, and she was the willful one when Jimmy hesitated, the positive one when he sagged. During campaign '80 Rosalynn Carter remained true to form: resolute, determined, and optimistic. And it was she along with Walter Mondale who bore the brunt of the actual campaigning. During the first nine months of 1980 she visited thirty states; on a two-day whirlwind tour of Pennsylvania she shook 10,000 hands. "I'm just so proud of Jimmy," she would say, "so proud that he is the President of peace, proud that he has gotten 80% of his legislation through Congress . . . proud that he has established an energy program . . . proud that his economic programs are beginning to beat inflation." Small wonder that when it was all over, her husband seemed less stricken than she. In Jimmy Carter's own words; "I'm not bitter. Rosalynn is, but I'm not."

It is true that Edith Wilson, Eleanor Roosevelt, and a few other First Ladies had a major political impact during the time of their husband's administrations. But one wonders if any other First Lady could fairly make the claim that without her, the man she married would never have become president in the first place, and without her, the shape of his presidency would have been altogether different.

A Second Self

There is a paradox in the relationship between the president and his Alter Ego. On the one hand, it is an equal bond. Certainly after 1960, John Kennedy never felt that Bobby was in any way his junior, and from the 1950s on, Jimmy Carter claimed that Rosalynn decided right along with him. On the other hand, it is the mission of Alter Egos to nurture, to protect, and to foster the career, the reputation, and the life of their partner. Within the relationship the two are equal; but the practical results of it are such that one appears to be sacrificing him/herself for the sake of the other.

To be sure, although Alter Egos are prepared to expend their last resource to benefit the president, they themselves are not without honor; to be called "the second most powerful person in America" is no mean tribute. But that title is almost an accidental by-product of their labors, for it is truly the case that Alter Egos have the president's best interest in mind in every single thing they do.

Why do they do it? What motivates Alter Egos to be so extraordinarily altruistic? How is it that they are willing, eager even, to do dirty work for the benefit of another?

The most obvious answer is love, the supposition being that Alter Egos love (and also, of course, respect) their presidential kin so much that they will move mountains for them, or at least try to. But is even an expanded notion of love enough to explain such devotion? I think not and offer, as a supplement, the following explanation:

For an Alter Ego relationship to exist at all, it must be reciprocal. The president depends on and values his Alter Ego as the Alter Ego depends on and values the president. The results of such a complete intermeshing of egos is that what happens to and is felt by one happens to and is felt by the other. That explains why, when John Kennedy agonized over the Bay of Pigs, Robert was equally disturbed; and it explains why, when Jimmy Carter tried against all odds to win the Democratic nomination for president in 1976, his wife struggled just as hard by his side. Alter Egos seem almost literally to become their president's second skin, and so whatever he experiences, for good or ill, they experience in more or less exactly the same way.

If this is the case, the concept of sacrifice is meaningless. It was no sacrifice for Bobby to work for Jack, or for Rosalynn to labor on behalf of Jimmy. By enhancing Jack and Jimmy, Bobby and Rosalynn were doing no less than enhancing themselves.

One caveat though: in order to render maximum service—and Alter Egos *are major political assets*—they must be something other than the president's mirror image. They must, if they are to give sound advice, retain their intellectual independence and a modicum of objectivity. By the same token, a wise president will not become overly dependent on his Alter Ego. For example, no one would disagree that President Jimmy Carter was lucky indeed to have such an ardent and competent counselor as his wife Rosalynn. But if in fact he came to lean on her too much because of his own inability to interact and feel comfortable with, win over, and (politically) use others, then his relationship to her may actually be said to have been *too* strong. It is significant that Jack and Bobby Kennedy saw each other only rarely during off hours, while Rosalynn was around her husband day and night, seven days a week. One cannot help but wonder if that was not too much of a good thing.

But our thoughts on Alter Egos ought not to end on a negative note. For there is no doubt that, unless excessive and obsessive, they render the president an invaluable service. All along it has been suggested that candidates and presidents with relatives to draw on have a tremendous resource. Whether it be expressed as John Kennedy's poignant "Thank God for Bobby," or as Jimmy Carter's more mundane "We have an absolutely unconstrained relationship," it should be apparent by now that those fortunate few who can draw on an Alter Ego-have the most precious resource of all.

CHAPTER 8

Skeletons

Skeletons embarrass the president. The reasons for this unease differ, but the net effect is always the same: a situation in which the Chief Executive tries hard to keep the offending kin hidden from public view.

The fact that the better part of this book is about such diverse assets as Decorations, Extensions, Humanizers, Helpmeets, Moral Supports, and Alter Egos might lead one to conclude that the political impact of the presidential family is by definition positive. Hardly. As the following sketches will show, it is not uncommon for the president to have a relative whom he considers an undesirable. Of Kennedy, Johnson, Nixon, Ford, and Carter, only Gerald Ford lacked such a Skeleton, and that may well be because only Gerald Ford lacked full siblings.

Skeletons are usually brothers or sisters. Sibling rivalry surely has something to do with the fact that of the last five presidents, two had brothers who were known alcoholics. (In light of this record the legendary vigor and fraternal support of the Kennedy clan are even more noteworthy.) There are clearly strains associated with growing up and old with a brother who has the makings of a president, strains that tear at individuals and at the fabric of the family itself.

In times past it was easier to conceal those kin who were

deemed a political liability. There was no television, no *National Enquirer,* less of an obsession with the "star" qualities of the Chief Executive, and above all there was, until very recently, a code of honor that tended to inhibit the press from revealing private embarrassments. Indeed, as we saw in Chapter 4, it was only with the advent of Betty Ford's "my life is an open book" style that some of the traditional barriers started to break down. In the last five years or so, the definitions of such terms as "privacy" and "good taste," as they apply to the president, have changed. We scarcely knew that Sam Houston Johnson even existed; but when Billy Carter entered a rehabilitation clinic for alcoholics, it was front-page news.

Still, the more things change, the more they stay the same. We did learn that Billy Carter was an alcoholic. Yet we learned it only *after* he began treatment for his disease, and only *after* the White House worriedly figured that some of his nasty habits had to be explained away. In other words, it was just as intolerable for President Carter to be saddled with a known but untreated case of alcoholism in his family as it had been for President Johnson. It is only that in one case the Skeleton was in the closet, and in the other, the more recent, he was out.

Skeletons and presidential kin who are political assets have their roots in precisely opposite phenomena: either there is something about skeletons that is (or is thought to be) an embarrassment instead of a glory to the family name, or their private relationship to the president is troubled, instead of excellent. Not surprisingly, the two negatives tend to go together; a brother who is a liability in public is not likely to be a favorite in private.

Of course the extent to which relatives, either through what they are or through what they do, can actually hurt the president is not completely clear. As we shall see below, Billy Carter was the only one of the Skeletons who did, it appeared, have the potential for causing his brother considerable political harm. But presidents are, above all, concerned about their image. To the extent that Skeletons can mar that image, they are kept, when possible, under wraps. For as we have already seen, families play symbolic roles. They help the president to come across as a part of a healthy unit. If any member of the family threatens to undermine this pretty picture, he or she, if past evidence is any indication, will be lied about, concealed from the public altogether, controlled by executive fiat, or maneuvered into treatment designed to alter the offending condition. In short, Skeletons out of the closet are simply not tolerated.

Rosemary Kennedy

The Kennedy family began to reveal the truth about Rosemary Kennedy only some two years after President Kennedy took office. All along it had been something of a family secret that Rosemary had been at Saint Coletta's school for the retarded in Jefferson, Wisconsin, since 1941. (The suggestion to send her there was Richard Cardinal Cushing's, who remembers that her father and mother were anxious "to have her live in a religious environment."[1])

In times past, a retarded child in the family was considered an object of shame. Mental disorders were thought to be primarily hereditary; if one person was afflicted, a child of the next generation might share a similar fate. The Kennedys, then, were not remarkable in trying to keep the condition of their eldest daughter to themselves. The parents set the example for their other eight children by never talking about it. One old family friend remembers that he heard of Rosemary in his family only "because my own wife and friends knew of Rosemary, but they rarely talked about it. . . . It would rarely be brought up by any of the children." Other acquaintences of the Kennedys were even more circumspect: "I first met Kathleen and then Rosemary, who was not well . . ." or ". . . I never really remember seeing Rosemary who was not very strong, was she?"[2]

If the Kennedys were keeping the facts of Rosemary's condition from their own friends, they were obviously compelled to play the same game in public once Jack Kennedy entered politics. Very simply, they misled the press. Books on the Kennedys that coincided with Jack's 1960 presidential campaign fictionalized Rosemary's fate. One described her as "shy and retiring" and claimed that she had devoted her life "to the sick and afflicted and particularly to backward and handicapped children." In another book on the family, *The Remarkable Kennedys*, which was also serialized in *Look* magazine, the author, Joe McCarthy, wrote that Rosemary was "teaching in a school for retarded children in Wisconsin." And the eminent historian James MacGregor Burns, in his biography *John Kennedy: A Political Profile*, reported that Rosemary was "a sweet, rather withdrawn girl, not up to the children's competitive life." Later he added that as an adult Rosemary went to St. Coletta, a Catholic school near Milwaukee, where she "helped care for mentally retarded children."[3] (By the time Burns got around to writing a biography of Edward Kennedy, he was able to be more open. Here he wrote that "Rosemary was sweet and quiet, and it was not until her parents discovered that she was slow in everything . . . that they realized she was retarded."[4])

Newspapers and magazines were equally erroneous in their reports. On July 10, 1960, the *New York Times* reported simply that Rosemary was "in a nursing home in Wisconsin," while *Time*'s issue of one day later wrote that "Rosemary, the eldest of the Kennedy daughters, was a childhood victim of spinal meningitis, [and] is now a patient in a nursing home in Wisconsin." Even more bizarre was a story in the *New York Times* of October 19, 1961. It was on President Kennedy's commitment to his panel on mental retardation. The president was quoted as saying that mental retardation "should be brought out into the sunlight and be given a full national commitment." But bringing the condition "out into the sunlight" apparently did not yet extend to members of his own family. The story went on to say that "much of the Kennedy family's interest in this subject stems from the fact that another of the president's sisters, Rosemary, suffered cerebral palsy in childhood. She is now doing some teaching in an institution in Illinois."

There was, in fact, a paradox: even while the Kennedys were still withholding the truth about Rosemary, they began a massive effort on the federal level to draw attention to the problem of mental retardation in America. The family's Joseph P. Kennedy, Jr., Foundation had given vast sums of money since as far back as 1946 to hospitals, day-care centers, and research projects in the field of mental retardation, and now that John Kennedy was president, they extended their efforts in this area still further. Eunice Shriver was the driving force here. Robert Cooke, a member of the Medical Advisory Board of the family foundation, recalls that even during the campaign she would urge him to submit ideas on programs that addressed the health and welfare needs of children. Once her brother was president, she pushed even harder—with, while he was still well, no small help from her father.

. . . I can recall at one or two meetings with the Shrivers discussing
the question of how attention could be drawn to the problems of the
retarded on a national level, and how the President could use the
authority of his office to call this to the attention of scientists and
important people of various disciplines as well as the general public. I remember very clearly the statement that Eunice made when
she talked with her father. Her father said they ought to use an approach similar to that of the Hoover Commission, and he was the
one who made a suggestion for the presidential panel. . . . And indeed Eunice and I went up to see Herbert Hoover and talked with
him before the creation of the panel to try to get some idea of what
sort of an organizational structure was needed to have a commission
like this.[5]

And so it came to pass that the President's Commission on
Mental Retardation was born well before the world learned why
he was so interested. Of the fact that John Kennedy's support for
this crash program grew out of his close connection to the problem there can be little doubt. When asked whether he would consider the retardation of the sister responsible for generating family interest in the subject, Stafford Warren, a special assistant to
the president for mental retardation, replied, "Well, one of the
things about the Kennedy family is they're exceedingly clannish,
and it's one for all and all for one. They're serious about this. It's
not just kind of a custom or anything. It's really a family tradition
that's very deep, and so I think that her problem was taken to
heart by the whole family as a problem. . . ."[6]

Theodore Sorensen wrote that President Kennedy had permitted photographers and cameramen to intrude into his office
and home "but never at the cost of his essential dignity and privacy." He remembered that as a senator Kennedy had been far
more sensitive, "and as a result more secretive, on stories about
his money and health, until he decided secrecy was causing stories far worse than the truth. He had also been far more sensitive
about stories on his sister Rosemary, until the whole family decided that a more matter-of-fact attitude better served the fight
against mental retardation."[7]

It was left to Eunice Shriver to execute the family's decision
to take a more "matter-of-fact" position on the long-held family
secret. She did so in an article written for the September 22,
1962, *Saturday Evening Post*. A story carried by the *New York*

Times four days earlier noted that Mrs. Shriver's statement was
the first public discussion of the "heartbreak her family under-
went with a retarded older sister who is in an institution."

Eunice wrote of how "early in life Rosemary was different.
She was slower to crawl, slower to walk and speak than her two
bright brothers. . . . Rosemary was mentally retarded. For a long
time my family believed that all of us working together could
provide my sister with a happy life in our midst. My parents . . .
rejected suggestions that Rosemary be sent away to an institution. . . . [But] in 1941 . . . Rosemary was not making progress but
seemed instead to be going backward. . . . She was becoming increasingly irritable and difficult. . . . My mother took Rosemary
to psychologists and to dozens of doctors. All of them said her
condition would not get better and that she would be far happier
in an institution . . . . It fills me with sadness to think this change
might not have been necessary if we knew then what we know
today . . . ." This discussion of Rosemary's fate constitutes a
rather small part of the article, which goes on to talk about the
problems brought on by the prejudices of the general public, the
opportunities that many of the retarded now have to live out useful lives, etc.

It is certainly true that Eunice's article broke ground. From
then on it was public knowledge that Rosemary suffered not from
a physical condition, but from a mental one. Gradually the matriarch herself, Rose Kennedy, started to talk about it as well. "It is
hard to talk about Rosemary," she said in 1963. "I could not do it
years ago. But I want people to know it should be talked about.
Not hidden. That there is hope now."[8]

It was also Rose Kennedy who, in her book *Times to Remember,* published in 1974, finally revealed the full story—which was
far more complicated than the one suggested by Eunice Shriver
in her 1962 article. Mrs. Kennedy told in considerable detail
about Rosemary's childhood and adolescence and about how difficult it was because she was neither normal nor blatantly unable
to function reasonably well. She wrote of how, when Rosemary
was about twenty-three, she became progressively more uncon-
trollable. "She was upset easily and unpredictably. Some of these
upsets became tantrums, or rages, during which she broke things
or hit out at people. . . . Her blows were hard. Also, there were
convulsive episodes. . . ." And finally she told about the medical
advice, "Rosemary should undergo a certain form of neurosur-

gery." The operation, which was a prefrontal lobotomy, "eliminated the violence and the convulsive seizures, but it also had the
effect of leaving Rosemary permanently incapacitated. She lost
everything that had been gained during the years by our own gal-
lant efforts and our loving efforts for her. . . . She would need
custodial care. . . ."[9]

Sam Houston Johnson

It is possible that in some bizarre way Sam Houston Johnson
played a functional role in the inner life of his brother, Lyndon
Baines. His slavish adherence to the will of the president, his
elder by six years, may well have satisfied a psychological need
on the part of both. But it is also true that Johnson consciously
saw his brother as a political liability, and that he tried his hardest to keep him concealed from everyone outside the immediate
family.

In the five years of the Johnson presidency his brother's name
appeared in the *New York Times* on only four occasions: once in
connection with a reported illness, twice because of auto accidents, and once as the subject of a story on a bounced check.[10]
This despite the fact that for most of Johnson's tenure in the
White House his brother lived there right along with him, and
despite the fact that on some occasions when LBJ was still a senator, he had referred to Sam Houston as "one of my close advisers."[11] To television correspondent John Cameron Swazey,
Johnson once even insisted, "Sam Houston is my chief political
adviser—always has been."

Lyndon Johnson's control over his younger brother was virtually total. It had been that way since childhood; Sam Houston
was always at Lyndon's beck and call. Doris Kearns suggests
that this early pattern indicates "the powerful position Lyndon
held in his family structure. . . . And when his father was away,
this position was strengthened: Lyndon was left in charge of the
household, responsible for taking care of his mother and delegat-
ing the daily chores to his sisters and brother."[12] But what is remarkable about this pattern is that it persisted, unchanged, all
through adulthood. At one point, Sam Houston was moved to
write, "I swear Lyndon has the most persistent 'big brother' com-
plex of anyone I've ever known. . . . Always checking on his three

sisters and only brother to make damn sure none of them get out of line."[13]

The earliest outside experiences mirrored what had already been firmed up in the home. Lyndon was the star, while Sam Houston watched and listened with "wide-eyed admiration." And from the beginning, the younger brother was pressed into the older brother's service. Throughout all the years of Lyndon Johnson's spectacularly successful political career, Sam Houston hung around. He referred to himself as "a political trouble-shooter," and "a sort of general overseer in [Lyndon's] office." And he remembered when, back in 1955, Lyndon instructed his staff, "Nothing goes out of this office, press release or anything else, without Sam Houston or me giving an okay."[14] But in the same paragraph Sam Houston noted mournfully that when the president asked him to move to Washington after his inauguration in early 1965, "his aides were wondering how I would fit into the picture."

The fact is that Sam Houston Johnson was utterly dependent on his older brother for everything. He never had an independent career; he had two failed marriages; he had no home of his own (in later years, when he was not living with his brother, Sam Houston lived with a sister); and he was an apparent alcoholic. This wretched state of affairs was to some extent wrought by both: all through the years, Sam Houston Johnson worked for his brother, lived with him in his various homes (albeit not without interruption), and allowed himself to be controlled by him. "I guess Lyndon wanted me close by so that he could keep a big brotherly eye on all my extracurricular activities," he ventured.

By the time Johnson was president, his brother's predilection for "going on a toot to get away from it all" probably played the major role in his desire to keep the black sheep locked in the barn. Sam Houston's penchant for the bottle had always (at least consciously) driven his brother to distraction. Sam Houston reported that on the one occasion when Lyndon got drunk, he summoned Sam Houston to see the wreckage: "I want you to take a damned good look at me, Sam Houston. Open your eyes and look at me. 'Cause I'm drunk, and I want you to see how you look to me, Sam Houston, when you come home drunk."[15]

There were, of course, many occasions on which Sam Houston lent his brother support. Over the years he did a million chores for him, joined him in countless games of dominoes (to soothe Lyndon Baines' ruffled nerves), and even, from time to time, gave good advice. At his best, mostly before LBJ became president, he was a go-between for those who wanted to get to Lyndon, and something of a sounding board for him, a sounding board from whom nothing needed to be hidden. But he almost never did anything without Lyndon's prior approval. The number of times on which he did were so few, in fact, that they were well remembered. As was the brother's wrath: "Damn you Sam Houston, I'm going to fire you one of these days" — to which Sam Houston writes he retorted, "You can't fire your own blood."[16]

By the time Lyndon Johnson reached the White House, the character of the interaction between the two brothers was engraved in stone: Lyndon, the all-powerful older brother who had merely fulfilled his manifest destiny in the presidency; Sam Houston, the sickly flunky whose behavior was deemed so erratic that he presumably needed no less than constant surveillance. (Sam Houston Johnson was indeed sickly; he suffered from a variety of physical ailments for many years. At one point he spent months in a body cast following surgery that left him with one leg 5 inches shorter than the other. On occasion he would try to use his illnesses. For example, Sam Houston recalled that he tried to get out of going to his brother's presidential inauguration on their account. But the effort failed: "How the hell will it look if my only brother doesn't show up?" Lyndon demanded.) Constant surveillance was just what LBJ provided. He was so anxious to keep his younger brother behind closed doors that during the Johnsons' stay in the presidential mansion Sam Houston was kept a virtual prisoner on the third floor. In one of the only published references to Sam Houston's stay in his brother's White House, J. B. West, for years chief usher there, makes the point:

> The White House served as a long-term way station for Sam Houston Johnson, the President's high-spirited brother whose exploits sometimes gained publicity that bothered President Johnson. . . . His principal activity was clipping newspapers, which the President told him would be useful for a future political campaign. It seemed, in fact, as if Sam Houston was under some sort of house arrest. At any rate, a Secret Service agent kept a log of his movements and visitors, and his contact with the world was pretty much limited to long conversations with Assistant Usher Nelson Pierce.[17]

It is in any case true that by "inviting" Sam Houston to live in the presidential mansion, Lyndon could maintain complete control over him. Sam Houston remembers that he "came to feel like an inmate on the third floor of the White House. My few visitors had to go through a security rigamarole—like gun molls visiting their husbands at Sing Sing. It was even worse when I stayed in the family quarters on the second floor—across the hall from Lyndon's room."[18] Of course, as even Sam Houston admits, Lady Bird and the Johnsons' two daughters were faced with some of the same restrictions. But one wonders if family members who did not feel themselves in some way coerced would refer to the building as a "penitentiary" and call their own quarters "as difficult to penetrate as the high-security cell block of a prison."[19]

The extent of Lyndon Johnson's mastery over his younger brother astonishes, as does the younger brother's submission to it.

> ... Lyndon had assigned me a very nice bedroom on the third floor of the White House and pointedly told me, "You're now sleeping in the room once occupied by Harry Hopkins, and I want you to act accordingly."
>
> In view of Hopkins' exalted status as Roosevelt's chief adviser, one might conclude that he had suddenly created a special job for me. Far from it. He was simply telling me that I had to behave, that I was expected to follow a straight and narrow path. . . . And to make damned sure I wouldn't stray too far off that terribly slender path, he assigned a Secret Service man . . . to hound my steps morning, noon, and night—especially at night. . . .
>
> Not that [the agent] actually stopped me from drinking or wenching; he never said a word of prevention. Yet I knew from long experience that Lyndon would be subjecting him to one of his grueling prosecutor's cross-examinations every day. "Where d'you and Sam Houston go yesterday? . . . Whom did he talk to? . . . What did he drink? . . . Who's he fooling around with? . . . When did y'all come home?"[20]

Lyndon Johnson did not always use intermediaries to do his monitoring for him. For example, when Sam Houston committed the cardinal sin of falling asleep with his light on, Lyndon himself would come into his room and shake his shoulder to wake him: "Goddamn it, Sam Houston, are you working for me or for the lousy power company?" Sam Houston remembers that nasty habit as one of the reasons he preferred to live on the third floor: Lyndon "still might come up to put off my light, but it would be a little harder on him." Still, the point was made. One evening when President and Mrs. Johnson had been out, they returned late to a pitch dark mansion. There was not a light on in the place—only a tiny flicker at the end of the long hall. It was Sam Houston, working at a desk, with only one small candle.[21]

Donald Nixon

At least one psychohistorian has postulated that Nixon perceived the birth of his brother Donald, only a little over a year after his own birth, as taking his mother away from him.[22] It is certainly true that although the brothers were very close in age, they were never close personally. As youngsters they worked side by side in the family grocery store; and it is said that when Dick was interested in a young school teacher named Pat Ryan, he kept Don up half the night talking about the types of engagement rings he had diligently investigated. Mostly, though, they went their separate ways, which, given their different personalities, was no surprise. Dick was moody and often silent; Don, who always took a back seat to his older brother, was more genial and relaxed.

David Abrahamsen, in his psychohistorical study of Richard Nixon, writes about resentment between Nixon and his brothers Donald; Arthur, (five years younger) who died when Dick was twelve; and Harold, (four years older) who died when Dick was twenty. Abrahamsen suggests that Donald and the others may have been vexed with Dick because they saw him as their mother's favorite, while Dick viewed them as competitors for his beloved mother's affection. Donald has recalled that "Dick used his tongue more than his fists. One time he lit into me and gave me a dressing down I'll never forget. I've forgotten what his beef was, but I had it coming. He didn't talk about the problem at the moment; he aired all his gripes of the past two or three years."[23]

As adults the three surviving brothers—Dick, Donald, and Edward, born when Dick was seventeen—remained distant. While Dick went into politics, Donald went into business. First he stayed behind in the family store; then he worked as a sales manager for Carnation Milk; and later he ran a small chain of quick-order California restaurants called Nixon's, featuring "Nixonburgers"! It was because of this last venture that he first became a political liability to his ambitious older brother.

"Nixonburgers" weren't selling well in the mid-fifties, and Nixon's was losing $5,600 a week. In a futile effort to keep the business solvent, Donald accepted a $205,000 loan from Howard Hughes. As security for the loan, he put up a vacant California lot that was owned by his mother, Mrs. Hannah Nixon, and leased to him. (In 1957 Donald subleased the lot to the Union Oil Company, which put a service station on it. The property increased in value from $52,000 to $163,000 some fourteen years later.) The loan was never repaid, and during the presidential campaign of 1960 questions arose about why Howard Hughes, a major manufacturer of defense components, might want to get in good standing with the Nixon family. Indeed, in October 1960 the family felt compelled to make a statement to the effect that there was no impropriety in the Hughes loan after nationally known columnist Drew Pearson, in what the family called a "political smear," charged that there was.

But the Hughes loan continued to haunt Richard Nixon. In his campaign for governor of California in 1962 the question came up again. At a joint appearance with his opponent, Pat Brown, before a group of California newspaper editors and publishers, he was asked whether he thought it "proper for a governor, morally and ethically, to permit his family to receive a secret loan from a major defense contractor in the United States." Nixon's reply:

> I welcome the opportunity of answering [that question]. Six years ago my brother was in deep financial trouble. He borrowed $205,000 from the Hughes Tool Company. . . .
>
> My brother went bankrupt six years ago. My mother turned over the property to the Hughes Tool Company. Two years ago in the presidential election, President Kennedy refused to make a political issue out of my brother's difficulties and out of my mother's problems, just as I refused to make a political issue out of any of the charges made against the members of his family.
>
> I had no part or interest in my brother's business. I had no part whatever in the negotiation of this loan. I was never asked to do anything by the Hughes Tool Company and never did anything for them. . . .
>
> Now it is time to have this out. I was in government for fourteen years as a congressman, as a senator, as Vice President. I went to Washington with a car and a house and a mortgage. I came back with a car and a house and a bigger mortgage.
>
> I have made mistakes, but I am an honest man. . . .[24]

(The Kennedys, incidentally, were not above at least trying to make hay out of a Nixon misdeed. Department of Justice files leaked to the *New York Times* showed that Robert Kennedy, in his capacity as attorney general, tried to develop evidence against the Nixon family on the basis of the Hughes loan. But, according to the article that appeared in the *Times* on January 24, 1972, the Department concluded that there was no basis for prosecution— even though it had examined the Nixons' income tax returns, the bribery statutes, and statutes governing political contributions.)

In the year that Richard Nixon was sworn in as president, his brother was hired by the Marriott Corporation in the 'field of catering." Apparently he was now transformed into a superb businessman, for a report carried by the *New York Times* on June 4, 1970, indicated that Donald Nixon "recently made a substantial commercial sale to Aristotle Onassis." It went on to say that he had concluded a deal under which Marriott would provide the in-flight catering for Olympic Airways, but that an associate of Mr. Onassis wished to assure everyone that the Marriott sale was "not the result of Mr. Nixon's White House connection."

For a short while the press left Donald Nixon alone, but in September 1973 the *Washington Post* broke the truce. It reported—and nobody really denied—that for more than a year during Nixon's first term in office he had the Secret Service tap his brother Donald's telephone. (The *Post* claimed "four highly reliable sources"; since then, not even Nixon's own *Memoirs* have contained a denial.) The most common conjecture was that Richard Nixon feared that some of his brother's financial activities might bring acute embarrassment to the Nixon administration— and then there was the still lively Hughes connection! The Secret Service declined any comment, but the White House saw fit to claim that if the Secret Service *had* tapped Donald Nixon's telephone, it would have been "related to the protective function of the Secret Service."[25] No mention was made of the fact that the mandate of the Secret Service was to provide protection only for the president's "immediate family"—and that this did not include siblings.

The Senate Watergate committee, however, decided not to pursue the matter. It claimed that the brotherly tap was outside its specific jurisdiction, and that, anyway, the surveillance "only confirms a pattern that we already knew existed. We knew [the brothers] didn't trust one another."[26] But the committee's appar-

ent equanimity in light of this new information did not signal the
end of the story. It came out that Nixon not only had tapped his
brother, but that in 1969 he had his trusted crony Bebe Rebozo
telephone Hughes' headquarters in Las Vegas and demand that
all of Hughes' associates stay away from Don. Rebozo's request,
though, was ignored, and during that same year Donald went to
the Dominican Republic with one of Hughes' top aides in an
apparently inconclusive effort to negotiate some mining deals.
(*Time* reported that upon their arrival in the Dominican Republic, Donald Nixon and his pal from the Hughes organization
were treated royally. "The government greeted them like poten-
tates and laid on a heavy military escort."[27]) Once again Rebozo
got on the phone to Las Vegas. This time Donald's traveling
companion was dismissed from the Hughes hierarchy; he was
subsequently indicted for income tax evasion.

By early 1974 an investigator for the Senate Watergate committee discovered that Donald Nixon's brother had also arranged
for physical surveillance. Quite clearly the Nixon White House
was obsessed with the possibility that Don's dealings would
prove embarrassing. In fact, a working document referred to as
"the Don Nixon book" was prepared for John Mitchell and John
Ehrlichman so that they would have a running account of all his
activities. As one Hughes insider put it, Don was not seen as
dishonest, but merely as a "very gullible fellow."[28]

There was more. It was rumored that the planned break-in
into the offices of Hank Greenspun, a Las Vegas newspaper publisher, by E. Howard Hunt and G. Gordon Liddy was aimed in
part at retrieving documents related to Donald Nixon. Moreover,
it had come out that Donald Nixon had another unsavory connection—this one to fugitive financier Robert Vesco, who was
under federal indictment on charges of illegally contributing
$200,000 to Nixon's 1972 campaign and conspiring to obstruct
justice, and who also stood accused of a $224 million stock fraud.
In 1971, Don's only son, Don, Jr., then twenty-four, was hired as
a personal aide by Vesco. The two got on smashingly: Vesco invited young Don Nixon to move into the family home in New
Jersey, while Don, Jr., took to calling Vesco his "best friend."
Donald, Sr., also stayed in touch with Vesco, and in that connection he was called on to testify for the government at the 1974
trial of former Nixon Cabinet members John Mitchell and
Maurice Stans (who were being charged with conspiracy, ob-

struction of justice, and perjury). Don Nixon tried to beg off testifying because of heart trouble, but after the judge ordered an examination by a physician, it was decided that Don could appear.

In court it came out that Vesco was indeed in touch with Don, Sr. Vesco had sent him a memo—which was, not so incidentally, intercepted by Mitchell—that warned that unless the Securities and Exchange Commission's investigation of his empire was stopped, his secret contribution to Nixon would be publicly disclosed; and he would also see to it that Generalissimo Francisco Franco of Spain would create "an international incident." If all of this sounds somewhat bizarre, that need not trouble us here. What matters is that Richard Nixon was preoccupied with his brother's shady connections, and determined that they remain under control and under wraps. Just how carefully the president kept his one-year-younger brother at arm's length from the White House was revealed by Donald's rambling, flustered performance in court. Said he, "John Mitchell is a man that I was delegated—that designated that I should talk to him about any matter pertaining to—in other words I never talk to my brother about anything, and John Mitchell was the man that I was assigned to."[29]

Billy Carter

By early 1979 Billy Carter's transformation from good ol' boy to national disgrace was complete. A commentator for CBS News in New York asserted that although other presidential brothers had embarrassed the president, Billy was the first to embarrass the whole nation.[30] But the jokes continued. To the question "Name three things that go to the bathroom outdoors," Johnny Carson's "Karnak" divined the answer, "A mule, a horse, and Billy Carter." And Dick Cavett volunteered that the producers of "Hollywood Squares" wanted Billy Carter for their show, but nobody would agree to sit under him.

Billy committed several sins at once: he did urinate outdoors, in public, at the Atlanta airport; he hosted a boisterous tour for Libyan businessmen and officials close to Libyan Colonel Muammar al-Qaddafi, the controversial leader of a government rich in oil but widely viewed as a bitter enemy of Israel and of Jimmy Carter's peace efforts in the Middle East; and he made a series of remarks that were interpreted as being anti-Semitic, such as "The Jewish media tears up the Arab countries full time, as you well know," and "There's a hell of a lot more Arabs than there is Jews." This series of transgressions caused a public uproar and made Billy into Jimmy's enemy number one.

Immediately the White House was put on the defensive. Press Secretary Jody Powell denied that the president shared any of Billy Carter's views that could "be interpreted as being anti-Semitic." "Yes," a presidential aide said, "the President is embarrassed by this, but it all comes back to a question of what the President can do about it. Everybody who has covered Billy knows he's not somebody we can give marching orders to. It's a problem. He has done this without consultation with the White House. . . ."[31]

But neither the public nor the press was about to be satisfied with what many saw as a lame excuse. The *New York Times* intoned that "there comes a time when private difficulties become the public's concern," and that even though Billy Carter was "obviously unstable in mind or character, he can no longer be dismissed as the family buffoon."[32] William Safire railed against the presidential claim that he had "no control" over Billy. He suggested that the president's fear that any public interference on his part would be "counterproductive" indicated that the White House was concerned about what Billy might reveal to the grand jury in the Bert Lance investigation. "What should be of concern is the reason behind the President's kid-glove treatment of his kid brother: What information, potentially incriminating to himself or his family, is Billy Carter concealing from the Lance grand jury?"[33] And Art Buchwald, although he took a typically humorous tack, nonetheless posed a central issue. Buchwald's friend from Georgia: "As President of the United States he can do anything he wants to except one thing—he can't control his own brother." Buchwald's reply: "If the President can't do that . . . , he's in a lot of trouble."[34]

Billy Carter was scheduled to explain himself on CBS's "Face the Nation" on February 11, 1979, but one day earlier, through his lawyers, the appearance was canceled. We got a hint as to why in President Carter's press conference of February 27.

> Q. Mr. President, your brother, Billy, has made some remarks concerning Jews, and I wonder, sir, if you deplore or condemn those remarks?

A. I might say first of all, I don't have any control over what my
brother says or what he does and he has no control over what I
say or do.

I know Billy and have known him since he was born and I know for
a fact that he is not anti-Semitic and has never made a serious critical remark against Jews or other people in our country. To the extent that any of his remarks might be interpreted as such, I certainly
do not agree and do not associate myself with them.

Billy is my brother; he's seriously ill at this point. I love him. I have
no intention of alleging to him any condemnation that I don't think
is warranted. And I would say that I disassociate myself and my
brother from any allegations or remarks that might be anti-Semitic
in nature.

Sick or not, though, Billy Carter was trouble now. The president was warned of this by his Jewish adviser for all seasons,
Robert Strauss,[35] and Jewish groups across the country were up
in arms. One letter of solicitation from a Jewish organization began like this: "THERE ARE MANY WHO WOULD LIKE TO
SEE US FAIL! In recent months, Jewry has been subjected to
Billy Carter's crude remarks, Iran's new anti-Israel government,
and a general strengthening of the Arab political and economic
condition. . . ."[36]

The Libyan connection—in April it was revealed that Billy
Carter's expense-paid trip to Libya the preceding September was
also the beginning of a plan for a corporate association with Qaddafi' s government—the alleged anti-Semitism, and the airport incident were in fact not Billy Carter's only problems. During the
spring of 1979 questions were being asked about the legality of
some of Billy's business operations as well. It started with the
grand jury investigation of the financial manipulations of Bert
Lance, for years the Carter family banker and early in the Carter
administration the federal budget director. The initial financial
support for Carter's early state campaigns came from the family
business. It also happened to be the case that when Carter decided to run for the presidency in 1975, he sought to increase the
size of the family peanut business by 300%. By 1977 Lance's National Bank of Georgia had advanced the Carters more than $6.5
million in credit—all this to the business that was now being
operated by Billy Carter. There was an implication that with the
knowledge and compliance of Billy, loan money had been diverted to cover expenses in Jimmy's campaign.

On one signal day in early March, some of the worst accusations against the Carter brothers came together with an excuse for at least some of Billy's behavior. Safire wrote in the *Times* of March 8, "Remember we are not dealing merely with charges against Billy Carter; we are dealing with potential fraud, conspiracy to misapply bank funds and tax evasion in a company 63 percent owned by Jimmy Carter." And in the *Times* of the same day, we learned that "Billy Carter . . . today began a program of group therapy sessions at the Long Beach Naval Regional Medical Center that are designed to help patients end their dependency on alcohol."

The fresh twist did not assuage everyone. Safire continued his assault against the Carters by suggesting that Billy was quite deliberately gotten out of the way. "You will recall how, only last month, Billy Carter was a loose cannon, spilling information to reporters. . . . Suddenly, for some unknown reason everything changed . . . . And when his doctor refused to attest to the seriousness of his illness, the man over whom the President claims 'no control' was sent to the naval alcoholic facility supposedly just for Government employees and their dependents. Under naval guard, he has become as incommunicative as Dita Beard."[37] And when a local news show in New York sent a reporter into the street to inquire of the man there whether the media should "ignore Billy Carter," the answers were mostly harsh: "It *is* hurting his brother," or "He's an idiot," or "He confirms the weakness in government."[38]

It appeared then that March 1979 was the low point. Americans are forgivers (and forgetters), and when Billy Carter emerged in April from Long Beach calling himself a "reformed alcoholic," sporting a new mustache and looking trim from the loss of weight, we were ready to pardon him. Indeed, Billy made it as easy as possible for us. He said that he had "never represented Libya in any way, shape or form," that he had been misquoted and misrepresented regarding his remarks about Jews, that he had not, earlier, realized that he was an alcoholic, and that when he went to a party on the preceding Saturday night, he "found one thing; I think it's almost as much fun to watch the drunks as to get drunk with 'em."[39] He asserted, moreover, that "not a dime" of the National Bank of Georgia loan money had ever been diverted to his brother's presidential campaign.

Most of us thought, quite reasonably, that now, after Billy's poor showing early in Jimmy's first term, he could and would be relegated to the back burner by his brother. He had brought the White House enough grief, and it seems a safe guess that they were relieved over on Pennsylvania Avenue when Billy's former agent announced in June that "it looks like Billy's show-biz days are over. . . . The travel and pressures are more than I feel Billy will ever voluntarily subject himself to ever again." But before you could Southern-drawl your way through "Jack Robinson," the new Billy made a lively, even witty appearance (along with his doctor from the rehabilitation center) on the "Phil Donahue Show," and he claimed to be having second thoughts about retiring from the celebrity circuit. From his home in Americus, Georgia, Billy said, "From the letters, I think there may be more interest than before."

The trouble was, there was. Although he had refused to register as a foreign agent, it was revealed that Billy had accepted over $220,000 in "loans" from Libya. The Republicans, smelling 1980 blood, wasted no time in calling for a prompt investigation.[40]

As it turned out, the "Billygate" story had only just begun. This time Billy escaped from the closet for keeps, and as *Newsweek* wrote in its cover essay on the subject (August 1980 saw Billy on the cover of *Time* as well), he was now "the center of a political hurricane that threatened his brother's already precarious White House perch."[41] The trouble was that this time around the bungling, the errors, the uncertainties with regard to matters of both propriety and law seemed to overflow into the Oval Office itself. Although Billy Carter's ties to the avowedly proterrorist Libyan government triggered the scandal, its life blood became the suspicion that Jimmy Carter and some members of his administration acted illegally at worst, unwisely at best. Questions included: Why was it necessary to use Billy Carter as an intermediary with the Libyan government in the matter of the Iranian hostages? (Ironically, the idea was said to have been Rosalynn's.) Did the White House act to enhance Billy's credibility with the Libyans? Was Billy warned about a break in the Justice Department investigation of his Libyan connection, and did he then receive favored treatment?

During summer 1980 the Billy Carter affair became and remained front-page news. A special Senate subcommittee was appointed to investigate the case; the president felt compelled to state that he was "eager to respond in person" to questions from the committee, and "the sooner, the better." No wonder. During July the president's political aides were advising him that it was important for him to disclose as much material as possible *before* the Democratic convention in order to limit the controversy as an issue on the floor,[42] for instead of receding, the scandal was growing. A sample of front-page *New York Times* headlines just before the Democrats met in New York: "CARTER SAYS HE TOLD BROTHER ABOUT CABLES ON LIBYAN TRIP,"[43] "CIVILETTI DISCLOSES HE SPOKE TO CARTER ON BROTHER'S CASE,"[44] "NEW CARTER EMBARRASSMENT: WHITE HOUSE FORECASTS PRESIDENT WILL SURVIVE BROTHER'S LIBYA TIE, BUT OTHERS FORSEE DAMAGE."[45]

There was little doubt that the president was being hurt. The Billy Carter scandal raised two serious questions about White House performance. First, there was the matter of integrity. Safire, who held on to the story like a terrier to a postman's leg, put it this way: "The issue is not whether our clown prince influenced his brother on Libyan policy, which is silly. The issue is why the President—knowing for three months that his brother was trying to squeeze money out of his demonstrated White House influence—was too blind or fearful to stop him."[46] Pollster Louis Harris was quoted: "The Billy thing puts President Carter on the defensive. He will not really be able to campaign in his favorite way with high moral dudgeon."[47] But perhaps the second question nagged even more: it was the question of good leadership, of competence. Even members of the president's own party addressed the issue out loud. Senate Majority Leader Robert C. Byrd stated that the president's performance in this matter was one of "bad judgment and rather amateurish" conduct of foreign policy.[48] Given the fact that doubts about Carter's competence had surrounded him throughout his tenure as president, he could ill afford the fresh crop raised by his participation, or lack of it, in "Billygate."

By early August the president was doing all he could to take the bull named Billy by the horns. He handed the Senate panel investigating the affair a 13,000-word report, including the texts of fifteen entries in his personal diary and the detailed recollections of several of his top aides. Moreover, he appeared in a one-hour (twice the normal length) televised news conference (his first in three months) in which he summarized the key points in his report to the Senate, recalled the Watergate case and his campaign for the presidency four years ago in which he promised to restore the confidence of the American people in their government, pledged that integrity would remain a "cornerstone" of his administration, and declared of his brother, "I love him, and he loves me."[49] By all accounts it was a strong performance, and by the time the Democrats met in New York the scandal had quieted somewhat.

The course of "Billygate" between the time of the president's news conference and election day was curious. On the one hand, the affair seemed to fizzle. Billy Carter's own performance before the Senate subcommittee was effective. In his opening statement he expressed the hope that "testimony will show in commonsense fashion that Billy Carter is not a 'buffoon,' a 'boob' or a 'wacko,' as some public figures have described him," and the consensus was that he got his wish. Moreover, although the Senate subcommittee concluded unanimously that the president and members of his administration had exercised poor judgment in the way they handled Billy Carter's relationship with Libya, the report cited no examples of "illegal or clearly unethical action on the part of government officials."[50] After the panel released its report, some senators seemed almost apologetic. Senator Claiborne Pell remarked that "in the beginning a lot of us thought we had a bear by the tail [but in the end] we really had a mouse." And even arch-Republican Robert Dole felt compelled to admit that there were "no parallels with Watergate."[51] Gary Trudeau's "Doonesbury" comic strip summed up the apparent anticlimax. In one panel a man addressing the subcommittee is saying, "A lot of people are wondering why nine U.S. Senators have been devoting their full energies to such a trivial affair." In the next panel two unseen senators are responding, "Uh. . . I didn't ask to be on this committee. I haven't even been paying attention," and "Me neither. I've been signing letters."[52]

On the other hand, "Billygate" dogged the Carter administration to the very end. The whole issue of the extent to which various members of the Carter family had overstepped the largely invisible lines of propriety and legality remained something of an open wound. It was revealed in August that Zbigniew Brzezinski had arranged for a National Security Council briefing for Ruth Carter Stapleton before she embarked the previous winter on a

Middle East tour (that was financed in part by an Arab businessman). And it was uncovered that same month that the president's
youngest son Jeff had been working since 1978 as a computer
consultant, and that among his clients were the World Bank and
the (authoritarian) government of the Philippines. In September—some would say too late in the game—the president issued a
memorandum to the heads of executive departments and agencies on how to deal with members of his family on business matters.[53] (*The New Republic* found this a "sorry gesture." "[The
president] reserved a right to continue using members of his family as his 'official representatives' and said no more than that
'there is a strong presumption against' members of his family
'seeking to do business with the government.' So, the humilia-
tion of issuing such guidelines now undergone, things remain
the same."[54])

Moreover, the Billy affair itself would not die. An article in
The New Republic of November 1 claimed that when "Billy
Carter was in Libya enjoying the hospitality of [Qaddafi] the
leading financier of international terrorism, he also met with two
of its leading practitioners: Yasser Arafat, head of the Palestine
Liberation Organization, and George Habash, leader of the most
extremist Palestinian group. . . ." The article went on to suggest
that Qaddafi's belief that he had succeeded in acquiring influence through Billy was, in fact, justified. Worse yet, a front-page
New York Times headline that appeared a mere two days before
the election, read, "JUSTICE AIDE FAULTS CARTER ON
INQUIRY." In other words, just before the first Tuesday in November 1980, fresh and urgent questions were being raised in an
internal Justice Department report about the president's role in
his brother's case. At best, the report (which was prepared by the
head of the department's office of professional responsibility)
charged, the president was uncooperative and unresponsive. One
example: "Regarding the President's diary and his personal
notes, we have not been granted the access we sought, despite the
President's public statements of total cooperation."[55] (The report
also accused Attorney General Benjamin Civiletti of deliberately
"dissembling.")

No one would claim that "Billygate" alone accounted for the
overwhelming defeat of President Carter at the polls. There is
widespread agreement, however, that it made what appeared to be
a sorry state of affairs considerably sorrier. Indeed, in a post-mor-

tem undertaken by White House and Carter campaign officials themselves, it emerged as one of eight main causes of the miserable outcome. (They saw the other seven as the president's poor performance in the preelection debate, his "Rose Garden" strategy, the March 1980 UN vote against Israel, his strident attacks on Ronald Reagan, his unsuccessful attempt to paint his opponent as a reckless warmonger, absence of vision, and efforts to keep discussion of "real issues" out of the campaign.[56]) It was Billy, though, typically and appropriately, who had the last word. "I'm willing to take some of the blame," he said on the day after the election, "but for sure not all of it."[57]

Black Sheep

The experiences of Rosemary Kennedy, Sam Houston Johnson, Donald Nixon, and Billy Carter lead to the conclusion that nowadays the only presidential relatives with the potential to cause significant political harm are those who commit what we can label "public sins." It is O.K. to be mentally retarded now, and it is probably even O.K. to be a drunk or a shady fiscal leech. What is intolerable is for a member of the president's family to run around the country spouting crude insults against a particular group, become involved in affairs of state as a representative of a foreign country, circumvent the law on matters of public interest, and/or involve the president in his own misdeeds.

It is clear, though, that even if public sins are finally the only ones that can quite literally be measured in terms of negative political impact, presidents are nervous too, very nervous, about the so-called private sins which have the potential of becoming public knowledge. The Kennedys went into public life determined that the American people would never learn the truth about Rosemary. And no wonder that we scarcely knew that Sam Houston Johnson even existed. Lyndon saw Sam Houston as a boozer who had, at all costs, to be kept in the closet. As for Richard Nixon, he kept tabs the electronic way; and he had his brother tailed to combat his "troublesome predilection for curious business enterprises with even more curious partners."

But if presidents are nervous about their errant kin, we can hardly blame them. We create a climate that assumes they should be. As Russell Baker noted during the brouhaha over Billy

Carter, the press and the public have an unfortunate penchant for
supposing that if a president can't make his family work right, he
is altogether incompetent.

> To a President, an independent relative can be almost as trouble-
> some as a telephone call in the night on the hotline from Moscow.
> This is because Presidents are victims of the foolish public notion
> that they ought to be able to control not only the Congress and the
> development of democratic institutions in distant and benighted
> principalities, but also the conduct of their own relatives. . . .[58]

All this, of course, is still another result of our tendency to idealize the president, who, in turn, feels compelled to try to live up to
what we concoct. His first impulse, then, to spirit the blemished
member from public view, is, under the circumstances, not un-
reasonable.

CHAPTER 9

The Family Legacy

And so it is that in presidential politics, too, blood is thicker than water. A couple of skeletons in the closet and out notwithstanding, *most relatives of presidents can be counted on to make some kind of a contribution to the political lives of their respective sons, husbands, fathers, and brothers.* Decorations, Extensions, and Humanizers take it upon themselves to "play to the public," while Helpmeets, Moral Supports, and Alter Egos "stand by the President."

Finally, we must ask ourselves "Why?" Why do the president's kin bother to assume political roles? Exactly who stands to come out ahead?

It turns out that this particular political game has up to four possible winners: the president, the press, the public, and the performer. When a presidential relative takes on a functional role vis-à-vis the great man himself, at least one of the four stands to gain. One way of looking at it is to consider each role performance as an exchange of sorts. A relative ends up filling one role rather than another (or none at all), because somebody's needs

233

are being met—by definition the president's (a role is "functional" in terms of what it does for the president), and also, more likely than not, the performer's, the press's, and/or the public's.

To illustrate what I mean when I say needs are being met, here are some of the benefits that await the four players:

1. The president receives varied, frequent, and benign publicity; loyal, shrewd, professional assistance; ardent political support (which, potentially, translates into votes); and personal devotion and substenance.

2. The press can count on increased sales and profits through the many stories in which kin are "stars." These range from simple gossip, to items or photos of "human interest," to hard news articles that cover legitimate political activities.

3. The public is accorded heroes, heroines, and scapegoats, figures who titillate, entertain, inspire, and intrigue us, and who—like other celebrities—lift us momentarily out of our own routinized lives. Sometimes we even get realistic role models who seem, by dint of the presidential connection, somehow above us and therefore worth emulating.

4. And the performer (kin) is in a position to gain fame, fortune (for example, Patti Davis, Ronald Reagan's long-struggling actress-singer-songwriter daughter, who in November 1980 found herself in sudden demand, "just about the hottest name in town"[1]), power, the gratification that comes from contributing to the success and fulfillment of a loved one, and also a vicarious esteem, an esteem that comes from being close to one who is esteemed.

Of course, there are also costs to this increased participation. Presidents are quick to perceive—sometimes with and sometimes without justification—political liabilities in their relatives. Even those kin who begin on the right foot in a functional role can turn the president into a temporary loser. Few of them are altogether immune from criticism. Thus, more likely than not, they will cast at least an occasional fleeting shadow over the White House. Decorations can be seen as too extravagant; Extensions as too spoiled, too pushy; Humanizers as too fresh and finally tiresome; Helpmeets as too manipulative; Moral Supports as filling the wrong role at the wrong time; and Alter Egos as altogether too powerful. For each of the roles bounds of good taste are set, implicit expectations. If these are not met, it seems to us to be the president's fault. Why couldn't Kennedy keep Jacqueline on a tighter clothes budget? Why couldn't Ford keep Betty from talking too much? Why couldn't Carter keep Rosalynn from taking over the presidency?

On this last question Johnny Carson once again threw the dart: "Did you know that when Rosalynn is out of the country, Jimmy is in charge?" During the height of campaign '80 it was clear that, for better or worse, Rosalynn Carter was being reigned in. Gone were the stories about her involvement in substantive decision making. What we had instead was a dutiful wife, laboring hard on the hustings, repeating over and over, "I'm just so proud of Jimmy." Mrs. Carter, though, was hardly the first First Lady to have been perceived as too equal. John Adams' political opponents had a field day asking pointed questions about "this unelected woman's influence over her husband." More recently, Eleanor Roosevelt worried constantly about encouraging the charge of "petticoat government."

The public also stands to lose through the political activities of the president's family. Kin contribute to the syndrome currently tagged "exaggerated expectations of presidential performance." Signs range from an early idealization of the president to a precipitous and profound disappointment, and the family plays its part by running around the country trumpeting its own virtue and by being, de facto, our only available royalty. In the act of selling themselves they seem to be promising something better, promising something they are, typically, unequipped to deliver. Then the man they espouse turns out *not* to be a miracle worker, and we painfully feel, at least partly correctly, that we have been suckered into buying a false bill of goods.

And as for the individual members of the president's family, surely most of them pay some price for their role playing. It is easy enough to imagine the hard parts of being a child or adolescent growing up in the White House, or of being the sibling of one who is getting *all* the attention, or of being the spouse of a man of whom it can be said that politics (sometimes among others) is his mistress.

The demands on the presidential family are, in any case, enormous. They live in a fishbowl, and there is not much time for family privacy. (President Carter may have paid a political price for his inclination to spend his weekends in seclusion at Camp David.) There are political affairs to attend, governmental ones, and social ones. Moreover, to appear is not enough. On any

public occasion members of the First Family are expected to appear well-nigh perfect—perfectly groomed and attired, perfectly
behaved. The adults must be prepared to speak, at least on occasion, and when they do, it should be with some minimal evidence
of poise, brains, and tact. Finally there is the matter of identity.
For some members of the president's family it has been a struggle
just to maintain a sense of self, to avoid becoming a mere shadow
of the presidential persona.

The newest First Family, Ronald Reagan's, is proving to be
an interesting case in point: political fame experienced as mixed
blessing. Although his four offspring are adults and therefore
less likely to feel the full brunt of their father's newfound global
prominence, each of them quickly felt the hot breath of media
attention, and each responded differently. During 1980 the older
two, Maureen and Michael, were forthcoming, apparently
pleased by their sudden fame; they campaigned eagerly on their
father's behalf. Maureen, who, we can speculate, will play the
role of a Humanizer, was notable primarily for her relative outspokenness, her willingness to disagree sharply with her parents
on several issues—especially in the area of woman's rights. ("I
am a feminist, and I say so," she asserted.) Michael acts the part
of an Extension. He worked steadily for his father, invariably es-
pousing the standard Republican line: "If we don't do the job to
help Ronald Reagan turn this country around and make it great
again, Americans 200 years from now may not have the freedoms
we cherish," he told a meeting attended by members from the
Montana, Wyoming, and Kansas delegations at the Republican
convention.[2]

But Ronald Reagan's younger children were leery of being
absorbed into their parents' political life. Indeed they have been
so cautious that it is difficult to predict with much confidence at
all what political roles they will play during the Reagan administration, if any. When Patti Davis, who has strayed furthest from
her parents' traditional values and mores, was asked if Ronald
Reagan weren't her father would she vote for him, she replied,
"Gee, uh, I don't know—maybe I wouldn't vote for anybody. I'm
really kind of apolitical. I just get the newspaper and turn to the
comics."[3] Ironically, though, since she stands to gain considerable professional success through her father's tenure in the White
House, she may, in spite of herself, end up playing some kind of a
political part—perhaps as Decoration.

Brother Ron politicked for his father in 1976 and, as long as he attended Yale, was a pride to the Reagan family and staff. But when he dropped out of college to become a ballet dancer, he made everyone nervous. In 1980, when asked, he was supportive, both of his father and of the Reagans as a clan: "Like any family, there are bad times and good times. . . . [But] there are lots of families that are more fragmented than we are."[4] And he appeared for family photos as needed. Mainly, though, he stayed separate, dedicated to his work. Tellingly, up to the point of election, his parents had not once seen him perform—the price, perhaps, paid by both parents and child for high visibility among a staunchly conservative constituency. (The *New York Times* dance critic reported that he was good: "You don't have to be a Republican to tell that Ronald Reagan is a very talented dancer."[5]) The pattern was maintained when Ron Reagan was wed to Doria Palmieri: the bride wore a black sweater and slacks and red cowboy boots; the groom donned a sweatshirt, jeans, and sneakers; and the parents were notified of the event via a long-distance telephone call.

Still, for all the sometime problems that are sometimes major—to wit "Billygate" in 1980—the benefits seem to outweigh the costs, and there is no doubt, in any case, that the political participation of the president's (and candidate's) family is here to stay. The changes that were discussed in Chapter 1.—the decline of the party, the increase in the number and importance of primaries, the trends of the office, the growing role of television, shifts in our social and political culture—are beginning to have a cumulative effect. The result: presidential politics is qualitatively different from what it was even two decades ago and is lending itself more than ever to a variety of public roles for kissin' kin. Indeed, the syndrome is spreading. Attractive relatives are valued now on every level of electoral politics, exploited if you will just like any other resource that can be parlayed into a powerful asset. When John Y. Brown, Jr., ran for governor of Kentucky in 1979, who was constantly by his side, hugging, nibbling, and kissing him? Why, none other than Phyllis George, glamorous television personality and Brown's brand-new wife. Ms. George candidly admitted that one of her main values to the campaign had been to draw crowds: "They used to call me Flypaper Phyllis," she said, "but what was John supposed to do, hide me in the closet?" It worked. "The John and Phyllis Show" took the

Bluegrass State by storm. Came November, Brown won handily. George's importance to her husband's success was acknowledged even by Brown's campaign coordinator, who went so far as to say that his man would never even have won the crowded Democratic primary in May without his wife's campaign help[6]— apropos the potential clout of a Decoration.

In fact, the word "attractive" is used very broadly here. In his successful effort to unseat incumbent Senator Jacob Javits of New York, little-known Alphonse M. D'Amato relied heavily on his avowedly middle-class ethnic-type mother—best described as a Humanizer. She became a regional celebrity through a string of television commercials on her son's behalf, commercials which were so effective that when the victorious D'Amato went back upstate to thank supporters, the question everyone kept asking him was "How's your Mom?"

There is also a new focus—triggered in good part by the activism of Rosalynn Carter—on the First Lady. Because of the aforementioned sociopolitical changes, most of our recent First Ladies have, at the least, pushed their own cause: Jacqueline Kennedy the arts, Lady Bird Johnson the environment, Betty Ford the Equal Rights Amendment, Rosalynn Carter the ERA and mental health. Moreover, without exception every First Lady since 1960 has been a highly visible part of the presidency and has done no less than help shape the mood, style, and character of her husband's administration.

We cannot know exactly what effect this heightened visibility has on presidential aspirants who are unmarried, or on those whose marriages are in trouble. Certainly politicians are no more and no less than a reflection of the society they represent. When the *Los Angeles Times* polled its readers on the burning question "If Governor Jerry Brown were to marry rock singer Linda Ronstadt, would that make any difference one way or the other?" Eighty-eight percent said that it would make no difference.[7] But how much further would Brown go with a winning wife and a child or two?) Moreover, some public figures seem to be able to sell their single status as something of an asset, for example, Ralph Nader. Their "unstated appeal is often that of the workaholic with no ties. Not only can such a politician claim that he/she is 'not beholden to special interests'—he/she can go further and appear free of all encumbering relationships."[8] (We can only conjecture about the impact of family themes on women candidates. Will we admit to the possibility of a woman being wife, mother, and president all at the same time? Or does any woman who hopes to be president have to be single—or at least past the age of active mothering?)

The hunch here is that for a time at least, the great American middle will feel more comfortable with presidents, and presidential candidates, with a First Lady alongside. Indeed, the importance that politicians who seek the presidency attach to the sacrosanct picture of a reasonably unified and reasonably stable family was vividly illustrated at the official start of Edward Kennedy's 1980 campaign. Although all who remotely cared knew by now that his wife Joan was living alone in Boston, trying hard after a bout with alcoholism to put her life in order, for the benefit of the announcement in front of the television cameras the nuclear family was carefully stitched back together. On the stage at Boston's historic Faneuil Hall were only five people: Teddy up front at the microphone, and to the back of him his wife and their three children. When Joan left her seat to make a nervous but solid statement of support for her husband, she brought the house down and received a long, lusty, and emotional ovation.

Kennedy's attempt to paint a tight family picture continued. His ads on local television just before the Illinois primary claimed that the series of Kennedy family tragedies had made the candidate "a more mature man." Of course, he was only countering a Carter commercial in which the president was seen sitting at a table with Amy and Rosalynn. The president's voice was heard: "I don't think there's any way you can separate the responsibilities of a husband and father and a basic human being from that of the President."[9] Finally, though, there was consensus that the Kennedys' marital problems showed, and hurt. (Indeed, in early 1981 they finally announced that they would seek a divorce.) In combination with Chappaquiddick they developed—with the help of the Carter campaign—into the "character" issue.[10] As one observer wrote of the 1980 presidential year, "the idea that there is a direct, easily understandable relationship between public and private behavior has never been more widely accepted."[11]

It is also true that during the tenure of Mrs. Carter, the institutionalization of the First Lady's role reached new heights. Mrs. Carter's chief of staff finally had the same rank and salary as the president's, Hamilton Jordan. (As of summer 1979 both received $56,000 annually.) In fact, the position of the First Lady's chief of staff was a newly created one. Until Edith J. Dobelle came to the White House, the head of Mrs. Carter's staff was Mary Finch Hoyt, who served simultaneously as press secretary. The fact that these two tasks were split into two salaried positions lends support to the theory that under Mrs. Carter the job of First Lady had not only increased personal importance but increased institutional importance as well. Dobelle attended the regular morning meetings of all White House senior staff, and there was every indication that both she and her brand-new position were taken seriously.

But we should note that the era of Rosalynn Carter gave us a skewed perception of the First Lady's role. During the Iranian crisis of late 1979 and in very early 1980 it was clear once again how accepting we had become of Mrs. Carter in the role of presidential surrogate. Even before the crisis hit, the First Lady had established her credentials as the top fund-raiser for the Carter-Mondale Reelection Committee. By September 1979 she had raised $850,000 for the effort—more than Vice-President Mondale or any of the Cabinet members. And after the Iranian students' capture of fifty American hostages kept the president from leaving Washington to take to the hustings on his own behalf, her efforts redoubled. In New Hampshire, for example, she and on occasion her mother-in-law, daughter-in-law, and husband's running mate's mate spent twelve-hour days getting to the grass roots. She continued, moreover, to act as emissary in areas of special presidential concern. It took Mrs. Carter's trip to the Thai camps for Cambodian refugees to put the United States government fully behind a relief effort on their behalf.

The thing to remember, however, is that the First Lady's tasks are, in large part, ones she assigns herself. To be sure, there are certain social obligations which any First Lady would be expected to at least oversee. And it is difficult now to envision a First Lady who is withdrawn from public life, a completely private person. But beyond that, *the position is what one makes it*. It is not possible to define the First Lady's "proper function," or to say with any consistency how much impact First Ladies *in general* can exert. Even in the age of increased institutionalization, the First Ladyship is malleable. Each time over, it is *sui generis*. The variety from which we could choose in 1980 was indicative. Candidates for the job ranged from Keke Anderson, of whom it was said that "nothing happens unless she approves,"[12] to Barbara Bush, who claimed she "had no influence whatsoever" on her husband.[13]

It is all the more remarkable, then, that the First Lady who has succeeded Mrs. Carter is, just possibly, also an Alter Ego—although I have tentatively projected her as a Helpmeet until it becomes clear just how politically involved she will be. Nancy Reagan has made her husband's career her own, participating in his bid for the presidency as both campaigner and adviser (albeit not nearly as extensively as Mrs. Carter). Well before election day, it was said that "if there ever is a Reagan administration in Washington, people who know him say, she will probably be the second most important person in it."[14] She is, in his words, "my best friend." (William Safire has suggested that such a succession of strong women in the White House is no coincidence. During the campaign of 1980 he considered the wives of the three leading contenders and concluded that "Rosalynn Carter, Nancy Reagan and Keke Anderson are all strong-willed women who have been urging their husbands to run. Whichever man wins, the First Lady will be assertive, influential and closely involved with the conduct of the presidency." Safire concludes that each has "heard the call of 'liberation' "—however differently they chose to interpret it, and however differently they manifest their taste for power.[15])

Once again, the First Lady's clout grows out of an extraordinary marriage. Nancy Reagan's tie to Ronald Reagan is legendary for its closeness, even to the point of excluding their children from the intimate circle of two. The press observed early on that while husband and wife were inseparable, the four children went their own ways. Indeed, there was a special irony here: family, along with neighborhood, work, peace, and freedom, had long been on Reagan's list of the core of Americans' "shared values." As the *New York Times* observed, "Mr. Reagan has long extolled the virtues of traditional family life and criticized nontraditional choices. But away from the cameras that focus on a smiling family unit, all the Reagan family seldom gathers together."[16] Still, the Reagans do attempt to present a proper façade. The family is united at the most important political moments, and in her autobiography Mrs. Reagan is careful to strike the right chords. Of herself she writes, "For me being a wife and mother is not ordi-

nary—it is an extraordinary and fulfilling way of life."[17] Of her
husband she says, "When one of our children has asked for his
help, he or she has always gotten it."[18]

And so it is to the romantic couple that the press turns: "To
see the Reagans together is to witness mad post-middle-aged
love."[19] Within a four-month period Nancy twice graced the
cover of *People* magazine; other covers, articles (the *New York
Times Magazine* had one called "The Biggest Role of Nancy's
Life"), and short items on anything you ever wanted to know
about Nancy (and could manage to find out) abound. Our curiosity about the president's wife continues unabated, and so the
inquiry ranges from the trivial (Nancy Reagan's conservative fa-
miliarity in matters of dress) to the not so trival: how much influence does Mrs. Reagan really have on her husband?

On this last question, there is debate only on the matter of
degree—debate fueled, incidentally, by Nancy Reagan's own
anxiety about the subject. When asked about her political role
she responds, "Well, I try to be supportive of my husband. I just
do whatever they tell me to do. That doesn't mean that we don't
talk politics all the time, because we do. And, um, it doesn't mean
that we don't influence each other. . . . But as far as real hard
decisions go . . . [her voice trails off]. My way certainly would not
be Rosalynn Carter's way. No, I would nòt be sitting on a power
base. No, no way."[20] Indeed, Mrs. Reagan makes a deliberate attempt to separate herself from her predecessor. She says that she
will not attend Cabinet meetings, nor will her husband send his
family abroad to represent the United States. It is a return to the
belief that for a woman to seem strong is to seem too strong, that
for a First Lady to exercise her influence overtly is worse than
improper: it is unseemly.

Her protestation notwithstanding, however, the indications
are that Mrs. Reagan does, explicitly and indirectly, have much
to say in all manner of matters with which her husband is concerned. "She often attends staff meetings, and her husband uses
her as a sounding board, discussing with her almost every important decision he makes. Because she is so finely attuned to her
husband's needs, she advises on his schedule. . . . She is also said
to have good instincts about people, and [her husband] pays close
attention to her judgments."[21] Moreover, she does not hesitate to
assert herself if her husband seems threatened. In a blunt and
unusual television advertisement that ran during the last week of

the campaign, Mrs. Reagan said in a quavering voice that she was "deeply, deeply offended" by President Carter's efforts to portray her husband as a "warmonger, as a man who would throw the elderly out on the street. . . ." She went on, "That's a cruel thing to do. It's cruel to the people. It's cruel to my husband."[22]

Perhaps the most economical way of viewing Nancy Reagan is to see her as a paradox. In part, she is an anachronism who appears for all the world to be living in a time when men ran things and women were less than equal, when they existed for and through their husbands. But she is also strong, opinionated, active, and fully participatory in her husband's political life. The woman who says forthrightly that "my life really began when I married my husband" is the same one who, when her husband was asked by a reporter why he did not support the Equal Rights Amendment, stepped firmly between her husband and the microphone and insisted that she be allowed to "speak to that."

Whatever the details, though, the overriding impression is of her single-minded devotion to her husband, and of President Reagan's fully equivalent devotion to her. As a friend of theirs observed, "They are joined at the hip."

But besides the greater political impact of the presidents' parents, wives, children, and siblings, we have other, related treats in store. We will, for example, be seeing more of the *extended* First Family—in-laws, aunts, uncles, nieces, nephews, cousins, and so on. (For instance, in his 1980 pitch Edward Kennedy got important help from nephew Joseph P. Kennedy III.) As politicians come to understand more fully the value of their families as both personal and political supports, they will quite naturally seek to maximize that resource, and that means drafting anyone who is in any way related.

We should also be looking forward to a new meaning of the term "political dynasty." There are indications that the enormously increased exposure of the president's family—which makes political stars of the president's offspring—will result in a situation in which the next generation also seeks to, and indeed does, gain political fame and fortune. In this mass-media era, merely carrying the family name is enough to ensure the younger set a hearing.

After Edward Kennedy has his moment in the White House sun, or tries to, there will be a fresh crop of young Kennedys—nieces, nephews, and perhaps his own children—ready, willing and able to walk into the political spotlight. The star of the Boston ceremony celebrating the opening of the Kennedy Library was none other than nephew Joe, who upstaged not only his uncle but also President Carter. Lyndon Johnson's son-in-law Charles Robb, currently serving as Virginia's lieutenant governor, is looking to take a step up in the 1981 election. His national reputation was guaranteed the second he said "I do" to Lynda Bird Johnson, daughter of the thirty-sixth president. And Mrs. Robb has herself recently entered political life; Jimmy Carter named her to head the National Advisory Committee for Women. (She was not, incidentally, any kind of recognized figure in the women's movement. Her chief credential was her family tie.) Had Nixon not become such a discredited figure, it seems safe to assume that either his daughter, Julie Nixon Eisenhower, or his son-in-law, David Eisenhower, or perhaps both, would have sought to enter politics early on. Given Watergate, they have retired now to lead a quiet life, but it is still probable that they will return someday to seek a political place. It is virtually certain that Jack Ford will someday seek political office; he has already spoken of running for a new House seat from San Diego in 1982, or possibly for California State Comptroller.

As for Jimmy Carter's four children, although it is too early to tell about Amy, two of his three sons have already made their political ambitions clear. Jack, the oldest, declared his candidacy for a congressional seat from Georgia, although later he withdrew. Chip, the second son, was employed by the Democratic National Committee, served frequently as his father's assistant and emissary, and regards himself now as a professional politician. (During 1980 he worked for the Carter-Mondale ticket at least twenty-four days out of each month.)

It is this steady stream of second-generation politicians that lends credence to the proposition that although presidents' sons with political ambitions have dotted our history, in the future they will abound. In the 1980s even daughters may be expected to enter the fray. In fact, before Ronald Reagan was even inaugurated, there was a rumor afloat that Maureen Reagan was interested in running for the Senate. She herself has fueled such talk. In July 1980, on NBC's "Tomorrow" and ABC's "Good Morning, New York," she said, "In years to come I might very well want to run for political office."

Our not so cloudy crystal ball tells us, then, that there will be more of the same, and more even than that. The president's family will continue to serve as Decorations, Extensions, Humanizers, Helpmeets, Moral Supports, and, on rare occasions, Alter Egos. Moreover, the day may not be far off when family assistance becomes increasingly legitimized in the form of salaried positions. (We saw an early sign of it in Chip Carter's slot at the Democratic National Committee.) Indeed, according to an October 1980 New York Times/CBS News poll, the majority of the American people think that the president's wife and family should help represent him in some official duties.[23]

Early in this book it was observed that until recently the activities of the First Family were thought irrelevant and innocuous (except in a few isolated cases), and were therefore almost invisible. Times have changed, though. Today the press makes the president's kin impossible to ignore; and now this book has taken the process a step further. It follows that an analysis such as this one has its practical aspects. Some lessons to be learned: (1) Politicians, and those who package, manage, and serve them, should confirm from the evidence that the public will resonate especially well to public figures with attractive, amusing, and interesting kin. (2) Candidates and presidents may reasonably be freshly appreciative of the value of relatives who assume along with them some part of their political burden. (3) The electorate should come to understand that a strong family is a source of emotional and intellectual support—as well as a potential political influence. (4) And the press might well benefit from the concepts underlying the functional roles, which help us to see both the whole and the parts with new precision.

From the president's (and candidates') point of view, it is certainly safe to say, the more kin to play out the functional roles, the better. By the same token, we are quite likely to continue to be suspicious of bachelor candidates, and candidates whose domestic lives appear to us to be in disorder. Indeed, for all the "progress" of the sixties and seventies, for all the talk about "changing life styles"—indeed, perhaps *because* of these—it is clear that Americans still see the family as a symbol of good old-fashioned virtue. And in politics as elsewhere this notion of virtue includes the traits of unity and stability. "How can a man

unite us if he can't so much as hold his own family together?"
"How can a man provide mature leadership if he can't so much as
lead a stable, decent family life?"

In any case we are stuck with it: both symbolically and practically the president's kin must now be considered a permanent
part of presidential government. It is true that for the president
and his family politics puts strains on "togetherness." And it is
also true that we are nagged by the feeling that his clan really has
no business meddling in matters best left to political professionals. Still, there is a logic to the prominence of the First Family, a logic that is strangely poignant in an era preoccupied with
the disintegration of the American family. Arthur Miller once
wrote on the interpenetration of self and world: "The fish is in
the water and the water is in the fish." The same can be said of
the president: he is in the family, and the family is in him. Indeed, in the last analysis, he is—in spite of his exalted position—
just another face in the family album.

Postscript on Method

The first methodological decision was to confine the more detailed investigation to the period Kennedy through Carter. The reasons for this focus on the period since 1960 are discussed in detail in Chapter 1. The Reagan family was not used for case-study material because President Reagan's administration is too new to determine role performance with certainty. The second decision involved largely eliminating from the discussion the political impact of more distant relatives such as cousins, aunts and uncles, nieces and nephews, and in-laws. Even though in some cases they played important parts (e.g., Stephen Smith, David Eisenhower, Hugh Carter), they did not do so often enough to make their detailed inclusion here—which would have resulted in a considerably more unwieldy product—justifiable. By narrowing the book to the five presidents' parents, wives, siblings, and children, the group to be considered was reduced to forty-two, the number of the five presidents' parents, wives, siblings, and children who were alive at the time their kin held the presidential office. The figures are as follows:

247

	Parents	Wives	Siblings	Children
Kennedy	2	1	6	2
Johnson	0	1	3	2
Nixon	0	1	2	2
Ford	0	1	6*	4
Carter	1	1	3	4

*Gerald Ford has one half brother and two half sisters by his father's second marriage and three half brothers by his mother's second marriage.

But although the great majority of those in this group had participated in one form or another in our political life, not all of them did (or if they did, there was no evidence of it). On that basis, some of the siblings of four of the presidents were also omitted from the discussion. These include the two sisters of Lyndon Johnson, Rebekah and Lucia; one brother of Richard Nixon, Edward; the six half brothers and sisters of Gerald Ford; and Gloria Carter Spann, the oldest sister of Jimmy Carter. The relationships between these siblings and their presidential kin vary, of course. Ford has had very little to do with any of his brothers and sisters, while Carter is said to be quite close to his sister Gloria. But even in this last case it did not seem that Jimmy saw Gloria enough for her to play any kind of a major role in his political life, nor was she at all visible to the public (possibly because during Carter's meteoric political ascent her son was serving time on a felony charge in a California prison). And so the group that would serve as the topic of this book was reduced still further—to twenty-nine persons who played functional roles and four who were dysfunctional to the candidacies and presidencies of their presidential kin, a total of thirty-two, not thirty-three, because Billy Carter was, at different times, functional and dys-functional.

Once the decision to focus on these thirty-two people had been made, the problem became how to do so without making each case *sui generis.* Some sort of categorization was needed if we were to be left with more than an amorphous collection of interesting facts. Ideally, imposing an order on the whole would be more than a way of organizing the materials: the ordering it-self would illuminate the phenomenon of the political impact of the presidential family.

But for natural patterns or groupings to emerge, facts must be accumulated, hordes of them. Thus the first task was to go through the available literature on the subject—such as it was (see Bibliography). Over 100 books were used, and current peri-odicals were also culled—from the *Ladies' Home Journal* to the *National Review.* In addition, the *New York Times* was an in-valuable source. An effort was made to balance the retrospective view, the mind's eye of the Monday morning quarterback, with what was experienced at the time of writing. Billy Carter is the prime case in point of the shift in perceptions that could result. It is actually hard to remember now that he once seemed hardly more than a wonderfully rambunctious country innocent.

In short, all of the parents, wives, siblings, and children who were considered to have had any political impact were thor-oughly researched in terms of how they were perceived by the public and also in terms of the relationship they had to their pres-idential kin.

Biographers, thoughtful ones anyway, give their methodology careful thought. Over and over again we hear judicious life histo-rians talk about suffusing themselves with the facts of the life, the details of it. We hear them speak of living with their subjects, of coming to adopt their personas almost like a second skin so that they can do more than just know about them—they can come to intuit about their lives and to feel what it was like to play their parts. To a lesser degree (this book is drawn on a larger canvas), the same process took place here. So much was read about the presidents' families that they gradually came to be completely familiar.

The more they were understood, the clearer it became that the logical method of categorization—according to each person's relationship to the president—would not do. Even the five wives, although buttressed by an institutional framework that called upon them all to play the same role of First Lady, were so radically different from each other, in their relationship both to the public and to the president, that to throw them in one pot would have resulted merely in a meaningless stew. There was precious little ground for comparing Jacqueline Kennedy with Rosalynn Carter, for example, even though, according to tradition, they had more or less the same privileges and responsibilities. In fact, there was no more reason to assume that they were cut with the same cookie cutter than there was to assume it of their husbands. Thus the main methodological task: how to impose the desired order? The answer to this question was to use the strategy of *role analysis.*

The word "role" has a particular meaning to sociologists, although it does not mean exactly the same thing all the time. Talcott Parsons asserts that role is the "organized system of participation of an individual in a social system."[1] Hollander and Hunt slant toward the social psychologist's view, defining role as "the behavioral expectancies usually associated with given positions and evoked by the appropriate symbols."[2] Roger Brown sees role as the norms that apply to categories of persons, norms that grow out of both prescriptions and expectations.[3] Daniel J. Levinson ties some of these several strands together, stating that role is often used to refer to what are really different phenomena, such as role demands, role conceptions, and role performance.[4]

Despite the differences in how "role" is defined, there *are* similarities. First, the concept of role is always tied to the concept of the institution. The terms used may range from "social system" to "position," but always there is the notion that a role is a part of an ongoing nexus of conduct. It is one role within a network of roles. Berger and Luckman go so far as to say that roles *represent* the institutional order, and that this representation takes place on two levels: (1) The performance of a role represents the role itself; for example, to "engage in judging is to represent the role of a judge." The judging individual is not acting on his own, "but qua judge." (2) The "judge stands in relationship to other roles, the totality of which comprises the institution of the law."[5]

The second similarity is that all sociologists agree that to fill a role properly, one must do so in reasonable accordance with certain expectations. These expectations can grow out of a variety of things, such as prescription, tradition, and prevailing codes of behavior; but once a role is assumed, so are a host of accompanying demands.

The only way "role" has ever been used to describe the president's kin has been with regard to "the role of the First Lady." This was not a social scientific application; rather it grew out of the assumption that, loosely at least, the president's wife was a part of the presidential institution, and that therefore there were certain demands that each of the wives faced in common. This assumption is of course true. But after studying the kin of Kennedy, Johnson, Nixon, Ford, and Carter more closely, it turned out that this particular truth was a trivial one. There were ways of looking at the political impact of the presidential family that were much more illuminating than the traditional ones. Thus, since it turned out that there were more similarities between the political functions of, say, Jacqueline Kennedy and Amy Carter than there were between those of Mrs. Kennedy and any of her successors, it seemed that a new way of defining these particular performances was called for.

But how, precisely, are Decorations, Extensions, and the rest "roles?" The answer follows from what is shared in all the definitions of "role." To begin with, the six functional roles exist as they do only within the context of the institution of the presidency. Whether we are talking of the first three roles, those that fall under the rubric "playing to the public," or of the second three, those referred to as "standing by the president," we are talking of sets of behaviors that grow out of the president's position within the executive branch. Such legitimacy as the president's kin do have in their roles grows out of their being a part of an institution that is headed by the one to whom they are related. The central position of the president as Chief Executive is the key to explaining the political impact of the presidential family, and it is the key to understanding why its members take on political roles of their own.

The second way in which family members can be seen to fill roles is by acting according to certain expectations. Of course, the First Family's choice of roles is not rigorously prescribed. There is more than one way of behaving as First Lady, and so *informal* influences are important, as are the *personal proclivities* of whoever is the First Lady at any given moment. But once a particular functional role is assumed, expectations arise, on the part of the public and the president, expectations that make it virtually incumbent upon the relative to continue to fulfill them. Once Betty Ford became a Humanizer, we all expected her to continue acting in a particular way. Had she not done so, had she withdrawn or turned traditional on us, there would have been political costs. By the same token, once Joe Kennedy had started to play Helpmeet, any alteration of that role for whatever reason would have made his relationship to his son, and even his son's continued political success, more difficult. When Billy Carter turned before our eyes from a Humanizer to something else altogether, the press and the public were upset and angry. Billy's switch also suggested that there are role strains associated with being a president's relative, strains that result, in large part at least, from a constant striving to meet all the private and public expectations.

This issue of expectations is a critical one. Early in the book it was observed that although being the president's kin had powerful advantages, there were constraints imposed as well. In particular, a certain *decorum* was demanded. Only under very special conditions was it O.K. to display bad manners or behave too wildly. This insistence on decorum combines with the pressure to perform politically in some fashion to make family members select those roles that meet the proper requisites while at the same time providing a comfortable fit with their own personalities.

What was most remarkable about the categorizing was that twenty-eight of twenty-nine functional kin fell so easily into one of six roles and stayed there. Clearly, there have been, since the administration of John Kennedy, at least six ways of responding to the demands and expectations of being a presidential relative that are routinely acceptable to all concerned. And, as we have also seen, once one of these roles is assumed, the way it is played by a wide assortment of persons is remarkably similar. Each of the functional roles, then, has characteristics (in the areas of norms, expectations, performance, etc.) that we can expect will continue to turn up in much the same way in the future.

Finally, we turn our attention to the matter of how the subjects of this book were assigned their roles. (Strictly speaking, I did not label the "dysfunctionals" as having any special "role," but the question remains the same: How was it decided that they were dysfunctional?) First, what was *not* done: what was not done was a quantitative content analysis. No effort was made to literally count the number of times Amy Carter served as a Decoration, or the Ford offspring performed as Extensions, or Billy Carter humanized the early Jimmy, or Lady Bird loyally helped Lyndon Johnson, or Julie Eisenhower came to the support of her father, or Robert Kennedy acted as his brother's Alter Ego. To have undertaken such an effort would have been to make a slightly ridiculous bow to what is in other kinds of studies perfectly reasonable precision in measurement.

For the same reason that political science has been stumped when it comes to imposing an order on the collective biographies of political leaders, the execution of this study of the presidential family had to be accomplished by relaxing the rules imposed by numbers. We were dealing here with a group of more than two score persons initially. That meant allowing for the fact that individuals do not always perform in exactly the same way. Imposing some organization on a group of this size necessitated an allowance for deviation and flexibility. Of course there were times when Rosalynn Carter was a Decoration, just as there were circumstances under which Jacqueline Kennedy served as her husband's Helpmeet. But primarily, most of the time over time, Rosalynn Carter was most accurately seen as an Alter Ego, and Mrs. Kennedy as contributing to her husband's administration by the visual impact she had on the American public.

And so it was that members of the First Family came to assume particular functional roles. The way in which the roles came into being in the first place was to look with great care at what it was the family actually did. Again, this grew out of a suffusion with the facts of the lives and the detection, then, of key regularities. Let me make explicit what is probably already clear: at the beginning of this study there was no such thing as a functional role. There were only forty-two members of presidents' families between the administrations of John Kennedy and Jimmy Carter. The roles grew out of the closest possible look at how the central thirty-two of these forty-two souls behaved—in both their public and private performance.

No claim is made to the effect that the six functional roles are all-inclusive. It is perfectly possible that some future member of the First Family will find a new way of helping the president, just as it is possible that presidential relatives will come along to give the term "dysfunctional" a new meaning. But for all practical purposes the scheme outline in this book should hold for the very large majority of the presidents' kin for some time to come.

Notes

Fuller titles and publishing data for works cited in the Notes will be found in the Bibliography. Cited interviews from the Oral History Program of the John F. Kennedy Library, Boston, are also listed in the Bibliography, with fuller identification of the interviewee and year of the interview.

Chapter 1: Presidential Politics as a Family Affair
(pp. 1–35)

1. As noted by Gene Smith in *When the Cheering Stopped*, p. 275.
2. The quote of Dr. Dercum and the quotes in the following paragraph are from Edith Bolling Wilson, *My Memoir*, pp. 285–289.
3. Smith, p. 125.
4. Milton Eisenhower, *The President Is Calling*, pp. 308–311.
5. Demaree Bess, Robert Donovan, and Fredrick W. Collins, quoted in Eisenhower, p. 314.
6. Stephen B. Oates, *With Malice Toward None*, p. 409.
7. All quotes in this paragraph are in Margaret Truman, *Harry S. Truman*, pp. 303–304.
8. Nelson Polsby and Aaron Wildavsky, *Presidential Elections*, pp. 125–126.
9. David Broder, *The Party's Over*, p. 22.
10. Martin Schram, *Running for President—1976*, p. 64.
11. Ibid., p. 169.
12. Jimmy Carter, quoted in ibid., p. 20.

13. Thomas Cronin, *The State of the Presidency*, p. 34.
14. George Reedy, *The Twilight of the Presidency*, p. 17.
15. The quotes in this paragraph are from Cronin, pp. 185–187.
16. *The Nation*, Sept. 30, 1978.
17. Eric Barnouw, *The Tube of Plenty*, pp. 276–277.
18. Jules Witcover, *Marathon*, p. 222.
19. Lyndon Baines Johnson, *The Vantage Point*, p. ix.
20. *New York Times*, Jan. 16, 1979.
21. *U.S. News and World Report*, Nov. 19, 1968.
22. Ibid., Dec. 30, 1974.
23. *New York Times*, May 29, 1977.
24. November 1976.
25. *Time*, Apr. 17, 1964.
26. *New York Times*, Dec. 26, 1965.
27. Ibid., Dec. 26, 1970.
28. Ibid., Dec. 26, 1977.
29. Theodore H. White, *In Search of History*, p. 524.
30. Aug. 7, 1966.
31. *U.S. News and World Report*, Dec. 30, 1974.
32. Edwin Newman, *Speaking Freely*, p. 71.
33. *U.S. News and World Report*, Nov. 19, 1968.
34. *McCall's*, May 1974.
35. May 29, 1977.
36. September 1974.
37. Dec. 20, 1976.
38. *Time*, July 19, 1976.
39. *National Review*, Aug. 29, 1975.
40. Oct. 17, 1977.
41. Aug. 18, 1975.

Chapter 2: Decorations (pp. 36–60)

1. Benjamin C. Bradlee, *Conversations with Kennedy*, p. 158.
2. Letitia Baldridge, *Of Diamonds and Diplomats*, p. 166.
3. White, *In Search of History*, p. 524.
4. Arthur M. Schlesinger, Jr., *A Thousand Days*, pp. 94–95.
5. Bradlee, p. 28.
6. Elizabeth Gatov, Oral History Program, John F. Kennedy Library (cited below as OHP), pp. 20–21.
7. See Theodore H. White, *The Making of the President—1960*.
8. Gordon Langely Hall and Ann Pinchot, *Jacqueline Kennedy*, p. 16.
9. Connie Berman, *The Two Princesses*, p. 39.
10. Stanley Tretick, OHP, p. 22.
11. Charlotte Curtis, *First Lady*, p. 125.

12. Baldridge, p. 40.
13. Quoted in Curtis, p. 47.
14. Quoted in ibid., p. 49.
15. Schlesinger, p. 667.
16. Quoted in Curtis, p. 93.
17. Mary Barelli Gallagher, *My Life with Jacqueline Kennedy*, p. 135.
18. Bernard Boutin, OHP, pp. 24 ff.
19. Sept. 1, 1961.
20. August Heckscher, OHP, p. 51.
21. Ibid., p. 12.
22. Schlesinger, p. 671.
23. Bradlee, p. 58.
24. Schlesinger, p. 352.
25. Mar. 23, 1962.
26. Mar. 30, 1962.
27. The quotes on Bourguiba and Abboud are from Curtis, p. 61, and those on Nehru and Khrushchev from Schlesinger, pp. 525 and 367 respectively.
28. Kenneth P. O'Donnell and David Powers, *"Johnny, We Hardly Knew Ye"*, p. 335.
29. Peter Lisagor, OHP, p. 75..
30. Belford Lawson, OHP, p. 11.
31. The quotes on the Texas trip are from O'Donnell and Powers, pp. 23–25.
32. June 8, 1962.
33. June Sochen, *Herstory*, p. 365.
34. Jimmy Carter, *Why Not the Best?* p. 79.
35. July 19, 1976.
36. *Time,* July 19, 1976.
37. *New York Times,* June 22, 1976.
38. Ibid., Oct. 31, 1976.
39. Schram, p. 192.
40. Article by Eric Foner, Dec. 21, 1976.
41. *New York Times,* Dec. 7, 1976.
42. Ibid., Jan. 25, 1977.
43. Ibid., Feb. 16, 1977.
44. Feb. 7, 1977.

Chapter 3: Extensions (pp. 61–87)

1. James Monaco, *Celebrity*, p. 3.
2. Sargent Shriver, quoted in Joan and Clay Blair, *The Search for J.F.K.*, p. 607.
3. Blair, p. 489.

4. William Kelly, quoted in ibid., p. 490.
5. Theodore Sorensen, *Kennedy,* p. 173.
6. O'Donnell and Powers, p. 181.
7. Peter Lisagor, Oral History Program, John F. Kennedy Library (cited below as OHP), p. 20.
8. O'Donnell and Powers, p. 180.
9. *Time,* Sept. 28, 1962. This item appeared during Teddy's first senatorial campaign.
10. James MacGregor Burns, *Edward Kennedy and the Camelot Legacy,* p. 66.
11. Oct. 12, 1959.
12. Aug. 22, 1960.
13. Aug. 1, 1960.
14. Don Bradley, OHP, pp. 7, 16.
15. Charles Garabedian, OHP, p. 14.
16. Mary Kelly, OHP, p. 8.
17. John Harlee, OHP, p. 12.
18. James Haught, OHP, p. 5.
19. Charles Love, OHP, p. 11.
20. Herschel Loveless, OHP, p. 25.
21. Walter Spolar, OHP, p. 5.
22. O'Donnell and Powers, p. 258.
23. Burns, p. 68.
24. *New York Times,* July 18, 1961.
25. Quoted in Milton Gwirtzman, OHP, p. 28.
26. Reproduced in Burns, pp. 80 and 95.
27. Bradlee, p. 70.
28. Gwirtzman, OHP, p. 29.
29. Burns, p. 77.
30. Bradlee, p. 104.
31. Nov. 7, 1962.
32. Quoted in Burns, p. 100.
33. *Time,* Dec. 13, 1973.
34. *McCall's,* May 1974.
35. Susan Ford in *Seventeen,* May 1975.
36. *Seventeen,* December 1974.
37. *Time,* Aug. 26, 1974.
38. *Ladies' Home Journal,* October 1974.
39. *Seventeen,* December 1974.
40. *Newsweek,* June 30, 1975.
41. *U.S. News and World Report,* Aug. 25, 1975.
42. *New York Times,* June 17, 1975.
43. Ibid., June 21, 1975.
44. In order, the columns mentioned are those of April, May, and June 1975.

45. Oct. 10, 1975.
46. *New York Times,* Oct. 5, 1975.
47. Ibid., Oct. 8 and 10, 1975.
48. Ibid., Aug. 12, 1975.
49. Betty Ford, *The Times of My Life,* pp. 113–114.
50. *Time,* July 21, 1975.
51. *New York Times Magazine,* Mar. 7, 1976.
52. Ibid.
53. Aug. 30, 1976.
54. Aug. 30, 1976.
55. Oct. 11, 1976.
56. Ford, p. 263.
57. Oct. 11, 1976.
58. The first on June 6, the second on June 17.

Chapter 4: Humanizers (pp. 88–114)

1. Victor Lasky, *J.F.K.; the Man and the Myth,* p. 151.
2. Rose Fitzgerald Kennedy, *Times to Remember,* p. 316.
3. Ibid., p. 363.
4. July, 1976.
5. July 19, 1976.
6. All quotes are taken from the *Westport News,* Oct. 11, 1978.
7. June 21.
8. *New York Times Book Review,* Aug. 14, 1977, p. 7.
9. Quoted in James Wooten, *Dasher,* p. 279.
10. *New York Times,* June 3, 1978.
11. Witcover, p. 287.
12. Ford, p. 158.
13. *New York Times,* Sept. 29, 1974.
14. Oct. 7, 1974.
15. Ford, p. 194.
16. *U.S. News and World Report,* Dec. 30, 1974.
17. Quoted in *New York Times Magazine,* Dec. 8, 1974.
18. Mar. 3.
19. *New York Times Magazine,* Dec. 8, 1974.
20. In order of appearance the quotes are from *New York Times,* Aug. 21, 1975; *Ladies Home Journal,* November 1975; *New York Times,* Aug. 12, 1975; William F. Buckley in the *National Review,* Sept. 12, 1975.
21. In order, Ford's statements in this paragraph are from the *New York Times,* Aug. 20, 1975, Oct. 8, 1975, Aug. 26, 1975, and Sept. 22, 1976.
22. September 1975.

23. *New York Times*, Dec. 17, 1975, and Nov. 11, 1975.
24. Dec. 29, 1975.
25. Ford, p. 207.
26. Ibid., p. 257.
27. *New York Times Magazine*, Mar. 7, 1976.
28. *U.S. News and World Report*, Oct. 18, 1976.
29. September 1975.
30. Dec. 29, 1975.
31. Ford, p. 280.
32. Jimmy Carter, p. 12.
33. Hugh Carter, *Cousin Beedie and Cousin Hot*, p. 7.
34. Jimmy Carter, p. 79.
35. Wooten, p. 273.
36. May 26, 1976.
37. P. 80.
38. *Time*, Dec. 20, 1976.
39. Dec. 6, 1976.
40. *The New Republic*, Sept. 25, 1976.
41. *Newsweek*, Dec. 20, 1976.
42. In order of appearance the first three quotes are from *New York Times*, Jan. 21, 1977; *New York Times*, May 21, 1977; and *Newsweek*, Nov. 14, 1977. The rest are from *Newsweek*, Feb. 21, 1977.
43. *New York Times*, Feb. 3, 1977.
44. All the quotes in this paragraph are from *Nation's Business*, May, 1977.
45. Aug. 29, 1977.
46. Aug. 29, 1977.
47. Oct. 17, 1977.
48. *New York Times*, Nov. 21, 1977.
49. Nov. 14, 1977.

Chapter 5: Helpmeets (pp. 115–149)

1. David Abrahamsen, *Nixon vs. Nixon*, p. 134.
2. Gary Wills, *Nixon Agonistes*, p. 32.
3. The quotes in this paragraph are from Blair, p. 369.
4. Richard Whalen, *The Founding Father*, p. 385.
5. Ibid., p. 396.
6. Mark Dalton, Oral History Program, John F. Kennedy Library (cited below as OHP), pp. 6– 12.
7. Whalen, p. 426.
8. Both quotes of campaign workers are in Whalen, p. 420. Whalen is the best single source on Joe Kennedy's role in Jack's early campaigns.

9. Edward McCormack, OHP, p. 2.
10. Hugh Sidey, OHP, p. 9.
11. George Smathers, OHP, p. 42.
12. Whalen, p. 443.
13. The Joe Kennedy quotes in this paragraph are from O'Donnell and Powers, pp. 147 and 160.
14. Whalen, p. 447.
15. O'Donnell and Powers, p. 173.
16. Whalen, p. 449.
17. John Kennedy's two remarks are in ibid., pp. 450, 451.
18. Charles Spalding, OHP, p. 64.
19. John Jay Hooker, OHP, p. 8.
20. Whalen, p. 452.
21. O'Donnell and Powers, p. 189.
22. Garrett Byrne, OHP, p. 27.
23. Frederick Dutton, OHP, pp. 22–25.
24. White, 1961, p. 160.
25. Spalding, p. 65.
26. All of Luce's quotes in this paragraph are from Henry Luce, OHP, pp. 9–12.
27. White, *Making of the President*, p. 321.
28. William O. Douglas, OHP, p. 21.
29. Arthur Krock, OHP, pp. 20 ff.
30. Whalen, p. 463.
31. Arthur M. Schlesinger, Jr., *Robert Kennedy and His Times*, p. 587.
32. Kennedy, p. 393.
33. Ibid., p. 394.
34. Victor Navasky, *Kennedy Justice*, p. 6.
35. Schlesinger, *A Thousand Days*, p. 142.
36. Schlesinger, *Robert Kennedy*, p. 231.
37. Lisagor, OHP, p. 56.
38. The quote is from Whalen and is in Navasky (p. 362), on which the Morrisey material is based. The Lewis and Katzenbach quotes in the next paragraph are on p. 363. Navasky's book also provided the information on the Landis case discussed immediately below—pp. 378–391.
39. Navasky, pp. 389–390.
40. Bradlee, p. 166.
41. *Time*, Aug. 28, 1964.
42. The quote is from Henry Brandon's article "A Talk with the First Lady," in the *New York Times Magazine*, Sept. 19, 1967.
43. Both quotes in this paragraph are from ibid.
44. Lady Bird Johnson, *A White House Diary*, p. 374.
45. Liz Carpenter, *Ruffles and Flourishes*, p. 57.
46. J. B. West, *Upstairs at the White House*, p. 325.

47. Brandon.
48. In order, the quotes in this paragraph are from Lady Bird Johnson, pp. 29, 172, 370, 59, 64, 45, and 254.
49. Joseph Califano, *A Presidential Nation,* p. 217.
50. Lyndon Johnson, p. 94.
51. Doris Kearns, *Lyndon Johnson and the American Dream.*
52. Ibid., p. 84.
53. Ibid., p. 83.
54. West, p. 330.
55. Kearns, p. 84.
56. West, p. 318.
57. Lady Bird Johnson, p. 319.
58. Brandon.
59. Carpenter, p. 115.
60. Ibid., p. 192.
61. Califano, p. 198.
62. Lady Bird Johnson, quoted in Carole Bannett, *Partners to the President,* p. 45.
63. Carpenter, p. 146.
64. Brandon.
65. Some of this information on the Lady Bird Special comes from Helen Fuller, "The Powerful Persuaders," in *The New Republic,* Oct. 24, 1964. For more on the tour, also see Carpenter, pp. 143 ff.
66. Lyndon Johnson, p. 108.
67. *Life,* July 22, 1966.
68. Helen Thomas, *Dateline: White House,* p. 78.
69. West, p. 329.
70. In order, the two quotes from the diary are from Lady Bird Johnson, pp. 329 and 369.
71. Jack Valenti, *A Very Human President,* pp. 30–31.
72. The text of the memo is in Lady Bird Johnson, pp. 138–139.
73. The note is in Kearns, p. 204. Also see Kearns for a psychological interpretation of Johnson's wavering in 1964.
74. Lyndon Johnson, p. 98.
75. Dec. 13, 1968.
76. *U.S. News and World Report,* Dec. 9, 1968.

Chapter 6: Moral Supports (pp. 150–166)

1. *McCall's,* February 1974.
2. Jules Witcover, *The Resurrection of Richard Nixon,* p. 53.
3. Dec. 8, 1969.
4. *Life,* July 19, 1968.
5. Ibid.

6. Richard Nixon, *RN*, p. 292.
7. Ibid., p. 687.
8. *Life*, July 19, 1968.
9. Ibid.
10. Sept. 27, 1968.
11. Bruce Mazlish, *In Search of Nixon*, p. 98.
12. Abrahamsen, p. 169.
13. *New York Times*, Oct. 5, 1968.
14. July 5, 1968.
15. Nixon, p. 334.
16. Ibid., p. 368.
17. *New York Times*, Dec. 1, 1969.
18. Dec. 8, 1969.
19. *New York Times*, Oct. 5, 1968.
20. Ibid., Apr. 12, 1970.
21. Nixon, p. 453. Nixon's *Memoirs* include a generous sprinkling of such private materials; Tricia Nixon's diary, for example, contributes significantly to his version of Watergate.
22. *New York Times*, Mar. 14, 1971.
23. Ibid.
24. Ibid., Mar. 30, 1971.
25. Ibid., Aug. 28, 1971.
26. Dec. 6, 1971.
27. Nixon, p. 708.
28. *New York Times*, July 11, 1973.
29. Nixon, p. 964.
30. All quotes in this paragraph are from *Time*, Nov. 5, 1973.
31. *McCall's*, February 1974.
32. The quotes in this paragraph are all from Nixon, p. 1022.
33. Maxine Cheshire, *Reporter*, p. 200. On this also see Bob Woodward and Carl Bernstein, *The Final Days*, pp. 164–166. They especially address Pat Nixon's drinking and her increasing distance from even her family.
34. Woodward and Bernstein, p. 167.
35. Ibid., p. 246. As described by either Brooks Harrington or his wife Carol, both of whom were present on that summer evening.
36. Ibid., p. 382.
37. The note and this reaction are in Nixon, pp. 1069–1070.
38. Quoted in J. Anthony Lukas, *Nightmare*, p. 764.
39. For both David and Julie's quotes in this paragraph, see *New York Times*, Sept. 13, 14, 17, and 18, 1974. The quote from Julie appeared on the 18th.
40. *McCall's*, August 1975.
41. Abrahamsen, p. 244.

Chapter 7: Alter Egos (pp. 167–208)

1. Lord Harlech in George Plimpton (ed.), *American Journey: The Times of Robert Kennedy*, p. 133.
2. Sorensen, p. 268.
3. *Time*, May 7, 1979.
4. Schlesinger, *Robert Kennedy*, p. 22.
5. Nancy Gager Clinch, *The Kennedy Neurosis*, p. 269.
6. Rose Kennedy, p. 457.
7. O'Donnell and Powers, p. 41.
8. Rose Kennedy, p. 322.
9. LeMoyne Billings, in Plimpton, p. 40.
10. Schlesinger, *Robert Kennedy*, p. 96.
11. Robert E. Thompson and Hortense Myers, *The Brother Within*, p. 26.
12. Schlesinger, *Robert Kennedy*, p. 133.
13. White, *Making of the President*, p. 246.
14. David Halberstam, quoted in David E. Koskoff, *Joseph P. Kennedy*, p. 443.
15. Jack Newfield, *RK*, p. 28.
16. White, *Making of the President*, p. 247.
17. Oct. 10, 1960.
18. Schlesinger, *Robert Kennedy*, p. 214.
19. Ibid.
20. O'Donnell and Powers, p. 220.
21. Richard Neustadt, in Plimpton, p. 128.
22. In order, the two preceding quotes are from Charles Spalding and Maxwell Taylor, in ibid., p. 128.
23. Peter Maas, quoting JFK, in ibid., p. 75.
24. Bradlee, pp. 138–139.
25. Schlesinger, *Robert Kennedy*, p. 228.
26. *New York Times Magazine*, May 28, 1961.
27. Nov. 23, 1960.
28. O'Donnell and Powers, p. 278.
29. Schlesinger, *Robert Kennedy*, p. 446.
30. Spalding, in Plimpton, p. 130.
31. Schlesinger, *Robert Kennedy*, p. 446.
32. In order, the quotes in this sentence are from Chester Bowles and Roger Hilsman, in Plimpton, p. 130.
33. O'Donnell and Powers, p. 321.
34. Schlesinger, *Robert Kennedy*, pp. 433–434.
35. Ibid., p. 439.
36. Navasky, p. xiv.
37. Ibid., pp. 329–330.

38. Robert Kennedy, *Thirteen Days*, p. 48.
39. McGeorge Bundy, in Plimpton, p. 132.
40. George Ball, in ibid., p. 134.
41. O'Donnell and Powers, p. 327.
42. *New York Times Magazine*, Apr. 7, 1963.
43. Schlesinger, *A Thousand Days*, p. 701.
44. *Time*, Feb. 16, 1962.
45. Schlesinger, 1978, p. 598.
46. O'Donnell and Powers, p. 321.
47. Schlesinger, *Robert Kennedy*, p. 599.
48. Robert McNamara, quoted in ibid.
49. Ibid., pp. 612–613. The "heart attack" observation was John Seigenthaler's.
50. Robert Kennedy, p. 88.
51. Jimmy Carter, p. 68.
52. Wooten, p. 181.
53. Jimmy Carter, p. 69.
54. Wooten, P. 220.
55. Hugh Carter, p. 186.
56. Wooten, p. 222.
57. Jimmy Carter, p. 78.
58. Wooten, p. 269.
59. Jimmy Carter, p. 115.
60. Witcover, *Marathon*, p. 118.
61. Schram, p. 171.
62. Witcover, *Marathon*, p. 222.
63. Schram, p. 172.
64. Witcover, *Marathon*, p. 606.
65. The quotes in this paragraph are from Hugh Carter, pp. 189–190.
66. *U.S. News and World Report*, Oct. 18, 1976.
67. *The New Republic*, June 18, 1977.
68. *Time*, June 13, 1977.
69. *Newsweek*, June 13, 1977.
70. The statements out of Peru, Venezuela, and Ecuador were in the *New York Times* June 14, 1977. The President of Costa Rica was quoted in *The New Republic*, June 18, 1977.
71. *New York Times*, June 14, 1977; *Time*, June 13, 1977; *Newsweek*, June 18, 1977; *The New Republic*, June 18, 1977.
72. June 13, 1977.
73. *Time*, Aug. 29, 1977.
74. *New York Times*, July 25, 1978.
75. Aug. 18, 1978.
76. ABC-TV interview, Dec. 12, 1978.
77. *The New Republic*, Aug. 19, 1978.

78. *Time,* May 7, 1979.
79. *New York Times,* June 3, 1979.
80. *Time,* July 31, 1978.
81. The sources for the preceding quotes are as follows: Kraft in *Time,* July 31, 1978; Jordan and Powell in *New York Times,* May 30, 1978; Caddell in *The New Republic,* Sept. 2, 1978; Kirbo, Strauss, and Randolph in *New York Times Magazine,* June 3, 1979.
82. *New York Times,* Feb. 8, 1979.
83. Ibid., Apr. 27, 1979.
84. *Time,* Apr. 23, 1979.
85. The information in this paragraph comes from a variety of media sources. The quotes are from the following: Rosalynn Carter on energy speech in *Time,* Aug. 6, 1979; Mary Finch Hoyt in *Time,* July 30, 1979; Rosalynn Carter on Camp David Cabinet changes in *Time,* Aug. 6, 1979; Tom Wicker in *New York Times,* July 24, 1979. The extent to which Rosalynn Carter was threaded through the events of the spring and summer of '79 is also carefully detailed in Elizabeth Drew, "A Reporter at Large—Phase: In Search of a Definition," in *The New Yorker,* Aug. 27, 1979.

Chapter 8: Skeletons (pp. 209–232)

1. Richard Cardinal Cushing, Oral History Program, John F. Kennedy Library (cited below as OHP), p. 2.
2. In order, the quotes in this paragraph are from Edward Gallagher, OHP, p. 18; Ralph Horton, OHP, p. 16; and Dinah Bridge, OHP, p. 2.
3. The quotes in this paragraph can all be found in Blair, p. 13. Also see James MacGregor Burns, *John Kennedy,* pp. 23 and 129.
4. Burns, *Edward Kennedy and the Camelot Legacy,* p. 27.
5. Robert Cooke, OHP, p. 27.
6. Stafford Warren, OHP, 1966.
7. Sorensen, p. 320.
8. *New York Times,* Oct. 31, 1963.
9. Rose Kennedy, p. 286.
10. The story of the bounced check appeared Oct. 24, 1964; the car accidents were reported on May 20, 1964, and Sept. 25, 1967, and Sam Houston Johnson's lung infection was reported on Aug. 26, 1964.
11. Sam Houston Johnson, *My Brother Lyndon,* p. 220.
12. Kearns, p. 37.
13. Sam Houston Johnson, p. 184.
14. Ibid., p. 148.
15. Ibid., p. 65.

16. Ibid., p. 245.
17. West, p. 340.
18. Sam Houston Johnson, p. 12.
19. Ibid., p. 138.
20. Ibid., p. 184.
21. This paragraph is based on ibid., pp. 63–64, and West, p. 341.
22. Mazlish, p. 22.
23. Abrahamsen, p. 59.
24. Nixon, pp. 242–243.
25. *New York Times*, Sept. 7, 1973.
26. Ibid.
27. Sept. 17, 1973.
28. *New York Times*, Feb. 4, 1974.
29. *Time*, Apr. 15, 1974.
30. Jan. 17, 1979.
31. *New York Times*, Jan. 12, 1979.
32. Jan. 15, 1979.
33. *New York Times*, Jan. 15, 1979.
34. *Boston Globe*, Jan. 18, 1979.
35. Elizabeth Drew, "Equations," *The New Yorker*, May 7, 1979.
36. The letter, dated Mar. 5, 1979, was sent out by the Jewish Federation of Greater Norwalk (Connecticut).
37. *New York Times*, Mar. 22, 1979.
38. NBC-TV.
39. *New York Times*, Apr. 24, 1979.
40. *New York Times*, June 26, 1980.
41. Aug. 4, 1980.
42. *New York Times*, July 30, 1980.
43. July 31, 1980.
44. July 26, 1980.
45. July 24, 1980.
46. Aug. 7, 1980.
47. *Time*, Aug. 4, 1980.
48. *New York Times*, Aug. 3, 1980.
49. Ibid., Aug. 5, 1980.
50. Ibid., Oct. 3, 1980.
51. Ibid., Oct. 4, 1980.
52. In the *International Herald Tribune*, Aug. 23–24, 1980.
53. The text is reprinted in the *New York Times*, Oct. 1, 1980.
54. Oct. 18, 1980.
55. *New York Times*, Nov. 2, 1980.
56. Ibid., Nov. 9, 1980.
57. *New York Post*, Nov. 5, 1980.
58. *New York Times*, Jan. 16, 1979.

Chapter 9: The Family Legacy (pp. 233–246)

1. *Time*, Nov. 24, 1980.
2. *Great Falls Tribune*, July 16, 1980.
3. *People*, July 21, 1980.
4. *New York Times*, July 15, 1980.
5. Ibid., Oct. 13, 1980.
6. Ibid., Oct. 30, 1979.
7. *Time*, Oct. 25, 1978.
8. *Boston Globe*, Dec. 6, 1977.
9. *New York Times*, Mar. 16, 1980.
10. For more on this see Elizabeth Drew's campaign '80 article in *The New Yorker*, June 23, 1980.
11. Susan Jacoby writing in the *New York Times*, July 10, 1980.
12. *Wall Street Journal*, Aug. 7, 1980.
13. *Los Angeles Times,* Apr. 6, 1980.
14. Robert Lindsey, in *New York Times Magazine*, June 29, 1980.
15. *New York Times*, May 19, 1980.
16. Ibid., July 15, 1980.
17. Nancy Reagan (with Bill Libby), *Nancy*, p. 19.
18. Ibid., p. 144.
19. *New York*, July 28, 1980.
20. *New York Daily News*, Nov. 11, 1980.
21. Lally Weymouth, in *New York Times Magazine*, Oct. 26, 1980.
22. *New York Times* Oct. 26, 1980.
23. *New York Times*, Oct. 28, 1980. But although 65% of those polled were in favor of family participation in official duties, 90% of the respondents said that a candidate's wife and family would not affect their vote. I am grateful to Henry Lieberman of the *New York Times* for this more detailed information.

Postscript on Method (pp. 247–254)

1. Talcott Parsons, *Social Structure and Personality*, p. 261.
2. E. P. Hollander and Raymond G. Hunt (eds.), *Current Perspectives in Social Psychology*, p. 256.
3. Roger Brown, *Social Psychology*, pp. 154–156.
4. Daniel J. Levinson, "Role, Personality, and Social Structure in the Organizational Setting," in Fred Greenstein and Michael Lerner (eds.), *A Source Book for the Study of Personality and Politics*, pp. 61–74.
5. Peter Berger and Thomas Luckman, *The Social Construction of Reality*, pp. 74–75.

Bibliography

It was noted in the Preface that the would-be student of the president's kin could not simply turn to the available presidential literature for data. There is a dearth there. For example, on the institution of the presidency the following three books are considered superior. All have stood the test of time, all are thoughtful and generally complete, and yet none even acknowledges the family as a political resource. Richard Neustadt's *Presidential Power* is a brilliant essay on the political and bureaucratic obstacles to presidential initiatives and a virtual instruction sheet on how these might be overcome. But there is no mention of the frequently built-in asset of the family, or of how it might be used to buttress the president's reputation and prestige and hence his power to persuade. Aaron Wildavsky's reader *The Presidency* is a splendid collection of articles on presidential "personality" and "power," the presidency and "the press" and "the people," etc., but not one of the forty-eight contributions mentions the president's family as having either personal or political importance. And although Thomas Cronin's text *The State of the Presidency*

269

examines some of the more elusive aspects of the office (e.g., there is an excellent chapter on the usually forgotten vice-president), in terms of the family it does no better. The family is excluded as though it did not exist.

Books on particular presidencies are much the same. Arthur Schlesinger's *A Thousand Days,* on Kennedy in the White House, mentions Jacqueline, of course, but although, for example, she is said to have had a profound effect on General Charles deGaulle, no serious political implication is drawn. Rather, the account of their acquaintance serves as, at most, a diverting aside. Jack Valenti's "intimate memoir" of Lyndon Johnson pays Mrs. Johnson her due, but only in abrupt passing. Valenti comments that if anything had happened to Lady Bird during her husband's career, "he would have been severely crippled" (p. 31). But the observation ends there, without the slightest hint of what *precisely* is meant.

Biographies and autobiographies follow the traditional pattern and the conventional wisdom. The books in both these genres could almost leave us wondering whether presidents have families at all. Doris Kearns' *Lyndon Johnson and the American Dream* is perhaps the most interesting case of all because the absence of the family in this portrait is particularly telling. The book purports to be "the story of his life," an "analysis of the private man," and a "fascinating story of the American political system." And in fact Kearns does capture unique insights into Johnson's private self. But how can we explain in a book of this sort the glaring absence of any discussion of the role of his wife and two daughters in Johnson's public and private lives?

The good psychobiographers will make more of an attempt to connect private relationships to public behavior than any other type of life historian (e.g., David Abrahamsen in *Nixon vs. Nixon*). But they tend to focus on the president's early life (rather than on ties to wife and children), and more often than not they will also ignore the political implications of having a public family. Thus even they provide only scant and scattered evidence.

Of course we do get some few insights from books written by those connected to the White House in less obviously political capacities. Liz Carpenter's *Ruffles and Flourishes* is such a book, as is J. B. West's *Upstairs at the White House.* (Carpenter was Lady Bird Johnson's press secretary, and West was long-time

chief usher at the White House.) And there are the life histo-
ries—the biographies of First Ladies, for example (though they
are almost always of inferior quality and addressed to a presumably female and indiscriminate audience), or the definitely more
rewarding autobiographies of presidential relatives, such as Rose
Kennedy's *Times to Remember,* Lady Bird Johnson's *A White
House Diary,* and Betty Ford's *The Times of My Life.* Still, by
and large, those who would wish to study the political life of the
president's family must depend heavily on materials from the
newsstand, in particular on magazines that cater to women. This
is reflected in the bibliography whose middle section is one of
useful magazines and newspapers. The other two sections list
books and particular articles, and interviews from the Oral History Program of the Kennedy Library, Boston.

Books and Articles

ABRAHAMSEN, DAVID. *Nixon vs. Nixon.* New York: Farrar, Straus & Gi-
roux, 1976.

ADAMS, ABIGAIL. *Letters of Mrs. Adams.* Boston: Wilkens, Corterolo,
1848.

ADAMS, CHARLES FRANCIS (ed.). *Letters of John Adams Addressed to His
Wife.* Boston: Charles Little and James Brown, 1841.

ALEXANDER, SHANA. "The Best First Lady." *Life,* Dec. 13, 1968.

BALDRIDGE, LETITIA. *Of Diamonds and Diplomats.* Boston: Houghton
Mifflin, 1968.

BANNETT, CAROLE. *Partners to the President.* New York: Citadel Press,
1966.

BARNOUW, ERIC. *The Tube of Plenty.* New York: Oxford University
Press, 1975.

BERGER, PETER, and LUCKMAN, THOMAS. *The Social Construction of Reality.* New York: Doubleday, 1966.

BERMAN, CONNIE. *The Two Princesses: Caroline Kennedy and Caroline
of Monaco.* New York: Popular Library, 1977.

BLAIR, JOAN and CLAY, JR. *The Search for J.F.K.* New York: Berkley
(Medallion), 1976.

BLOUNT, ROY, JR. *Crackers,* New York: Knopf, 1980.

BRADLEE, BENJAMIN C. *Conversations with Kennedy.* New York: Norton,
1975.

BRANDON, HENRY. "A Talk with the First Lady." *New York Times Magazine,* Sept. 10, 1967.

BRODER, DAVID. *The Party's Over.* New York: Harper & Row, 1971.

BROWN, ROGER. *Social Psychology.* New York: Free Press, 1965.

BURNS, JAMES MACGREGOR. *Roosevelt: The Lion and the Fox.* New York: Harcourt, Brace & World, 1956.

BURNS, JAMES MACGREGOR. *John Kennedy: A Political Profile.* New York: Harcourt, Brace & World, 1959.

BURNS, JAMES MACGREGOR. *Edward Kennedy and the Camelot Legacy.* New York: Norton, 1976.

BUTTERFIELD, L. H., et al. (eds). *The Book of Abigail and John: Selected Letters of the Adams Family 1762 – 1784.* Cambridge, Mass.: Harvard University Press, 1975.

CALIFANO, JOSEPH. *A Presidential Nation.* New York: Norton, 1975.

CARPENTER, LIZ. *Ruffles and Flourishes.* New York: Doubleday, 1970.

CARTER, HUGH. *Cousin Beedie and Cousin Hot.* Englewood Cliffs, N.J.: Prentice-Hall, 1978.

CARTER, JIMMY. *Why Not the Best?* New York: Bantam, 1976.

CHESHIRE, MAXINE. *Reporter.* Boston: Houghton Mifflin, 1978.

CLINCH, NANCY GAGER. *The Kennedy Neurosis.* New York: Grosset & Dunlap, 1973.

CRONIN, THOMAS. *The State of the Presidency.* Boston: Little, Brown, 1975.

CURTIS, CHARLOTTE. *First Lady.* New York: Pyramid, 1962.

DANIELS, JOSEPHUS. *The Wilson Era: Years of War and After, 1917 – 23.* Chapel Hill: University of North Carolina Press, 1946.

DAWSON, RICHARD, PREWITT, KENNETH, and DAWSON, KAREN. *Political Socialization.* Boston: Little, Brown, 1977.

EDELMAN, MURRAY. *The Symbolic Uses of Politics.* Urbana: University of Illinois Press, 1964.

EISENHOWER, DWIGHT. *Mandate for Change.* New York: Doubleday, 1963.

EISENHOWER, JOHN. *Strictly Personal.* New York: Doubleday, 1975.

EISENHOWER, MILTON. *The President Is Calling.* New York: Doubleday, 1974.

EPSTEIN, EDWARD. *News from Nowhere.* New York: Random House, 1973.

EVANS, ROWLAND, and NOVAK, ROBERT. *Lyndon B. Johnson: The Exercise of Power.* New York: New American Library, 1966.

FORD, BETTY. *The Times of My Life.* New York: Harper & Row, 1978.

FORD, GERALD R. *A Time to Heal.* New York: Harper & Row, 1979.

FULLER, HELEN. "The Powerful Persuaders: Lady Bird's Trip Through the South." *The New Republic,* Oct. 24, 1964.

GALLAGHER, MARY BARELLI. *My Life with Jacqueline Kennedy.* New York: McKay, 1969.

GEORGE, ALEXANDER and JULIETTE. *Woodrow Wilson and Colonel House.* New York: John Day, 1956.

GLAD, BETTY. *Jimmy Carter: In Search of the Great White House.* New York: Norton, 1980.

HALL, GORDON LANGLEY. *Lady Bird and Her Daughters.* Philadelphia: Macrae Smith, 1967.

HALL, GORDON LANGLEY and PINCHOT, ANN. *Jacqueline Kennedy.* New York: Frederick Fell, 1964.

HESS, STEPHEN. *Organizing the Presidency.* Washington, D.C.: Brookings, 1976.

HOLLANDER, E. P., and HUNT, RAYMOND G. (eds.). *Current Perspectives in Social Psychology.* New York: Oxford University Press, 1963.

HUGHES, EMMETT JOHN. *The Ordeal of Power.* New York: Atheneum, 1963.

JOHNSON, LADY BIRD. *A White House Diary.* Holt, Rinehart and Winston, 1970.

JOHNSON, LYNDON BAINES. *The Vantage Point.* New York: Popular Library, 1971.

JOHNSON, SAM HOUSTON. *My Brother Lyndon.* New York: Cowles, 1969.

KEARNS, DORIS. *Lyndon Johnson and the American Dream.* New York: Harper & Row, 1976.

KELLY, KITTY. *Jackie Oh!* Secaucus, N.J.: Lyle Stuart, 1978.

KENNEDY, ROBERT. *Thirteen Days.* New York: Norton, 1969.

KENNEDY, ROSE FITZGERALD. *Times to Remember.* New York: Doubleday, 1974.

KOENIG, LOUIS. *The Chief Executive.* New York: Harcourt Brace Jovanovich, 1975.

KOSKOFF, DAVID E. *Joseph P. Kennedy: A Life and Times.* Englewood Cliffs, N.J.: Prentice-Hall, 1974.

LASH, JOSEPH. *Eleanor and Franklin.* New York: Norton, 1971.

LASKY, VICTOR. *J.F.K.; the Man and the Myth.* New York: Macmillan, 1963.

LEVINSON, DANIEL J. "Role, Personality, and Social Structure in the Organizational Setting." In Fred Greenstein and Michael Lerner (eds.), *A Source Book for the Study of Personality and Politics.* Chicago: Markham, 1971, pp. 61–74.

LEVINSON, DANIEL J., et al. *The Seasons of a Man's Life.* New York: Knopf, 1978.

LINK, ARTHUR. *Wilson: Confusions and Crises 1915–16.* Princeton, N.J.: Princeton University Press, 1964.

LINTON, RALPH. "Status and Role." In Talcott Parsons, Edward Shils, Kasper D. Naegle, and Jesse R. Pitts (eds.), *Theories of Society.* New York: Free Press, 1961.

LUKAS, J. ANTHONY. *Nightmare.* New York: Viking, 1976.

MAZLISH, BRUCE. *In Search of Nixon.* New York: Basic Books, 1972.

MCELROY, ROBERT. *Grover Cleveland: The Man and the Statesman.* New York: Harper, 1923.

McGINNISS, JOE. *The Selling of the President 1968.* New York: Simon & Schuster, 1969.

MONACO, JAMES. *Celebrity.* New York: Dell (Delta), 1978.

MONTGOMERY, RUTH. *Mrs. LBJ.* New York: Holt, Rinehart and Winston, 1964.

NAVASKY, VICTOR. *Kennedy Justice.* New York: Atheneum, 1970.

NEUSTADT, RICHARD. *Presidential Power.* New York: Wiley, 1960.

NEVINS, ALLAN. *Grover Cleveland: A Study in Courage.* New York: Dodd, Mead, 1932.

NEWFIELD, JACK. *RK: A Memoir.* New York: Dutton, 1969.

NEWMAN, EDWIN. *Speaking Freely.* Indianapolis: Bobbs-Merrill, 1974.

NIXON, RICHARD. *RN: The Memoirs of Richard Nixon.* New York: Grosset & Dunlap, 1978.

NOVAK, MICHAEL. *Choosing Our King.* New York: Macmillan, 1974.

OATES, STEPHEN B. *With Malice Toward None.* New York: Harper & Row, 1977.

O'DONNELL, KENNETH, and POWERS, DAVID. *"Johnny, We Hardly Knew Ye."* Boston: Little, Brown, 1972.

PARSONS, TALCOTT. *Social Structure and Personality.* New York: Free Press, 1964.

PLIMPTON, GEORGE (ed.). *American Journey: The Times of Robert Kennedy.* New York: Harcourt Brace Jovanovich, 1970.

POLSBY, NELSON, and WILDAVSKY, AARON. *Presidential Elections.* New York: Scribner, 1976.

POMPER, GERALD, et al. *The Election of 1976.* New York: McKay, 1977.

RANDALL, RUTH PAINTER. *Mary Lincoln: Biography of a Marriage.* Boston: Little, Brown, 1953.

REAGAN, NANCY (with Bill Libby). *Nancy.* New York: Morrow, 1980.

REEDY, GEORGE. *The Twilight of the Presidency.* New York: New American Library (Mentor), 1970.

ROOSEVELT, JAMES. *My Parents: A Differing View.* Chicago: Playboy Press, 1976.

ROSS, ISHBEL. *The President's Wife: Mary Todd Lincoln.* New York: Putnam, 1973.

ROSSITER, CLINTON. *The American Presidency.* New York: Harcourt Brace Jovanovich, 1956.

SCHLESINGER, ARTHUR M. JR. *A Thousand Days.* Boston: Houghton Mifflin, 1965.

SCHLESINGER, ARTHUR M., JR. *The Imperial Presidency.* New York: Popular Library, 1973.

SCHLESINGER, ARTHUR M., JR. *Robert Kennedy and His Times.* Boston: Houghton Mifflin, 1978.

SCHRAM, MARTIN. *Running for President—1976: The Carter Campaign.* Briarcliff Manor, N. Y.: Stein & Day, 1977.

SHORTER, EDWARD. *The Making of the Modern Family*. New York: Basic, 1975.

SIDEY, HUGH. "The Presidency." *Life*, July 22, 1966.

SMITH, GENE. *When the Cheering Stopped*. New York: Morrow, 1964.

SMITH, MARIE. *The President's Lady*. New York: Random House, 1964.

SOCHEN, JUNE. *Herstory: A Woman's View of American History*. New York: Knopf, 1974.

SORENSEN, THEODORE. *Kennedy*. New York: Harper & Row, 1965.

STAPLETON, RUTH CARTER. *Brother Billy*. New York: Harper & Row, 1978.

THOMAS, HELEN. *Dateline: White House*. New York: Macmillan, 1975.

THOMPSON, ROBERT E., and MYERS, HORTENSE. *The Brother Within*. New York: Macmillan, 1962.

TRUMAN, MARGARET. *Harry S. Truman*. New York: Morrow, 1973.

TUMULTY, JOSEPH PATRICK. *Woodrow Wilson as I Know Him*. New York: Doubleday, 1921.

VALENTI, JACK. *A Very Human President*. New York: Norton, 1976.

WEST, J. B. *Upstairs at the White House*. New York: Warner, 1974.

WHALEN, RICHARD. *The Founding Father: The Story of Joseph P. Kennedy*. New York: New American Library, 1964.

WHITE, THEODORE, H. *The Making of the President—1960*. New York: Atheneum, 1961.

WHITE, THEODORE, H. *In Search of History: A Personal Adventure*. New York: Harper & Row, 1978.

WHITNEY, JANET. *Abigail Adams*. Boston: Little, Brown, 1947.

WILDAVSKY, AARON (ed.). *The Presidency*. Boston: Little, Brown, 1969.

WILLS, GARY. *Nixon Agonistes*. Boston: Houghton Mifflin, 1969.

WILSON, EDITH BOLLING. *My Memoir*. Indianapolis: Bobbs-Merrill, 1938.

WITCOVER, JULES. *The Resurrection of Richard Nixon*. New York: Putnam, 1970.

WITCOVER, JULES. *Marathon: The Pursuit of the Presidency 1972–1976*. New York: Viking, 1977.

WOODWARD, BOB, and BERNSTEIN, CARL. *The Final Days*. New York: Simon & Schuster, 1976.

WOOTEN, JAMES. *Dasher: The Roots and the Rising*. New York: Summit, 1978.

YOUNG, JAMES STERLING. *The Washington Community 1800–1828*. New York: Harcourt, Brace & World, 1966.

Magazines and Newspapers (1960–1980)

Ladies' Home Journal, Life, Look, McCall's, The Nation, National Journal, National Review, The New Republic, The New

Yorker, Newsweek, Saturday Evening Post, Seventeen, U.S. News and World Report, Time, Vogue.
   The *Boston Globe*, the *New York Times*, the *Washington Post.*

Interviews from Oral History Program, John F. Kennedy Library, Boston

Bradley, Don, California political figure, 1966.
Boutin, Bernard, administrator, General Services Administration, 1964.
Bridge, Dinah, Kennedy family friend, Great Britain, 1966.
Byrne, Garrett, Massachusetts political figure, 1967.
Cooke, Robert, member, Medical Advisory Board, Joseph P. Kennedy, Jr., Foundation, 1968.
Cushing, Richard Cardinal, Archbishop of Boston, no date.
Dalton, Mark, Massachusetts political figure, 1964.
Douglas, William O., Supreme Court Justice, 1967.
Dutton, Frederick, special assistant to President Kennedy, 1965.
Gallagher, Edward, Kennedy family friend, 1965.
Garabedian, Charles, Massachusetts political figure, 1964.
Gatov, Elizabeth, California political figure, Treasurer of the United States, 1969.
Gwirtzman, Milton, presidential adviser, 1966.
Harlee, John, Kennedy associate, 1964.
Haught, James, West Virginia legislator, 1964.
Heckscher, August, special consultant to the president on the arts, 1965.
Hooker, John Jay, member, JFK presidential campaign, no date.
Horton, Ralph, Kennedy associate, no date.
Kelly, Mary, Oregon political figure, 1966.
Krock, Arthur, correspondent, *New York Times*, Kennedy family associate, 1964.
Lawrence, William, journalist, *New York Times*, 1966.
Lawson, Belford, presidential adviser on civil rights, 1966.
Lisagor, Peter, correspondent, *Chicago Daily News*, 1966.
Love, Charles, West Virginia political figure, 1964.
Loveless, Herschel, governor of Iowa, 1967.
Luce, Henry, editor-in-chief, Time, Inc., 1965.
McCormack, Edward, Massachusetts political figure, 1967.

Sidey, Hugh, Washington correspondent, *Time*, 1964.

Smathers, George, senator from Florida, 1964.

Spalding, Charles, Kennedy friend and campaign aide, 1968.

Spolar, Walter, presidential campaign organizer, 1966.

Tretick, Stanley, *Look* photographer, 1966.

Warren, Stafford, special assistant to the president for mental retardation, 1966.

Index

Index